PREDICTABLE WINNERS

Predictable Winners

A Handbook for Developing,
Forecasting, and Launching
New Products and Services

STUART E. JACKSON
and
ILYA TRAKHTENBERG

STANFORD BUSINESS BOOKS
AN IMPRINT OF STANFORD UNIVERSITY PRESS • STANFORD, CALIFORNIA

Stanford University Press
Stanford, California

Special discounts for bulk quantities of Stanford Business Books are available to corporations, professional associations, and other organizations. For details and discount information, contact the special sales department of Stanford University Press by emailing sales@www.sup.org.

ISBN 978-1-5036-3885-3 (cloth)
ISBN 978-1-5036-4212-6 (electronic)

Library of Congress Control Number: 2024047845

Library of Congress Cataloging-in-Publication Data available upon request.

Cover design: Martyn Schmoll
Cover art: iStock
Typeset by Newgen in 10/15 Minion Pro

Contents

PART II

Developing Product and Service Concepts

Proven low-cost approaches are available to identify high-potential innovation concepts worth further assessment. Digital businesses have unique product development requirements, while most traditional businesses can enrich innovation with digital. Large organizations can take steps to ensure that breakthrough innovation ideas are not stifled.

PART III

Forecasting Revenue

A compelling revenue forecast and business case for a new product or service concept are critical to winning support from investors and other stakeholders. A rigorous research and forecast development process covering opportunity size, target customers, realistic adoption expectations, competitive threats, and pricing will generate conviction in a revenue forecast and lay the groundwork for a successful commercial launch.

PART IV

Ensuring Commercial Success

A deep pre-launch understanding of customer decision-making and adoption barriers is critical for the successful launch of a new product or service. Creating a flexible but sufficiently detailed launch plan that proactively aims to overcome adoption barriers is well worth the effort. This launch plan needs to incorporate decisions on the right scale of launch and the right channels to reach customers. Finally, configure the organization optimally to execute a successful launch.

PART V
Creating Long-Term Value

Traps that cause many organizations to destroy value after the first launch can be avoided, while incremental innovation can be used to build on the success of a breakthrough in the long term. The requirements for driving sustainable success from innovation vary for different types and scale of businesses.

Acknowledgments

The journey of writing a book is in many ways like the journey of creating a successful innovation—things have to go right at each step along the way and you need the right people alongside you. And there have been many people alongside us on this journey, helping make this book a reality.

We are indebted to all those who have made it possible for us to earn a living doing what we love: helping companies create value through innovation and growth. We would like to thank our clients, who have supported us, often over ten or twenty years, covering hundreds of different initiatives. In addition to our clients, we would like to thank the board members, investors, advisors, and L.E.K. Consulting colleagues whom we have had the privilege of working alongside, and who have all contributed to the body of knowledge that forms the basis of this book. A special thanks is due to those who contributed ideas and examples to this book, including John Goddard, Pierre Jacquet, Rob Rourke, Harsha Madannavar, Darren Perry, Eileen Coveney, Jeff Marrazzo, Erin McCleave, Gil Moran, Andrew Rees, Hatem Sellami, and Craig Wills. Additionally, a wide range of colleagues served as sounding boards as we iterated on the many topics in this book, including Rob Haslehurst, Dominic Perrett, Katlin Erines, Nathalie Herman, and Matt Taylor. It was humbling to have the unconditional support of such a brilliant set of colleagues and friends on this journey.

In turning our ideas into a book, we would like to thank Geoff Gill and John Nichols-Daly for their research support and enthusiasm and our editor, Jeff Cruikshank, for his tireless efforts to make sure the book "delivers" for our readers. Further, a heartfelt thank you to our reviewers Paul LaViolette, Ed Keller, Alan Lewis, and Dan McKone, who provided invaluable feedback for which our readers will certainly be grateful. A special thank you goes to Richard Narramore for giving us the encouragement to take on this project and guiding us along the way.

Finally and most importantly, we want to share our deep gratitude to our families, especially our stalwart champions Marisa and Marina, who patiently provided support, understanding, and encouragement, both in the writing of this book and on our broader journeys. Thank you for making this book possible.

Stuart Jackson and Ilya Trakhtenberg

PART I

Configuring for Success

Eighty to ninety percent of new product and service innovations fail. But these long odds can be improved with a systematic approach at each step of the innovation journey, constant reevaluation of the opportunity in light of new information, and the right leadership mindset.

ONE

Use a Systematic Approach
to Beat the Odds

"Innovate—or die trying!" has become the watchword for many organizations, as the lifespan of companies on the S&P 500 has plummeted from sixty years in the late 1950s to under twenty years as recently as a decade ago.[1] For this reason and others, organizations today are making tremendous efforts to become more innovative.[2] Globally, some 3.4 million patents were filed in 2022 alone, including more than 650,000 in the United States. So by this measure at least, companies have embraced the innovation imperative.

Why Investing in New Products Is so Difficult and so Important

But here's the rub: It turns out that creating a sense of urgency about innovation and generating new ideas toward that end are not where companies are truly struggling. The *real* problem they face lies in generating an attractive return on their investments in product and service innovations.[3] The track record is daunting. Between 1926 and 2019, fewer than 0.2 percent of businesses accounted for 40 percent of all value creation.[4] According to the late Harvard Business School professor Clayton Christensen, there are more than thirty thousand new product launches each year, on average. Of those, something like *95 percent* fail. True, other studies aren't quite as gloomy; even so, they generally peg the failure rate at between 70 and 90 percent. Successful launches are particularly difficult for those new-to-the-world breakthrough innovations that potential customers may not even know they need. In recent years, this has become only more difficult given the growing complexity of products, the ever-increasing sophistication of customers, and the extraordinary ballooning of data available to inform (or confuse) decision-making.

And finally, the odds are even more stacked against new market entrants. For example, as we pointed out in an earlier book, the success rate in grocery product introductions was *seventeen times higher* for large companies than for smaller players.[5]

To balance the need for innovation against its obvious risks, many large companies seek to improve their odds by focusing their innovation on close-in product extensions and variations, which leverage existing customers, production processes, and sales channels. There are well-established approaches to managing this type of innovation, most notably the Stage Gate Process first adopted in the 1980s and 1990s. But as highlighted by the work of Christensen and many others, organizations that focus only on incremental innovations sooner or later face the risk of being disrupted by a challenger.

How Risk and Uncertainty Can Be Systematically Managed

Fortunately, there are better solutions. This book describes evidence-based insights and perspectives on how successful companies embrace the need to go beyond incremental product and service innovations while still maintaining attractive investment returns. The approach we advocate is to systematically identify and retire risk at each step of the innovation journey from concept development to commercial launch and beyond. Importantly, success requires getting not just one or two steps right, but all the steps right along this journey. This approach and our perspectives in this book are grounded in a vast body of insights derived from thousands of growth-oriented projects the authors have led for hundreds of management teams over several decades at L.E.K. Consulting, as well as the experiences of numerous successful practicing innovators and dozens of case studies in the public domain. At the same time, we draw lessons from several proprietary L.E.K. resources and analyses. These include

(a) a ten-year "look-back" database covering over one hundred innovations with more than $20 billion in peak revenues; (b) a longitudinal analysis of public company performance following their first product launch; and (c) evaluations of the role and share of new innovations in different sectors of the economy. This unique base of material allows us to compare, for example, the systematic disaggregation and management of risk in the biotech industry with the value of lean prototyping in digital innovations. It allows us to objectively contrast the role and value of internal versus external (acquisition-based) innovation, and it helps us to explain why most successful first-launch companies fail to create value in subsequent years. Many of the insights shared throughout the book synthesize lessons from this dataset with a wide range of case studies.

So, how does it work?

First, successful companies embrace what might be called an agnostic approach to internal or external ideas. In other words, they focus on *finding the best ideas*—wherever they come from—and helping those ideas take root and flourish. They seek early customer feedback on new concepts through rapid prototyping to define a minimum viable product and then validate, refine, or let it fail fast. They then use quantitative tools to disaggregate and manage distinct risk factors in concept development, revenue forecasting, and launch planning. They thereby not only develop a much more realistic assessment of a new product's true potential but also define the kinds of requirements that are needed to overcome critical areas of risk and uncertainty.

What else? They maintain a focus on capital returns and value creation by managing innovation spending through a series of value-inflection points, with a focus on the costs, benefits, and option value of getting to the next milestone. They look beyond the first product and keep an eye toward continuing launches that can turn a one-hit wonder into an enduring franchise. This includes maintaining a healthy view of internal and external value-maximizing opportunities *after* product launch, as well as before. The importance of this kind of post-launch handholding cannot be overstated. For example, according to a 2022 study by our L.E.K. colleague Pierre Jacquet, over the past two decades more than 50 percent of public biopharma companies with a single product destroyed value in the first twelve and twenty-four months after product launch. We argue that in many cases, it didn't—and doesn't—have to go that way.

The Benefits of a Systematic Approach

In our experience, most companies can eliminate many of the potential sources of failure and, by so doing, *achieve a success rate for innovation well above 50 percent.* This means *constantly tilting spending toward innovations in which risk factors are being successfully managed.* To illustrate the point: if a company's innovation success rate is 60 percent but spending is three times higher on the winners, then more than 80 percent of spending is going toward successful innovations.[6]

Who This Book Is For and What You'll Find Inside

This is not a book for dreamers wishing they could come up with the next brilliant new product or service idea. It is for people whose livelihoods depend on being able to take on all the uncertainties related to launching new products and services and turning them into *predictable winners.* They may be entrepreneurs, product developers, R&D directors, marketing directors, business development leaders, business unit heads, CEOs, and investors. They are people who recognize that for most breakthrough concepts, there are multiple inventors with similar ideas, most of which will fail. The winners are those who can manage the risks and eliminate the sources of failure at each of the key steps in the innovation journey that are covered in the five parts of this book:

1. **Configuring for success.** Embracing a systematic approach to managing every step of the innovation journey, with constant reevaluation in light of new information and with the right personal mindset on the part of those leading innovation teams.

2. **Developing product and service concepts.** Sourcing and developing high potential innovation ideas, taking advantage of lean approaches to concept development and assessment, including tactics large organizations can use to embrace breakthrough innovation.

3. **Forecasting revenue.** Developing a realistic forecast and business case for an innovation—including understanding opportunity size, target customers, adoption expectations, competitive threats, and optimal pricing and pricing models. If the forecast isn't robust enough to convince management or investors or if the necessary product or service concept doesn't appear to be achievable, then you're better off walking away at the outset.

4. **Ensuring commercial success.** Taking the key steps and overcoming the hurdles involved in going from fully developed concept to successfully launching and generating revenue, including proactively identifying and addressing adoption barriers, creating a launch plan, and preparing the organization for successful launch execution.

5. **Creating value for the long-term.** Avoiding the traps that cause many organizations to destroy value after the launch and using product innovation as part of the broader corporate development agenda for different types of organizations.

Figure 1.1 provides an overview of the topics we will cover in this book and serves as a systematic checklist of the key steps to maximizing success along the innovation journey. Depending on whether you are the person responsible

Innovation Journey Checklist

Configuring for Success
- ❑ Use a systematic approach to reduce failures at every step of the innovation journey
- ❑ Manage risks by evaluating multiple indicators of success
- ❑ Avoid the seven behaviors that reduce the odds for many innovators

Developing Product and Service Concepts
- ❑ Look for what's broken, who's not being served, and how to leverage your strengths
- ❑ Take advantage of direct market feedback and rapid prototypes
- ❑ Embrace continuous upgrades and lean development for digital-led businesses
- ❑ Move up the Detect-Analyze-Act pyramid to enrich products using digital
- ❑ Use a start-up mindset for breakthrough innovation in large companies

Forecasting Revenue
- ❑ Build a business case to avoid the product graveyard
- ❑ Size the prize and identify the customers you will win
- ❑ Gather customer insights, not "voice of customer"
- ❑ Never take market research at face value
- ❑ Assume competitors are at least as smart as you
- ❑ Price to unlock the full value of your innovation
- ❑ Build a high-confidence revenue forecast
- ❑ Create a bulletproof business case

Ensuring Commercial Success
- ❑ Identify and lower the biggest barriers to adoption
- ❑ Plan enough but not too much, creating a "living" launch plan to ensure smooth execution
- ❑ Take the shortest path to value by optimizing launch scale and picking the right channels
- ❑ Prime the organization for a successful launch by tailoring capabilities and nurturing alliances

Creating Long-Term Value
- ❑ Turn a single success into an enduring franchise
- ❑ Make use of acquisitions and partnerships to accelerate innovation value
- ❑ Embrace proven pathways for long lead-time innovation
- ❑ Use incremental developments to complement breakthrough innovation
- ❑ Turn gaps into strengths for start-ups and entrepreneurs

for making your organization more innovative, sourcing new ideas, assessing product potential, or overseeing the whole enterprise, you may pay more attention to some sections than others but we expect everyone to benefit from understanding what's involved in the complete innovation journey.

Throughout the book, we will use the terms *product* or *product development,* but this is meant to encompass both products and services. We'll also reference many real-world situations—both reassuring and cautionary—to make our points. One particularly notorious example demonstrates the overarching premise of getting things right along the entire innovation journey. In the mid-1980s, in major metropolitan areas, cell phones were starting to take off. Motorola, a proud company with an enviable history of innovation and already one of the leaders in communications technology, came up with an amazing new product concept: *Iridium.* Iridium would provide cell phone–style communications anywhere on earth using seventy-seven low-earth-orbit satellites, to be launched at a cost of $5 billion. Motorola did its upfront research, interviewing more than twenty-three thousand people from forty-two countries and surveying more than three thousand corporations.[7] Then came a full decade of development, with key constituencies, particularly international business executives, continuing to support the concept. Launched in the late 1990s, the newly spun-off Iridium Communications saw its stock price triple in less than a year. There was much fanfare. Vice President Al Gore made the first Iridium call—to Gilbert Grosvenor, the great-grandson of Alexander Graham Bell and the chairman of the National Geographic Society.

The sky was the limit—or so it seemed. But as soon as Iridium's commercial service was launched, worrying shortcomings began to pop up, quickly reaching critical mass. A year later, in 1999, the spun-off company filed for bankruptcy.

What went wrong? Well, during those ten long years of development, the world changed, with cell phone service becoming available in most countries, including much of the developing world. Cell phones offered smaller handsets, better indoor service, lower pricing, and more agile service operators than Iridium. For Motorola as a whole, the failure of Iridium proved to be a devastating blow, and the parent company has never fully recovered from the episode.

With the benefit of hindsight, Motorola got one thing right and many things wrong. It started with a brilliant concept that filled a gap in the market and was rigorously tested by market research. But it failed to think through how, in real time, expanding cell phone usage would shrink its base of target customers—namely, underserved international executives. As a leading technology supplier to the cell phone industry, Motorola knew that competitors were expanding their capabilities. But it failed to link that awareness to its implications for Iridium. For its sales channel to customers, moreover, Motorola relied on legacy telecom partners that were slow to embrace and promote Iridium. The ten-year development cycle and associated capital costs made it very challenging to deliver an attractive investor return. Finally, even with Motorola's intimate knowledge of mobile communications technologies, Iridium failed to anticipate demand for next-generation products with broadband streaming capabilities. To summarize, Motorola got it right in terms of embracing the initial concept, but it failed to anticipate and manage the full suite of risks from concept to launch.

Of course, sometimes expectations are wrong in the opposite direction. The Merck oncology drug Keytruda was originally discovered by accident as scientists looked for a way to block the PD-1 (more formally known as "programmed cell death protein 1") part of an immune response for patients with autoimmune disease. The scientists noticed that adjusting PD-1 unlocked the potential for the body to fight cancer using its own immune system. But it was originally seen as a long shot, and the program barely survived through two mergers. After Merck acquired it in 2009, the company—not having cancer as one of its priority disease areas—put it on the out-license list. Only after seeing early results from a similar program by cancer specialist Bristol Myers Squibb did Merck, at the last minute, pull the term sheet. By 2023 Keytruda was already the world's top-selling drug; it is expected to continue growing annual revenues to exceed $30 billion by 2028.

This book is aimed at all those people who have found themselves involved in difficult decisions about planning or investing in product and service innovation and have wound up wondering: *Is this worth the risk? What am I missing?* And maybe it includes *you*—in your current role or in that job you're aiming for. While this book may not give you the answer to what you're missing in a specific circumstance, it *will* give you the right questions to ask and the right tools to use. In the following chapters, you will find what adds up to a handbook for how to systematically manage innovation risk for all types of products and services at every stage of the innovation journey—concept evaluation, target customers, potential adoption, pricing, revenue forecasting, investment funding, sales planning, promotion, and next-generation products.

We are well aware that specialized texts and other resources exist in each of these areas, and many of them are outstanding. But this book complements those resources by providing a holistic, sequenced overview—one that will help you understand and navigate the full range of issues and challenges involved in translating product and service ideas into successful revenue-generating businesses.

How Did We Come to Be Leading This Tour?

So how did the authors get to the point where we can offer these sweeping prescriptions?

The authors—Stuart Jackson and Ilya Trakhtenberg—have spent their entire careers as growth-focused consultants, acting as coaches, advisers, and researchers working alongside hundreds of different management teams. Stuart Jackson joined L.E.K. Consulting when it was a ten-person start-up in 1984 and helped it grow into one of the world's leading growth-focused management consulting firms, with more than two thousand professionals and a global network of twenty offices when he stepped down as chairman nearly forty years later. Ilya Trakhtenberg is a leading partner in several L.E.K. industry practices who joined the firm more than fifteen years ago and brings special expertise in the fast-growing areas of healthcare, product launch excellence, and sustainability. L.E.K. Consulting first developed a reputation for new product forecasting in the 1990s. The Human Genome Project was underway, prompting massive investments in biotechnology. But as we saw it, the approach by most investors—of applying a 30 or 40 percent discount rate to optimistic projections—made no sense. L.E.K. therefore pioneered the use of quantitative tools for concept and clinical risk (what are the odds of a drug candidate moving from Phase 2 to Phase 3?), customer risk (what is the potential patient population if the drug only applies to non–small cell lung cancer discovered before it metastasizes?), competitive risk (what share of the market can we expect to retain if there are drugs with similar attributes launching two to three years later?), and capital risk (how long will it take to reach commercialization and how will value change during that time?). This last question apparently was one that Motorola never asked during its ten years of Iridium product development.

This rigorous approach created demand for much more in-depth assessment of biotech investments, to the extent that savvy clients began joking that we had created a brand-new market for ourselves. Since then, L.E.K. has applied the same rigor to innovation investing across almost all sectors—including technology, consumer products, media, and industrial goods—and often embracing new approaches to product forecasting and risk management. These have included, for example, developing revenue forecasts for new high-speed rail networks using geolocation data from mobile phones, projecting revenues from next-generation lightweight wallboard by assessing building practices and potential labor savings, and many, many more.

We—your authors—have more than fifty years of combined experience with the firm.[8] We have advised on hundreds of client situations involving more than a thousand new or recently launched products. Many times, we have advised clients to walk away—sometimes to run away!—from opportunities despite the sunk costs and strong statements of commitment from those involved. Other times—happier times, such as the Merck situation—we've been able to tell clients that the product they were ready to write off has great untapped potential, if they choose to commit to a different approach.

As part of the research for this book, we have taken a detailed look back at over one hundred new product or service forecasts developed by our firm between 2010 and 2020 and compared them to real-world results. We have incorporated insights from this research throughout the chapters in this book, but some important overarching lessons are worth sharing here at the outset:

- Overall, these new products and services represent a huge success, with a combined total of more than $25 billion in peak annual sales.

- For products and services that meet technical targets but underperform expectations, the two key drivers are underestimating competitors and taking longer than expected to bring the product to market (often linked).

- For innovations that exceed expectations, the key driver is failing to anticipate expanded opportunities beyond the initial target market.

■ Execution is as important as the product attributes; management teams can make or break a product, with outsized impact on both under- and overperformers.

The point we hope to make with this short list is that some guidelines are enduring and helpful. At the same time, the great thing about new products and services is that, by definition, *every situation is new*. While we have the insights that come with long experience, we continue to learn from every new concept, and we approach each with the same trepidation and careful consideration: *Is this opportunity as good as it sounds? What are we missing?*

We know that applying a systematic approach to looking at each step in the innovation journey will deliver the best possible outcomes in an uncertain world—and that's what we hope to deliver in this book.

EXECUTIVE SUMMARY

Use a systematic approach to reduce failures at every step of the innovation journey.

■ Between 70 and 90 percent of new product innovations fail to achieve market success and profitable returns.

■ There is no single ingredient that guarantees success; even the best ideas will fail if other elements of the innovation journey are not executed successfully.

■ Improve the odds of innovation success by taking a systematic approach to reducing risk *at every step* in the innovation journey, from initial idea to commercial launch and on to second-generation products.

TWO

Manage Risks by Evaluating Multiple Indicators of Success

One proposed solution to the low odds for success with new products is the concept of "fast-fail" product innovation. The idea is that rather than putting everything into one big product launch and risking one big failure, it's better to de-risk product development with multiple smaller launches to see what works and what doesn't work and modify things as you go along.

This concept is closely linked to the process of validated learning and iteration popularized in Eric Ries's bestseller, *The Lean Startup*. Ries's book advocates building a minimum viable product (MVP) good enough to solicit customer reactions, testing it in the market, learning from this real-life customer feedback, and repeating this loop until you either achieve a strong product/market fit—that is, a compelling product customers want to buy—or realize that the product won't work. The goal is to maximize the amount of learning in the least amount of time to avoid wasting scarce resources.

Benefits and Challenges of Fast Fail Innovation

There are certainly benefits to this approach. For example, potential product flaws become more apparent with each successive generation of the working prototype. This is demonstrably true for software applications, which have used their version of this approach for many years. Increasingly, it's also true for physical products, especially since 3D printing began to make short production runs more cost-effective. So on balance, yes—constantly reevaluating and "failing fast" is a good discipline for all kinds of situations. Returning to the example from the last chapter, it would have been far better for Motorola if they had talked to 2,300 potential customers each year over Iridium's ten-year product development cycle, rather than all 23,000 upfront. We are big believers in the value of **gathering early market feedback through fast-fail or other lean approaches**, a topic we discuss further in Chapters 5 and 6.

That said, there are many situations in which the low-investment version of "fast-fail" is *not* a viable approach. If you want to launch a new cancer immunotherapy that appears to have the potential to increase five-year survival rates from 50 to 70 percent, there's no way around it: you're going to need a clinical trial involving hundreds of patients over at least a five-year period at a cost of many hundreds of millions of dollars.

Barriers to Change for Established Companies

In the context of many large organizations, even making small changes is a complex task. When a yogurt lover pays a visit to the Minneapolis headquarters of General Mills—the parent company of Yoplait, one of the world's leading yogurt brands—he or she may eventually stumble upon a painful question: "How did all of these thousands of talented marketers, brand managers, and product developers miss the Greek yogurt trend?"[1] After all, Greek yogurt, which is strained to make it thicker and creamier and which also has a higher protein content, would seem to be a natural extension of the Yoplait product line.

The unhappy truth is that launching a "fast-fail" Greek yogurt version of Yoplait in the United States back when Chobani was just getting started in 2005 would have been just that: a fast failure. Why? Because nobody in the General Mills Yoplait organization would have wanted it to succeed—not production management, which wouldn't want a more complicated process; not the sales organization, which wouldn't welcome the task of convincing supermarkets to commit precious shelf space to an unproven product; and not brand management, which wouldn't like the idea of a product with higher ingredient costs and lower gross margins. Branded consumer products companies spend decades building trust and consumer confidence in their brand promises. If you want to launch something new, you had better do your homework and be sure your new entry meets customer expectations and enhances your precious brand. And you had better build allies in the organization—allies who understand that sometimes incumbents need to have the courage to attack themselves.

For General Mills, the stakes couldn't have been higher for its fastest-growing division. In 2012, Chobani opened a $750 million plant in Twin Falls, Idaho, which eventually grew into the world's largest yogurt-producing facility, and in 2017, Chobani beat out Yoplait to become the second-largest yogurt producer in the world (both behind Dannon). In the twelve years between 2005 and 2017, Greek yogurt's share of the U.S. market grew from less than 1 percent to more than 50 percent.[2] While leading the market with a "fast-fail" experiment in Greek yogurt would have been very difficult for General Mills, the company could have done a better job of monitoring and reacting to industry developments. The market was providing a powerful indication that consumer tastes were changing, but for many years this information did not figure into the plans for Yoplait.

For an example of how "going fast" sometimes creates its own problems, consider the Boeing 737 MAX, launched in 2017 to meet demands from airline customers for longer range and better fuel efficiency for their narrow-body jets. Rather than design a new aircraft from scratch, Boeing took the expedient route of adding advanced new engines and aerodynamic modifications to the long-in-the-tooth 737 platform, which made possible an accelerated time-to-market. What happened next? You know the terrible outcome: two catastrophic crashes and the subsequent grounding of the entire 737 MAX fleet, which cost Boeing not only an estimated $20 billion in fines, compensation, and legal fees but also indirect losses of more than $60 billion from 1,200 cancelled orders.[3]

Lack of Resources for Entrepreneurs and Emerging Businesses

Back down at human scale, the average entrepreneurs behind start-up businesses feel lucky if they have the funds needed to cover, say, eighteen months of operating losses. They don't want "fast failures"; they need demonstrated progress to entice new investors and keep prior investors happy with a higher valuation for the next funding series. That doesn't necessarily have to translate into an out-of-the-park home run, but it *does* mean demonstrating progress toward the next milestone, whether that milestone is technical or commercial.

The investors' influence on these calculations shouldn't be underestimated. If you're an investor considering the acquisition of a high-growth new technology business, then fast fail is not on your agenda. You need to have confidence that the business potential and payback from the business is sufficient to deliver an attractive expected return from the upfront investment you're going to have to make.

So there are two bottom lines on fast fail. Yes, it's a valuable concept, to which we will return later. Its power lies in the fact that it is based on actual customer behavior rather than stated intentions. At the same time, **multiple indicators can provide powerful insights into the future success of a new concept**, including the success of related products and in-depth research on customer intentions and priorities. Relying on any single indicator is insufficient for many situations that demand a well-developed product concept, a robust business case, and a fully developed launch plan before the product or service can be tested in the market.

The Catch-22 of New Product Investing

This brings us to what we call the Catch-22 of new product development, which we'll summarize as follows: You need to thoroughly evaluate and prepare high-potential products prior to launch. But you also need to be willing to kill low-potential product concepts early, before they consume too much in the way of time and resources. But wait: how do you know which products are high- or low-potential if you haven't yet thoroughly investigated them?

The short answer is that **prioritizing product and service opportunities is not something you do one way or one time**. You need to be open to different indicators of future success, and you need to be constantly evaluating and reevaluating them throughout the journey, from concept to launch, matching the scale of investment to confidence in the final product concept.

Let's look at two examples: a cautionary tale from what now feels like ancient history—the mid-1990s—and a more recent and happier story.

We've learned to think of Apple as a bulletproof innovator. But this wasn't always the case. Our unhappy story focuses on Apple's failed personal digital assistant (PDA), the Newton, which hit the market to great fanfare in 1993. The Newton was a handheld device that supposedly combined high-end computing and communications capabilities. Unfortunately, its vaunted handwriting-recognition skills were woefully inadequate, it weighed about a pound—not so portable!—and it cost $700 (more than $1,500 in 2024 dollars). Steve Jobs, the founding visionary then in exile from the company, scoffed that at that price point, Apple could never hit the volume needed to sustain the product. He was right. Newton was quickly chased out of the PDA market by, among other less expensive entries, Palm's Pilot organizers.

One subplot of the Newton story was that it reflected the determination of Apple's management to innovate in Jobs's enforced absence. CEO John Sculley's 1991 corporate plan, for example, called for new products to be developed and introduced *each quarter.* The company thus spent scads of money on the front end of R&D but committed scant resources to follow through on its innovations. Apple's Pippin game device, introduced in 1995, met the same fate as Newton. It sold—or actually, *didn't* sell—for $600, compared to Sega's competing system priced at $300, even though Pippin had real advantages, including a highly sophisticated network computer as its engine.[4] Pippin was pulled off the market after only a year.

Our second and happier example of applying this discipline comes from Tesla's journey to launch a mass-market electric vehicle. Rather than undertaking the huge investment to take on the legacy automakers from the start—a mountain that over the last century-plus almost no one has climbed successfully—Tesla's first vehicle launch in 2008 was less of a frontal challenge and more of a proof of concept. That first vehicle, an electrified version of the Lotus Elise roadster, found only about 2,450 customers between 2008 and 2012. But it established as viable the concept of a lithium-powered electric vehicle with a range of more than two hundred miles.

This success cleared the path for the Model S, launched in 2012, with sales surpassing 250,000 units by 2018. The Model S was a huge leap forward, giving Tesla increased confidence and a growing fan base of loyal customers (whom the company reached by selling direct, rather than through dealers).

Finally, in 2017, Tesla tackled the mountain: it launched its first mass-market electric vehicle, the Model 3, designed to go head-to-head with the major automakers. Since 2018, the Model 3 has been the best-selling electric vehicle in the United States and in many markets around the globe—including Europe (2019) and China (2020). In 2020 it became the best-selling electric car in history.[5]

You get the idea: It's about **delaying the biggest spending while creating room to experiment and learn**. In Part 2, we will introduce a range of cost-effective approaches to identifying high-potential opportunities that justify the thorough investigation that many products need prior to successful launch.

EXECUTIVE SUMMARY
Manage risks by evaluating multiple indicators of success.

- Avoid fixating on a single approach to assessing product potential. Leverage multiple sources of evidence such as product analogs, market research, and live trials.

- Be aware of the strengths and prejudices of your own organization. Just because you have a strong market insights group or a world-class rapid prototyping team does not mean that you should ignore other sources of information.

- Take time to experiment, but make sure those experiments translate into actionable insights.

THREE

Avoid the Seven Behaviors that Reduce the Odds for Many Innovators

As with most things in life, success in product innovation and launch is not just about what you do. It's as much about what you *don't* do. We've worked with hundreds of innovators across many companies and observed best practices among those who succeed far more often than the odds might predict. In this chapter, we share some of the behaviors that those successful innovators tend to avoid. Whether your role is as an investor choosing between investment opportunities or a senior manager making strategic bets, use this chapter as an introduction to the kinds of behaviors you want to look out for—and to avoid. In subsequent chapters, we'll provide more detail on the practices that great innovators embrace.

A comment in advance: Some of the cautions on our list may appear to be internally contradictory. But we make no apology for that. After all, success is partly about effectively balancing competing demands.

Overrelying on Intuition, Rather Than Objective Evidence

Intuition can play an important role in helping you grasp ideas and convert them into product concepts. But beyond that, it can get in the way of absorbing evidence that runs counter to the original idea—and that's a problem. Yes, the best product managers are passionate about the innovation they hope to bring to market, but at the same time, they're constantly looking for new evidence that supports or refutes their hypotheses.

Very often, unexpected news is not necessarily *bad*, just different, something that requires an adaptation or a reworking of the solution. If it really is bad news—perhaps in the form of a critical product failure, or a competitor's leapfrog development—then better to take that news on board and, if necessary, abandon the project and look for other opportunities.

Failure does not happen just because of bad luck. But it does not necessarily imply incompetence, either. **Every product or business failure is a learning opportunity. But that kind of learning can only take place if those involved first acknowledge the reality of what happened, why it happened, and what they could have done differently.** One of us served on the board of a start-up business providing a software as a service (SaaS) solution to identify and rate recruiting candidates for management positions. The real underlying problem was that potential customers could not get comfortable with letting go of their traditional approaches for senior hiring. But the CEO always had some other excuse for why the service wasn't working. He spent another five years refining the concept, knocking on more doors, and burning through resources before finally admitting defeat. Who knows what might have been accomplished in those five years if the CEO had learned from the feedback, rather than coming up with rationalizations for why it still made sense to continue down the same path.

Rushing into New Areas Where You Have No Right to Win

Successful innovators focus on areas they know. They look for areas where they have some special advantage in terms of expertise, customer relationships, or industry connections. Product managers or entrepreneurs who pile into new high-growth areas often find much more competition than they bargained for, forced to face others with more expertise and experience.

In contrast, the sleepiest and most mature businesses are often fertile fields for new thinking and ideas by people who really understand their customers. There was a time when all sorts of utility companies—electric, gas, water companies—decided it would be a good idea to expand into unregulated businesses. After all, they had seen the success of Enron with its "asset light" model. Why limit yourself to a cost-of-capital regulated rate of return when there were riches to be found in new business areas—telecommunications, energy services for homes and businesses, and warranty services, among others? There was even a major consulting firm that advised clients on "how to be more like Enron."

An extreme example was the French water utility Compagnie Générale des Eaux (later renamed Vivendi), which diversified into film and TV entertainment. Nearly all the expanded company's product launches and acquisitions ended up producing major losses: perhaps not a surprise, given the fairly dramatic lack of fit with the company's established capabilities.

Fearing Failure If Products Are Not "Absolutely Perfect"

You will never have the perfect product. The iPhone was perhaps the most brilliant innovation of the last twenty years, but it was far from perfect when its design was being wrapped up in 2006. (The story goes that Steve Jobs, the CEO of Apple, was annoyed to discover that his car keys had scratched the plastic screen of the prototype he had been carrying in his pocket, and so he decided then and there to switch to a glass screen.)[1] And as we all know, the iPhone has since gone through extraordinary transitions and upgrades.

You need to launch a product that can succeed *now*; the pursuit of perfection can come later. Why? In part because you will never have perfect information. You're guessing today, and you'll be guessing tomorrow. In subsequent chapters, you'll find tools and techniques to give you the best insights possible for the resources available, but those tools can only take you so far. In the end, there will still come a point where you need to make your best judgment, taking account of the information available.

In most business roles, fear of failure is an important ingredient in getting people to focus on what needs to be done and avoid errors or omissions. But in the same way that strikers on a soccer team need a different mentality than defenders, the most successful product innovators focus on success. If something doesn't succeed, it is treated as a "missed shot" and a learning opportunity rather than a personal failure. Psychology is surprisingly important. Everyone knows there are tough odds against innovation, especially breakthrough innovation in small businesses. The best leaders imbue a sense of confidence in their teams, raising expectations and often convincing them that they are better than they think they are.

Prioritizing Product Features over Customer Needs and Solutions

The best innovators start with a *relentless focus on unmet customer needs and potential solutions to those problems.*

This sounds straightforward, but in fact it has many implications. For example, innovation rarely takes place in a corporate vacuum. Sometimes an organizational commitment to an existing product feature—a legacy love story, if you will—gets in the way of prioritizing the kinds of new features that the market is now demanding. BlackBerry found itself in this situation when, in early 2007, Apple introduced the iPhone, already mentioned, with its revolutionary touchscreen technology. BlackBerry had achieved a dominant market position with a smartphone based on a tiny, but full, QWERTY keyboard and keys that clicked audibly when pressed. BlackBerry users, who tended to be tech-savvy business professionals, proudly referred to themselves as "thumb jockeys," and the device's addictive quality earned it the dubious nickname of the CrackBerry.[2] All well and good—but the iPhone appealed to a much broader base of consumers, in part because the device lent itself to use by gamers, web surfers, and members of mobile social networks. The writing quickly appeared on the wall: BlackBerry's U.S. market share declined from 45 percent in 2006 to 40 percent the following year—mainly due to the iPhone's astounding success in its first six months on the market.[3]

But BlackBerry couldn't quite say goodbye to its clicks. Instead, in 2008, it came up with a halfway-there technological response: the BlackBerry Storm, with a larger screen that was itself a giant button, with that legacy mechanical switch beneath, which when pressed delivered that beloved *click*. This "SurePress" display was a bad idea, at best—much slower than its BlackBerry predecessors and much less versatile than even the first-generation iPhones, which quickly got better (and were soon joined by Google's Android). The "SurePress" lasted only two years.[4] By 2016, BlackBerry's share of the global smartphone market was barely measurable.

The point? **The customer is always right—and this may be especially important when (1) the customer base is a moving target and (2) evolving technology is driving that movement.**

We should also note that in some cases, *product features may be secondary to the problem your company is trying to solve.* For example, the movie-recommendation feature on Netflix was not something that customers were demanding from the company in the early years of its existence, when it was only a mail-order DVD subscription service. Back in those days, Netflix simply couldn't afford to keep enough of the movies that customers most wanted in stock, because that demand understandably centered on new releases. So the recommendation feature was a way of getting customers to appreciate the breadth of the Netflix catalog—and take some of the pressure off the most popular titles. This turned out to be the solution that allowed the company to grow into a subscription movie service that worked both internally and for its customers.

Focusing Only on the Short Term or the Long Term

Success often takes time—sometimes up to a decade or more. When you focus on what needs to be done this week or this month, it is important to keep the long-term goal in mind. As noted in Chapter 2, Tesla fueled its unlikely dream of selling millions of electric vehicles and competing with the largest car companies in the world by entering the market with a niche sportscar that ultimately sold only a few thousand units: a proof of concept on the way to success. Staying aligned on the long-term goal—in Tesla's case, "to accelerate the world's transition to sustainable energy"—helps maintain priorities and serves as important reinforcement for the product team, management, and the investors who are supporting the project.[5]

But if you only dream about the long term without delivering on short-term priorities, then you may never get there. Think back to the Motorola story in Chapter 1, in which that innovative company spent a full decade developing a cell phone–style communications system that might have been competitive had it arrived in Year One, but had been effectively bypassed when it was finally launched, in Year Ten. Whether you are a team inside a large organization or an entrepreneur working with independent investors, **you need** milestones—both to show progress along the way and to keep a wet finger in the winds of the marketplace—and you need to hit those milestones. If you can prove technical success, win support from a marquee account, or even secure interest from future customers, then getting the next round of support will be easy. Without evidence of success, you risk a downward spiral of trying to gain momentum with fewer and fewer resources. As Theodore Roosevelt advised, "Keep your eyes on the stars but your feet on the ground."

Trying to Own It All

The most consistent innovators recognize that they can't do it all themselves. They look for help anywhere they can to access the best ideas and expertise. They work tirelessly to build support from key stakeholders who are critical to success, whether these are outside investors or internal sales, marketing, finance, and manufacturing teams. Most are generous in giving credit to all involved and modest about their own roles. If they are entrepreneurs, they prioritize securing the funding and future of the business over limiting their ownership dilution. If they are corporate leaders, they recognize the importance of building a strong team and are generous in sharing success with others. An example of how *not* to comport oneself comes from Jean-Marie Messier, the corporate leader in the Compagnie Générale des Eaux-Vivendi example cited earlier. In part through his overreaches in the United States and Canada, he earned the unwelcome nickname "J6M": Jean-Marie Messier Moi-Même-Maître-du-Monde, or "Myself, Master of the World." Messier became the epitome of the domineering CEO and ended up making a series of irrational and risky acquisitions that led to $100 billion in debt and a collapse in the value of the company.[6]

Interestingly, experienced entrepreneurs tend to give up more of their company's equity in early-stage fundraising than first-time entrepreneurs, but they more than make it back with higher valuations and less dilution in later stages.

Failing to Flex

Along the product journey from concept to launch, new information will come to light. The best innovators welcome this. **Change is not necessarily bad. In fact, external change often creates new opportunities, which means that your internal priorities can and should change**. Going back to the BlackBerry example, how different things might have been if only they had recognized that their tiny click-action keyboard, brilliant though it was in its time, had been surpassed by touch-screen technology.

By the time your product or service comes to market, the chances are that your original plan is already out of date. That does not make it worthless—but it may need to be adapted in light of the new market context. If you have prepared your plan well (see Parts 3 and 4 of this book) you shouldn't come up against large and unpleasant surprises. Nevertheless, some things will be different. For major product launches—see Chapter 18—you should already have a plan for tracking the leading indicators of performance.

EXECUTIVE SUMMARY

Avoid the seven behaviors that reduce the odds for many innovators.

- Know your own strengths and weaknesses, particularly as they relate to the seven behaviors described in this chapter.

- When needed, deliberately emphasize actions that run contrary to your natural tendencies (e.g., if you love technology features but not gathering customer insights, force yourself to go talk to potential customers).

- Build a team with complementary skills and backgrounds and empower its members with the mandate to challenge ideas and learn from failure.

Part 1: Configuring for Success Checklist

Configuring for Success

- ✓ Use a systematic approach to reduce failures at every step of the innovation journey
- ✓ Manage risks by evaluating multiple indicators of success
- ✓ Avoid the seven behaviors that reduce the odds for many innovators

Developing Product and Service Concepts

- ☐ Look for what's broken, who's not being served, and how to leverage your strengths
- ☐ Take advantage of direct market feedback and rapid prototypes
- ☐ Embrace continuous upgrades and lean development for digital-led businesses
- ☐ Move up the Detect-Analyze-Act pyramid to enrich products using digital
- ☐ Use a start-up mindset for breakthrough innovation in large companies

Forecasting Revenue

- ☐ Build a business case to avoid the product graveyard
- ☐ Size the prize and identify the customers you will win
- ☐ Gather customer insights, not "voice of customer"
- ☐ Never take market research at face value
- ☐ Assume competitors are at least as smart as you
- ☐ Price to unlock the full value of your innovation
- ☐ Build a high-confidence revenue forecast
- ☐ Create a bulletproof business case

Ensuring Commercial Success

- ☐ Identify and lower the biggest barriers to adoption
- ☐ Plan enough but not too much, creating a "living" launch plan to ensure smooth execution
- ☐ Take the shortest path to value by optimizing launch scale and picking the right channels
- ☐ Prime the organization for a successful launch by tailoring capabilities and nurturing alliances

Creating Long-Term Value

- ☐ Turn a single success into an enduring franchise
- ☐ Make use of acquisitions and partnerships to accelerate innovation value
- ☐ Embrace proven pathways for long lead-time innovation
- ☐ Use incremental developments to complement breakthrough innovation
- ☐ Turn gaps into strengths for start-ups and entrepreneurs

PART II

Developing Product and Service Concepts

Proven low-cost approaches are available to identify high-potential innovation concepts worth further assessment. Digital businesses have unique product development requirements, while most traditional businesses can enrich innovation with digital. Large organizations can take steps to ensure that breakthrough innovation ideas are not stifled.

FOUR

Look for What's Broken, Who's Not Being Served, and How to Leverage Your Strengths

This is not a book about generating innovation ideas—because in many ways, that's the easy part.

As we described in Chapter 1, millions of patents are filed every year, and those filings represent only a fraction of the universe of new product ideas. The difficulty comes in finding which of these potential new products or services can be successfully launched, winning enough paying customers and avoiding the "product graveyard" that we will describe in later chapters. Throw into the mix the added challenge that for every one of your great ideas, there are usually several companies exploring similar concepts (or who will leap to do so as soon as they hear what you're working on). This means that you need to find concepts that your company, in particular, can be successful with, rather than simply serving as a door-opener for some other player in the marketplace.

Having worked with and observed hundreds of new product and service situations, it's clear to us that **breakthrough concepts share several critical ingredients:**

1. **Something is seriously broken or missing in today's version** of the customer experience of a given product or service.

2. **There are potential customers who are not being served today** because existing offerings aren't configured or priced to meet their needs.

3. **The innovating company has a unique capability or competitive advantage** when it comes to providing the product or service solution.

In this chapter, we'll show how to apply these tests.

What's Broken?

Is there something wrong with an existing product or service, or the way people buy it, or the way it is paid for?

Or, conversely, does the product work fine, and your innovation amounts to adding new features that the customer doesn't really need or value? This approach might be summed up as "uneconomic differentiation"—and it's definitely *not* the zone you want to be in.

Are you *fixing* something? In our experience, this is a great first test. There are plenty of things out there—products and services—that are broken in one way or another, and there's more broken stuff showing up every day.

This breakage emerges even in sectors where you might not expect it. For example, in recent years, the seemingly slow-moving service economy has been a particularly fertile ground for innovation. Remember taxi services in big cities before Uber? Because of widespread rationing of taxi licenses, service was overpriced. Drivers often only accepted cash, which meant you had to carry enough cash around for what could turn out to be a hefty tab. When you ordered a cab, you couldn't be sure if it was really coming at all, since the quality of independent cab companies varied wildly. Trying to get a taxi at peak times or in bad weather was often difficult. Even if you were willing to pay a premium for premium service, there was no easy way to do so.

Uber and Lyft fixed all these problems by taking advantage of simple geolocation and communications technologies. Similarly with Airbnb: Yes, even before this breakthrough concept, you could find short-term rentals—but it took a lot of digging through local agencies, independent websites, and classified listings. Often renters and hosts ended up using word of mouth, because that was pretty much the only way to gain any confidence about the reliability of both the property and the renter. Airbnb solved these problems with a single searchable source and standardized reviews and ratings for both properties and renters. It conducted surveys of user preferences to refine the platform so that it could provide exactly the information that most renters wanted.

If you are an established company, one way to look for what's broken is to follow the complete customer journey, including before and after interacting with your product or service. One company that has done this very well is Hertz. The company was founded way back in 1918, when it rented a fleet of twelve Ford Model T vehicles. Hertz introduced the first airport rental service in 1932 at Midway Airport in Chicago. We now take it for granted, but someone had to be the first to dream it up. The focus on removing hassles in the customer journey took a big leap forward in 1989 with the introduction of Gold Plus Rewards—an express rental arrangement that allowed enrolled customers to skip the rental counter and go directly to the vehicle lot, pick up their car, and drive off. In 1995, Hertz gave many drivers their first experience with GPS navigation when it introduced the NeverLost system in most of its fleet. Overnight, the company eliminated the biggest drawback of renting a car versus relying on taxis: getting lost in an unfamiliar city. In 2016, Hertz introduced Ultimate Choice, allowing Gold Plus Rewards customers to browse the Hertz parking lot at the airport and choose their own vehicle from a selection within their specified grade.[1]

Often, what's "broken" doesn't *appear* to be broken until the moment someone comes up with a clever way to fix it. *Of course* you have to stand in an endless, slow-moving line at the car-rental counter—until the day that you don't. *Of course* you have to take the car that's been assigned to you and none other—until the day that the IT team figures out how to inject enough flexibility into the checkout system to allow you to pick the car that appeals to you. Applying our first test, Hertz fixed clear unmet needs for rushed business travelers with Gold Plus Rewards and with NeverLost (years before GPS became ubiquitous in smartphones).

Who's Not Being Served?

Is there a group out there that either doesn't like how an existing product is configured or doesn't want to pay a high price for the configuration they want? If so, can you do better?

Payment processor Square, founded in 2009, spotted such an opportunity in the form of small business customers who were not being served well by the then-dominant payment services. For many part-time merchants and sole operators, the hardest part of doing business was getting paid without having exorbitant service fees imposed on them. Square provided a solution for that with web-based credit-card payment processing through a simple device that can be attached to any smartphone while also providing systems to support in-person and self-service kiosk payments. Solutions to other chronic challenges—such as customer data security and payment card industry (PCI) compliance—were included in Square's packages. Even before it established a dedicated sales team, Square enrolled one hundred thousand monthly users through word-of-mouth referrals alone. By 2022, the company reported $17.5 billion in revenue and was employing more than twelve thousand people.[2]

Another great example of identifying an underserved community comes from Dollar General, which recognized the retail gap that existed for low-income consumers in rural and suburban areas, especially in towns lacking a Walmart or other major grocery store. To excel in these underserved communities, Dollar General crafted its business strategy around compact stores with a cost-effective operational model. Averaging 7,400 square feet and requiring an average investment of $250,000, their low-cost approach (again, coupled with operational efficiency) facilitated rapid expansion.[3] The number of stores grew from approximately 8,000 in 2008 to roughly 19,000 in 2022, with profits surging from $110 million to an impressive $2.4 billion.

Our second test requires asking questions like who's unhappy out there, and why? What group are they a part of, and how big is that group? Can you improve the quality of their home or work life and perhaps save them money at the same time?

How Is Your Company Special?

Now, we come to the final test: *differentiation*. Does your company have special—and, ideally, unique—capabilities for bringing this new product or service to market?

Applying this test is not always straightforward. The authors have both hosted workshops with a company's senior management to discuss unique capabilities that could form the basis of successful growth initiatives. "We have world-class marketing," a person asserted at one of those workshops. "We have a strong employee culture with great people," said another. Well, obviously, these kinds of general capabilities are good things to have, but that's not what we're talking about here. What you're looking for are *specific, distinctive* capabilities that truly set your organization apart—capabilities that no one else (or almost no one) would be able to claim in a similar workshop at a competitor.

We attended a presentation by 3M that hinged on a novel proposition: *We're best at products that are thin and flat.* No, we wouldn't normally build a description of capabilities on something like product dimensions, but if you think about that innovative company's products—whether it's abrasive papers, Nexcare medical dressings, Post-it notes, adhesive tapes, or specialty sheeting—the characterization mostly works and can in fact be built upon. While 3M recently spun off its healthcare business, it continues to provide a strong example of a large and diversified corporation that still has a clear understanding of its "permission space"—that is, the sphere of activities where it has a proven track record of success and in which it feels comfortable looking for new opportunities.

Sometimes capabilities can take a company in a very different direction. The company that is now known as Iron Mountain started out as a mushroom-farming operation that acquired a depleted iron ore mine in which to cultivate its product. When the mushroom market shifted in 1951, the company began looking for other opportunities and eventually hit upon a business opportunity based on protecting valuable corporate information. Iron Mountain first persuaded banks in New York City to store microfilm copies of deposit records and signature cards in its underground facility. Then, in the late 1980s, Iron Mountain ventured into records management and, thanks in part to a strategic acquisition, emerged as the nation's largest records-management company. It has continued to add new services—among them, secure shredding and cloud storage/migration—and also continues to benefit from the ever-expanding volume of corporate records and information.[4] In 2023, Iron Mountain reported revenues of over $5 billion, with a large portion of that coming from new services in document shredding and digital records management.

For an equally colorful example of using capabilities to enter unrelated new markets, we can look back more than three hundred years to the early history of Lloyd's of London. In the late seventeenth century, Edward Lloyd owned a coffee house in London that was popular with ship owners and captains returning from voyages. Seeing an opportunity, Lloyd began renting out "boxes" (tables) where entrepreneurial businessmen could sell insurance to ship owners against the unhappy event their ships did not return. The insurance business soon overshadowed the coffee operation, with the Lloyd's organization becoming the center of merchant-related insurance underwriting for the next three hundred years. Along the way, of course, it benefited from the continual expansion of global trade and a broadening set of use cases for insurance.

Yes, both Iron Mountain and Lloyd's were "lucky," but as the saying goes, luck favors the prepared mind. In both cases, the leaders of these companies were prepared to take advantage of an opportunity that presented itself and that built on their existing skillsets and assets.

The "Edge Strategy": Leveraging Unique Capabilities

Sometimes organizations stumble across new business opportunities, as was the case with Iron Mountain and Lloyd's. Another approach is to do a thorough evaluation of the opportunities that may be adjacent to a business's current operations. A detailed explanation of how companies can systematically seek out new product or service opportunities that leverage existing capabilities can be found in the book *Edge Strategy* by our colleagues Alan Lewis and Dan McKone.[5]

They describe three kinds of "edges" that are adjacent to the company's current offering:

- **Product edge.** Capturing incremental growth by slightly altering the elements and composition of a core offering to customers.
- **Journey edge.** Earning new growth by adjusting your role in supporting the customer's journey to and through your offering (like Hertz).
- **Enterprise edge.** Unlocking new value from resources and capabilities that support your core offering by applying them in a different context for a different offering or a different set of customers (similar to Lloyds or Iron Mountain).

If you look hard enough, **there is almost always something broken or missing about the customer experience in some area related to where your**

business operates. The likelihood is that, sooner or later, someone will figure out a way to address that gap in the market. If it's a problem serious enough to make customers willing to pay for it to go away and if you can find a solution that uses some part of your company's unique capabilities to fix at least part of what's broken or to serve customers who aren't being well served, you may well have uncovered a high potential new service or product.

EXECUTIVE SUMMARY

Look for what's broken, who's not being served, and how to leverage your strengths.

- Create breakthrough innovations by solving a problem in the customer journey and/or targeting customers not being served today.
- Ensure that you are competitively advantaged to successfully provide this innovation.
- For existing businesses, be creative in identifying innovation opportunities that leverage your unique capabilities by looking at the "edges" of your business activities.

FIVE

Take Advantage of Direct Market Feedback and Rapid Prototypes

When researchers at Denmark's Novo Nordisk were testing a new diabetes drug in 2016, they noticed an interesting side effect: the subjects in the test all seemed to be losing weight.

A further trial in 2021 showed a 14 percent weight loss for patients with high body mass index. In the years since then, the company has been able to track the benefits of reducing heart disease as patients lost weight, demonstrating a 20 percent reduction of heart attack, stroke, or death from heart disease compared to those on placebo. With that kind of data, it was obvious that the two formulations of the drug—Ozempic for diabetes, Wegovy for weight loss—were going to be huge. In the first few months after the news was released, there were more than 273 million views on social media. As of this writing, more than a dozen companies are working on therapies that target the same Glucagon-like peptide-1 (GLP-1) pathway that helps people feel full and reduces appetite.

The market is expected to reach $100 billion by 2030. By 2023, Novo's market capitalization had risen to *75 percent of Denmark's GDP*—an astounding figure.

Of course, it is rare to get an early signal of future demand as powerful as the one seen by Novo. The authors are strong advocates for in-depth market research as a prerequisite to positioning, forecasting, and launching break-through new products and services. But research can be expensive. At the early stages of concept development, there is often not the time or budget for more than very limited research, so direct market feedback takes on greater importance. For clarity, we define direct market feedback as any form of market insight based on consumers' unprompted behaviors and revealed concerns rather than stated priorities and intentions in response to market research. **Direct behavioral feedback is often key to establishing both the extent of the unmet need and the effectiveness or acceptability of the potential solution**. In later chapters we discuss how these observed behaviors can be combined with market research to develop robust insights.

Let's look at a couple of new product innovations that had different signals from the market as they were being developed.

The Value of Early Market Feedback

For the first example, consider the humble bicycle. The bicycle was invented 140 years ago, around the same time as the first cars were being developed. But while the car has seen all sorts of safety innovations—crash-absorbing body structures, padded interiors, head restraints, seat belts, airbags, ABS brakes, collision-avoiding radar—the bicycle has seen next to nothing (other than the bike helmet). Not surprisingly, fatal accident rates for cars have been gradually declining, whereas those for bikes remain stubbornly high.

One of the critical safety issues for bikes is that their high center of gravity makes them susceptible to over-the-handlebar accidents when the front wheel locks (during braking) or the bike hits an obstacle. So when some respected companies—including Blubrake/Shimano and Bosch—came out with anti-lock braking systems (ABS) for bikes, one might have expected them to have a ready market. The cost of the ABS was around $500 when they were introduced around 2023—a hefty premium when you consider that entry-level bikes often cost less than $250. But on the other hand, there are estimated to be 1 billion bikes in the world, including 100 million in the United States. Among this group are millions of serious cyclists, many of whom are happy to spend $1,000 or more on a performance bike with special features. In short, it seemed like there were plenty of potential customers.

But there was a problem, which quickly became apparent on social media. When rumors of the ABS brakes started to appear, the feedback among cycling enthusiasts was almost uniformly negative. Why? Because they viewed braking accidents as something that happens to beginner cyclists who don't have the benefit of good technique. In other words, the target market of enthusiastic cyclists willing to buy premium bikes and features was the same one that felt ABS brakes were an unnecessary complication. Maybe opinions will change over time, but it seems it will be a tough slog to build acceptance. In the meantime, manufacturers have switched their attention to e-bikes. Being heavier, these are less prone to over-the-handlebars braking accidents, but they have the advantage of a higher price point, which brings with it a greater ability to absorb the premium for ABS. Perhaps future regulation will play a part, as it did with automobile safety features. We shall see.

Our second example involves litter trays for indoor pet cats. As the Whisker company describes:

> It was 1999 after a long workday and Brad Baxter—inventor and founder— was down in his basement cleaning the mess his 2 inherited cats had made. As he bent down and scooped he started thinking, "How can I make this easier for myself and better for the cats?"[1]

The eventual result was an automatic self-cleaning litter box: the Litter-Robot. The key innovation was a sifting rotational action that filtered clumps into a waste drawer with collection bags and left behind a clean bed of litter every time. A large and sophisticated device, it would need to command a retail price of around $500. Could it succeed in achieving wide adoption at the same price point that presented such problems for bike ABS? As with bikes, there is a huge potential customer base, with an estimated 220 million pet cats in the world, including 58 million in the United States. Unlike cycling, though, owning a cat is not cheap, with the average owner spending between $500 and $1,000 per year on food, litter, toys, and veterinary visits.

The answer? Unlike the ABS brake, the Litter-Robot has been a huge hit on social media, boasting more than 32 million Instagram followers in 2023. (By comparison, Blubrake had fewer than 1,000.) The sales success of the Litter-Robot has followed a similar trajectory. By 2023, just three years after launch, Whisker was employing some four hundred people and had been named one of the top 2,000 growth companies by *Inc.* magazine.

Litter-Robot enthusiast Katherine Dudley helps explain the phenomenon:

> Not only was the experience of cleaning out a regular litter tray multiple times a day unpleasant, but you also have to factor in the amount of litter you are wasting each time. Although the Litter-Robot seems crazy expensive, I figured our cat is going to live fifteen years and so it will easily pay back. After three years it has probably paid back already. Not only that, we save money on Febreze by not having a stinking cat litter tray.[2]

The two examples are instructive in different ways. In both cases, the developers had done their homework in identifying an unmet need with millions of potential customers. **The difference was whether there were enough potential customers who considered the problem worth solving and were willing to spend $500 on a solution.** A quick scan of social media would have shown that cycling enthusiasts are much more interested in weight savings and comfort than they are in safety innovations. On the other hand, prior to the Litter-Robot cat owners had clearly been unhappy with the existing waste solutions. No, initial perspectives from potential customers are not always right, but they do provide an indication of whether building a market will be a downhill sleigh ride or an uphill slog.

Whatever business you are in, there are always ways to get some early indications of the likely interest in and effectiveness of your new concept.

Benefit from Lean Development and Low-Cost Prototyping

As will be discussed in Chapter 6, **many lean innovation teams today target the creation of a rapid prototype or mock-up in a matter of weeks (or even days).** This is new. Historically, in most large organizations, the nexus of power for new product development has been the marketing group. This is still true in many organizations. Marketing teams do extensive research on consumer segments with different attitudes and needs, and then the marketers use this information to come up with concepts that engineers and designers turn into products.

To some extent, it's a productive model, with good things popping out of the chute now and then. One problem with the approach, however, is that the marketing team lacks the technical capabilities of their design-engineer colleagues, who might come up with a product more or less out of the blue: "Here's an interesting thing we could do. Maybe customers would like this?" A second problem is that the marketing group tends to lack the intimacy with customers that the sales team enjoys. A salesperson is well positioned to say, for example, "Here's an idea that customers say would fix this issue they are worried about."

This brings us back to prototyping. Today, even some of the largest organizations—including, for example, Procter & Gamble—are embracing the lean approach, which translates into an attitude of *let's take ideas from anywhere, create rapid prototypes, and get them in front of a few customers to test reactions.* In some industries such as food, retail, or software as a service (SaaS), the rapid prototype may be fully operational; in others, it may be more of a mock-up that is just real enough that potential customers can grasp and evaluate it.

Because companies are testing more ideas, the development of each needs to be low-cost; this is the "lean" part. They end up failing most concepts—in part because there are not enough resources to fully develop and launch all of them—but the ones that *do* make it have already had some testing. Again, this is in sharp contrast to the traditional approach, in which ideas are not tested until *after* they are fully developed, by which time it's far harder to accept negative feedback. This explains how we end up with products that have huge resources behind them but that nobody wants to buy—with Crystal Pepsi, the Apple Newton, the McDonald's Arch Deluxe, and Google Glasses being prime examples.

What about smaller businesses? They may not have to worry about strange ideas from teams in ivory towers. Indeed, the marketing department, the design team, and the sales department may all be the same person—or at least a group of people sharing the same lunch table. But they can still apply the disciplines of getting customer feedback early.

Leverage a Variety of Early Signals to Assess Potential

For the consumer packaged goods (CPG) industry, test markets can provide accurate feedback. CPG is an example of an industry in which direct pre-market testing is often used, usually in one or more test-market geographies carefully selected to be representative of tastes in the country as a whole. Sometimes these test markets exist across all outlets in selected cities. Alternately, the company may select just a few target outlets for testing and monitoring. At still other times, companies may test reactions at special events such as promotions in bars (for alcoholic beverages) or presentations to special interest groups for foods that are targeted at people with specific dietary requirements.

3D-printed prototypes can prompt reactions to a product's look and feel. For example, entrepreneur Kate Hansen and her husband developed the Ergo Spout, which turns any mason jar into a pourable jug. They tested the product by creating a 3D-printed prototype that they then took to a local farmers' market to get feedback. They came back with not only suggested changes but also sixty email addresses from people interested in buying the product when it was ready.

Unfortunately, not very many established companies have learned these fairly basic techniques. Although 3D printing (also called "additive manufacturing") has dramatically lowered the cost of producing parts that have complex shapes in small volumes, most large companies we work with have failed to take advantage of this to get feedback on early-stage product concepts and designs. They thereby miss out on opportunities to address potential product shortcomings and to build alliances and a sense of shared mission with current and future customers.

Social media can be a powerful tool to gather early market feedback. As we saw with the bike ABS braking and Litter-Robot examples, social media interest can be strongly correlated with eventual sales. Innovators are often reluctant to go public about potential new products before they are ready. Either they want to avoid creating a cycle of negative feedback by releasing a concept that is not fully formed, or they want to avoid tipping off competitors about their plans. These are valid concerns, but there are ways to mitigate them. You can discuss the "problem" without revealing your proposed solution upfront. Do people care about the problem? Is resolving it something people are willing to spend money on? Are millions of people interested in the solution or just a few hundred?

Sometimes your whole business can be a rapid market-feedback tool. Based in Spain, Zara is a renowned and highly successful fashion retail brand that has become synonymous with the concept of "fast fashion." Founded in

1975 by Amancio Ortega, Zara has a global network of nearly three thousand stores across ninety-six countries. Zara's nimble response to fashion trends is facilitated by its small-batch production, which reduces overproduction risks and enables quick experimentation with new designs. If an item underperforms, it can be promptly withdrawn from stores to make room for fresh products.

The brand also maintains flexibility through in-house production, reserving 85 percent of factory capacity for in-season adjustments. Zara commits to just 15 to 25 percent of a season's line six months in advance, with 50 to 60 percent finalized at the season's onset, allowing for up to 50 percent of clothing to be designed and manufactured during the season itself.

Zara also employs a strategy by which it manufactures trendier and riskier items—which require testing and piloting—in Spain. Conversely, it outsources the production of more conventional designs with predictable demand to countries like Morocco, Turkey, and Asia to optimize production costs. This dual approach allows Zara to **balance innovation and cost-effectiveness** in its supply chain. Zara also draws upon the insights of its sales associates and store managers, who actively interact with customers and collect real-time feedback. Zara's design teams reinforce this customer-centric strategy by **tracking Instagram influencers and visiting popular venues** (e.g., university campuses, night clubs) to observe fashion trends firsthand.

Some industries, such as the life sciences, can't use rapid prototyping and must look for other indicators. Most pharmaceutical innovations don't start with a truly lucky break, like the Novo example cited at the beginning of this chapter; it is far more common to begin with painstaking research into the proteins or other "targets" that are associated with making a particular disease or syndrome better or worse. Historically, the pharmaceutical industry has then used high-throughput screening of thousands of compounds to test whether they produce a signal with these targets before undertaking the much higher costs associated with human clinical trials. Increasingly, however, pharmaceutical companies are designing biologic drugs directly using mRNA technology, as was the case with Moderna and BioNTech's COVID-19 vaccines. Researchers looking for early indicators can also take advantage of what is generally a more open culture of research publishing, covering both successes and failures. We will dig deeper into pharmaceuticals and other industries with long lead-time innovation in Chapter 24.

Analogs can be another powerful early market indicator. General Mills could be very confident in the success of Cheerios Berry Burst fruit cereal, given the direct analog of Kellogg's successful Special K Red Berries fruit cereal—an example we will discuss later in the book. But even if such a direct analog does not exist, there are often indirect analogs that can be useful. When Edwards Lifesciences was developing its SAPIEN transcatheter heart valve for treatment of aortic valve disease in the early 2000s, there were those who questioned whether it would enjoy broad acceptance. In contrast to the established approach of open-heart surgery, the transcatheter valve is inserted into the heart through a blood vessel, starting in the leg or chest. While the procedure was low-risk, it showed a slightly higher rate of repeat procedures when compared to surgery. Initially, therefore, the procedure was only indicated for extremely frail patients considered too high-risk for open surgery.

But Edwards' management had observed how stenting procedures had been broadly adopted as an alternative to open surgery for coronary artery disease, even though the stents, too, often required repeat procedures. The analog proved a powerful one. Most patients and doctors would rather take a lower-risk transcatheter procedure (less than 1 percent mortality) and accept a slightly higher probability of reoperating than go for a higher-risk open surgery procedure (usually still less than 3 percent mortality). Sales of transcatheter heart valve devices have far exceeded early expectations, with 2023 revenues approaching $4 billion for Edwards.

Collecting pre-launch deposits confirms interest and generates cash. The electric aircraft company Bye Aerospace has collected more than nine hundred deposits for two-seater, four-seater, and eight-seater electric aircraft that are all still under development. This effectively provides Bye with an interest-free loan over a multi-year development cycle. It has also created what amounts to more than a billion dollars in orders before the first certified aircraft has been completed, providing assurance to suppliers and financial backers.

This is a proven technique for capital goods that has been used frequently by established aircraft manufacturers—and other industries are now taking notice. With its direct-to-consumer sales model, Tesla has taken advantage of customer deposits far more than any other automotive manufacturer, using the mechanism to gauge demand even for vehicles not yet launched. As of June 2023, the company was holding more than a billion dollars in customer deposits, providing both cheap funding and an accurate indication of which vehicles enjoy the strongest demand.

For lower-cost consumable products or services, collecting deposits is generally less feasible. But businesses can still collect email addresses or social media followers with a tailored invitation—for example, "Register here to be first to know about product updates and availability in your area!"

It's great to have a large potential market—but that's just the first hurdle. The more difficult question is, **what proportion of potential customers are likely buyers?** Is it one in a million, like ABS brakes for bikes? Or is it more like one in a hundred, like Litter-Robot? **You need to find lean, low-cost ways to get an early read** on that question. Doing so will put you well on your way toward fielding a predictable winner.

EXECUTIVE SUMMARY

Take advantage of direct market feedback and rapid prototypes.

- Whatever business you are in, there are always ways to get early indications of interest in your new concept.

- Use direct behavioral feedback as a cost-effective way to gauge early market signals before investing substantial resources in development and customer research.

- Take advantage of direct market feedback through tools such as low-cost and rapid prototypes, test market trials, social media, and analogs.

SIX

Embrace Continuous Upgrades and Lean Development for Digital-Led Businesses

Nowhere is innovation happening faster and with more impact than in the world of software and digital products. Consider just one part of the digital economy: the Apple and Android app stores. As of 2022, there were something like 4 million distinct apps, generating revenues exceeding $129 billion. Including associated in-app purchases and advertising revenues, the app economy was estimated at more than $6 trillion in 2021,[1] involving something like 6 billion smartphone users.[2] In the broader tech space, there are estimated to be more than 116,000 technology-based start-ups in the United States alone.[3]

The app economy has created an attractive channel to market and has reduced barriers to entry for many digital start-ups—good news for the new entrants, of course, but it also means that established businesses must constantly innovate and improve if they are going to stay ahead of the game. There is also fundamental platform change happening throughout the software industry, with text-based software continuing the long-term trend to graphical user interfaces (GUI), on-premise solutions shifting to cloud-based SaaS, and the rapid adoption of artificial intelligence (AI).

All of this means that digital businesses must be prepared for a rate of innovation that is faster than in any other industry. The good news is that once companies achieve success in this market, digital product sales tend to be highly profitable, with very low variable costs. But the associated challenge is to constantly roll out competitive new products without going broke under the weight of development costs.

The answer is to **use lean approaches to developing new digital products**: narrowing the initial solution to tackle the essence of the customer problem, sprinting to develop prototypes in days or weeks rather than months or years, and launching and refining products based on direct customer feedback. But how do companies do that without disappointing customers by selling them incomplete or unrefined products? In this chapter, we discuss a range of approaches used by digital companies to manage these difficult tradeoffs.

Design Sprint for New Concept Development

The five-day sprint (Google Ventures calls it the "Design Sprint") is a quick way to create and validate ideas by fostering collaboration, innovation, and user-centered design. Many organizations use it to speed up product development and problem-solving. As the name implies, the process involves designing, preliminary prototyping, and gathering feedback from customers in a process as short as five days.

For the Design Sprint to be effective, you should probably plan a week or two of preparation in advance. You want to have a deep understanding of the business context and who you are designing for. Ideally, you would create customer personas for the team to ideate against.

Figure 6.1 illustrates a typical five-day sprint timeline. The key to the process is engaging a cross-disciplinary team to develop the ideas and concept sufficiently far to get meaningful feedback from customers on whether the proposed app has real potential.

FIGURE 6.1. Five-Day Sprint Timeline

Understand	Diverge	Prioritize	Prototype	Validate
• User attributes • Unmet needs • Substitutes	• Ideate • Envision • Multiple solutions	• Rankings • Storyboarding	• Illustrative model • Clear functionality	• External customers • What does/doesn't work

Trialing the User Experience

The five-day Design Sprint should give you enough output to determine whether your direction "has legs." To revert to more formal business language, you should wind up with some clear key performance indicators (KPIs) to give you a sense of whether the direction is worth pursuing. Of course, at this early stage there are still a lot of stones left unturned—it's highly unlikely that you'll design and test all the relevant nuances in five days—but you can get a good initial indication, typically at the propositional level. You might set out things like *desirability* (do people respond positively?), *feasibility* (is it technically doable?), and *viability* (is it going to be good for the business?). If you investigate all that and the results are good, you can progress to a deeper prototype, building on and expanding the initial validation. By so doing, you will develop a new set of KPIs related to the stage you're in—for example, products that use established technology to put together information in a new way to help consumers succeed or fail, depending on the user experience.

Craig Wills, CEO of digital innovation agency Hi Mum! Said Dad, describes how a rapid prototyping approach can work:

> Suppose a business has its sights set on developing a Personal Finance Management app designed to help consumers navigate loan interest, insurance options, and asset management. Rather than diving headlong into a comprehensive specification, a lean approach is employed.
>
> This methodology assembles stakeholders, end users, and subject-matter experts in a series of workshops alongside our design and technology teams. It compresses the time it takes to gather the necessary context and aims to have SMEs directly apply their expertise to the evolving solution. The lean approach doesn't skimp on rigor, but provides a dynamic platform for continual insights and validation at each stage before progressing.
>
> In the early phases, the focus is on generating visual outputs or conceptual sketches rather than a working prototype. These initial visualizations are summarized in a Product Canvas, which outlines the vision, target audience, financial pain points to address, proposed solutions, business goals, and potential questions for future exploration. The canvas acts as a synthesized record of the collective insights gathered through this design thinking process.

If, and *only* if, these initial steps confirm the project's desirability, feasibility, and viability, a rapid prototype can then be developed. While this prototype may lack full data integration, it should feature a complete, interactive user interface that closely emulates the final product. This allows for more comprehensive testing of functionality and user experience, identifying winning designs, and dealing with any lingering obstacles.[4]

The benefit of getting a working prototype into potential customers' hands early is that it can provide specific and actionable feedback on the product. In the case of the hypothetical financial management app discussed by Wills, for example, the working prototype would pose and elicit answers to critical questions about the product. For example, which features drive the most value for users? How much information are users willing to share about themselves? Are users willing to link access to their own accounts?

Once you have a working prototype, diary studies can be used to gauge user response in their own homes or workspaces over an extended period—perhaps twenty to thirty days. For instance, assume that you're developing a language learning app, and you've determined that daily usage is a key success criterion. A diary study allows you to gauge if the experience drives engagement and repeat usage, or if user enthusiasm dwindles after a certain point. You could interview users after the testing period, moreover, and get much deeper feedback than from, for example, a test conducted over a few hours in your offices.

Sometimes this kind of feedback identifies a serious flaw in the concept—an up-to-the-minute example of "fast fail." Sometimes the flaw can be rectified, and early tweaks can change a likely failure into a successful product launch. Other times, of course, the flaw turns out to be fatal—but if so, at least the investment in the product will have been purposefully limited.

Proof of Concept for AI Products

For advanced digital solutions, in which the feasibility of the technology poses the greatest risk to the concept proposition, the most important test is whether the application can be made to work effectively. In most AI applications, for example, the first task is to review and select the most appropriate LLM or "large language model." Examples include OpenAI's ChatGPT, Oracle's Cohere,

Google's Gemini, and Meta's Llama. Each has tradeoffs in terms of data privacy, cloud availability, features, licensing costs, and integration capabilities.

Once the LLM is selected, the next step is creation and validation of the proof of concept. Typically, this starts with prompt optimization (optimizing the AI instructions), then the use of various approaches for fine-tuning, followed by validation against training data. In many situations, these steps can be completed in a period of five to ten weeks.

For example, one multi-channel information company came up with the idea of a new offering on its app that would allow consumers to ask questions like, "What can we make for dinner?" The app would come up with dinner options and help plan future food shopping for consumers, using "smart refrigerators" that track food inventory by taking pictures of the fridge contents every time the door is opened. The app used object recognition from Clarified and Google Image AI to analyze the fridge contents and return a list of items in it. The only way to determine whether the idea could work in practice was to build a proof of concept and gauge the extent that the AI models could be trained to accurately detect and list items. But here you should conjure up an image of the chaotic real-world context for this proposed innovation: fridges in our houses and yours, full of items stacked on top of each other, often in unlabeled containers.

The conclusion? The fast-fail test showed that the concept could be made to work but only in controlled conditions. In that chaotic real-family refrigerator, the results were not accurate enough to carry the concept forward, at least not without the introduction of manual corrections that most consumers would find unacceptably tedious. Yes, with broad adoption and millions of corrections to improve accuracy, it was theoretically possible that the errors could be gradually eliminated. In terms of today's technology, however, it didn't seem possible to achieve the level of adoption needed.

Again: **In the case of a disappointing outcome, fast-fail concept testing can at least mitigate the costs.**

Use Platform Customers for B2B Solutions

For many B2B digital solutions, the innovation challenge is complicated by the fact that there may not be millions of potential customers. Instead, there may be only a few thousand—or, in some cases, just a few dozen. For example,

Atlanta-based Cognira is a developer of advanced solutions for very large and complex retailers, typically with several billion dollars in sales. CEO Hatem Sellami describes the challenge of getting his new company and product off the ground:

> We have maybe a hundred or so potential customers. They are like a small club who all talk to each other, and businesses like us are considered only as good as our last product. We could not afford to fail; we knew our first product needed to be a big success.[5]

Cognira's approach, therefore, was to start with a narrow application—advanced analytics to optimize retail promotions—where they knew there was a gap in the market. But how to develop, refine, and launch such a complex product from scratch? The company knew it had to **find a platform customer to partner with**. Ultimately, that partner turned out to be a very successful regional supermarket chain that had previously relied on home-grown solutions. Certainly, the fact that such a customer was willing to partner with Cognira served as solid confirmation of the gap in the market around advanced promotions management.

Manage Risks for B2B Customers

Business customers are naturally risk-averse, and this is particularly true for customers of software and digital products. It used to be said in business that "nobody gets fired for hiring IBM." Today's equivalent might be, "Nobody gets fired for using SAP or Oracle."

Given this risk-averse reality, how do you secure a platform customer—especially when you don't yet have a product you can show them? Sellami describes what Cognira did:

> Our approach was to break the problems down into modules requiring around six months each, and then guarantee the success of each module before moving on to the next. This reduced risk and gave the customer more control over the process. We were adamant about retaining ownership of the IP from the work, but flexible on all other aspects of the contract. Now,

several years after the original launch, we have a complete solution around retail promotions and have an expanding customer base with a pipeline of software solutions for other areas of retail.

Network Benefits for Digital Businesses

Everyone understands the network benefits for digital businesses such as Facebook, Instagram, WhatsApp, Snapchat, YouTube, TikTok, Waze, LinkedIn, and X (formerly Twitter). The more users you have, the greater the advertising revenues or data benefits, the more content you are likely to have access to, and the stronger your app's attraction for users. Seen in this light, it's easy to see why Meta acquired potential challengers Instagram and WhatsApp, why Google acquired YouTube and Waze, and why Microsoft acquired LinkedIn.

Assessing network benefits is an important part of determining the potential of digital businesses. Very few companies can hope to emulate the extraordinary success of Facebook or YouTube, but all kinds of digital businesses need to consider whether their business can be configured to take advantage of network effects.

Exocad—a digital dental company based in Darmstadt, Germany—was founded in 2010. The company spotted an opportunity when it realized that dental restorations were increasingly no longer being made from physical molded impressions of a patient's mouth but instead were being generated through digital imaging and production. The leading dental companies at that time were promoting closed systems involving their proprietary scanners, computer-aided design (CAD) tools, implants, and lab communications. This made sense for the big manufacturers, but less so for dentists who did not want to be locked into a single system.

Exocad created an open communication platform allowing dentists and labs to share patient images and files from multiple manufacturers. The network benefit was that the more dentists and labs used the software, the more powerful the demand would be for manufacturers to make their products compatible. Exocad was acquired by Align Technology in 2020 for more than $400 million; by 2023, Exocad software solutions were being used in more than 150 countries.

A Special Context for Innovation: Leaner, Faster, and Networked

In this chapter, we don't attempt more than a brief overview of innovation in the digital space. Each of the topics we touch on here could be the subject of entire books—and in fact, many already are.[6]

But in summary, digital and software businesses are different from the rest of the economy. They don't have physical products or showrooms that customers can visit. Many do not even have a sales force. Yes, **digital businesses own software code, but their most important assets are (1) their product performance, and (2) their network of customers, suppliers, and partners**.

As more and more products and services within the global economy acquire digital elements, they increasingly show attributes associated with those digital components. The only way to maintain leadership is through a continuing process of reinvention—made possible by lean development tools, constant vigilance, and many of the other tools and techniques described in this book.

EXECUTIVE SUMMARY

Embrace continuous upgrades and lean development for digital-led businesses.

- Digital-led businesses, such as software companies, often face low barriers to entry, constant challenges from new entrants, and the need for continuous, rapid innovation.

- Just as mature manufacturing businesses compete on the basis of low-cost manufacturing, digital businesses need to configure themselves for low-cost innovation and development.

- There is a range of proven approaches that digital businesses can employ to deliver rapid, low-cost product development, including design sprints, AI tools, partnering with platform customers, and exploiting network benefits.

SEVEN

Move Up the Detect-Analyze-Act Pyramid to Enrich Products Using Digital

Sometimes it seems hard to point to any corner of the economy that is untouched by digital applications—whether they make sense in those corners or not.

Let's assume that in your personal life, you're on the upper end of the tech scale. If so, your toothbrush may be teaming up with your smartphone to tell you how well you're brushing and how you might do better. When you want to retrieve the results of a biopsy from your dermatologist, you may have to download an app and create a profile and a password. When you are riding your electric bike, it may be that the only way to know how much battery charge you have left is to use an app on your phone that connects to the bike via Bluetooth.

Now let's look at a very different, less personal realm: the world of drones and what's called "action cameras." These technologies require a mass storage device, a high-resolution display, and a way of sharing and editing images and video. The user leverages each of these capabilities through a smartphone connection.

Aside from context, the difference between the first set of examples and the second is that in the first, digital is an add-on feature to the service or product, and one that may or may not be valued by the customer. In many cases, the appeal of this add-on is no sure bet. At least *some* customers would prefer to track their own tooth-brushing, would prefer to get a call from the dermatologist's office, or would like to have a charge-indicator gauge mounted on the handlebar of their bike for easy reference.

By contrast, in the second example, we have what is genuinely a better customer solution. Yes, these systems require a phone, an app, and a Bluetooth connection to make things go, but that makes *sense*, because the alternative—building those capabilities into a self-contained device—would make that resulting device heavy, unwieldy, and far more expensive.

So the first question you need to ask about a proposed digital innovation is, *Is this really an enhancement?* Does the new technology or technological overlay really improve the customer experience enough to offset any related learning curves, inconveniences, and cost bumps? To use a medical analogy: "First do no harm."

But you should be able to do much better than that. Figure 7.1 shows a framework we use to help companies identify and develop opportunities to grow their businesses and serve their customers better using digital technologies.

The bottom left quadrant is about expediting the use of digital technologies to enhance the current customer experience and defend the current franchise. The chances are that your competitors are already working on ways to upgrade the customer experience through digital. If your business is not at least matching that, then there is a risk of falling behind and losing share. These opportunities should have the highest near-term payback.

The upper left corner is where companies can often find opportunities to develop digitally enabled new products or services that build on existing services and capabilities. These should also offer good near-term payback, while allowing the company to learn and develop as an organization.

Finally, on the right-hand side we have opportunities that involve entering new markets and developing entirely new capabilities. These will have a longer-term payback but will often provide a stepping stone into entirely new areas of growth.

Applying the Framework: Collins Aerospace

We can apply the framework by looking at one company that has a long history of asking these questions—and, as a result, of effectively using digital technologies to improve the customer experience: Collins Aerospace, now part of

FIGURE 7.1. Digital Innovation Framework

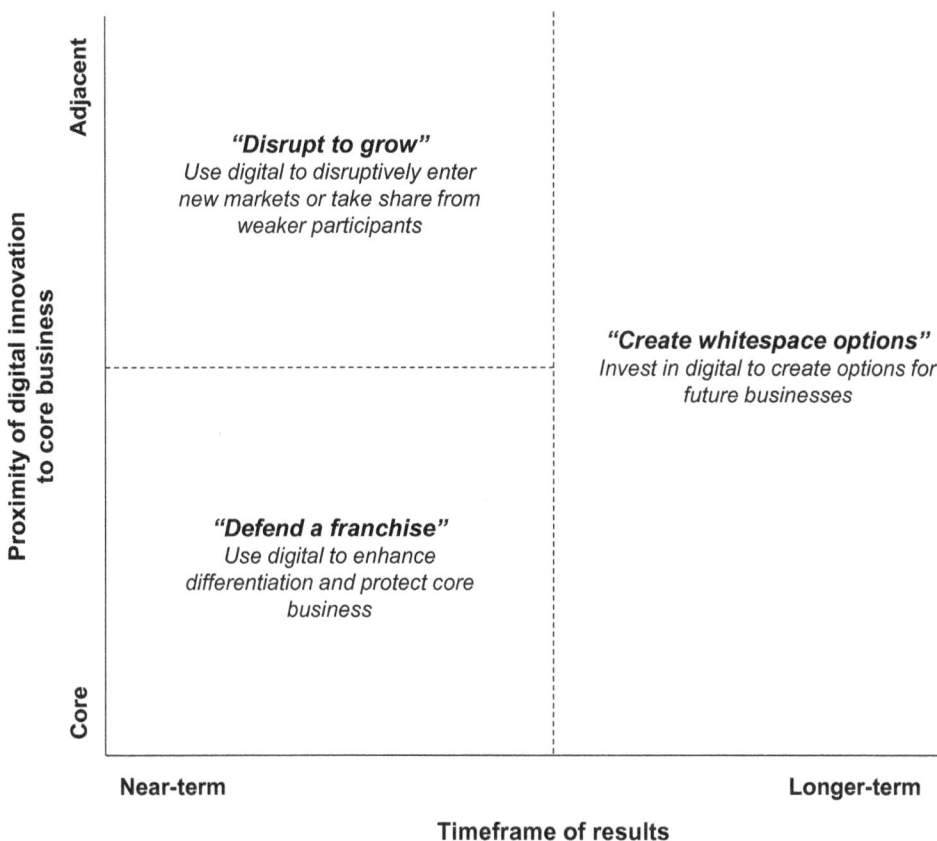

"Disrupt to grow"
Use digital to disruptively enter
new markets or take share from
weaker participants

"Create whitespace options"
Invest in digital to create options for
future businesses

"Defend a franchise"
Use digital to enhance
differentiation and protect core
business

Adjacent

Core

Proximity of digital innovation to core business

Near-term   **Longer-term**

Timeframe of results

RTX.[1] Collins Aerospace was formed when UTC acquired Rockwell Collins in 2018, merging it with UTC Aerospace Systems.

Rockwell Collins started out as the Collins Radio Company in Cedar Rapids, Iowa, in 1933, making shortwave radio equipment. It developed a reputation for producing high-quality flight-control instruments and radio communication devices and was a key supplier to the NASA space programs in the 1960s and '70s.

In 2000, Collins introduced the Pro Line integrated avionics system for business aircraft cockpits. Before this innovation, pilots had to scan six key flight instruments to maintain safe flight: airspeed, altitude, attitude indicator, compass, vertical speed, and slip-skid indicator. The Pro Line 21 used digital display technology to combine all of this information into a single primary flight display as well as provide other situational awareness capabilities with checklists, terrain maps, airport maps, and the like. This made flying both easier and safer, especially for single-pilot operations. In the years immediately following its introduction, this much-improved user experience led to rapid adoption by most leading business aviation manufacturers, and it proved to be the beginning of what has become a revolution in the way pilots and their aircraft interact. The plethora of round "steam gauges" that once made aircraft cockpits so complex and intimidating are now found only in older-generation or vintage aircraft. Today, almost all new aircraft are delivered with flat-screen primary flight displays—and the reaction of pilots experiencing the new displays for the first time tends to be amazement at the way so much information can be packed into a single two-dimensional image.

Our point: The Pro Line 21 integrated avionics launch is a perfect example of using digital technology to defend the core business and get ahead of competitors. Collins got there first, with a great product, but competitors were also working on their own versions of the same thing. Sometimes the difference between success and failure is all about speed to market.

More recently, Collins Aerospace has broadened the scope of how it thinks about using digital technologies to improve customer outcomes. Rather than simply focusing on how to make their existing products better, the company took a fresh look at the most pressing needs their customers were facing and how it might help address those needs. It began with the recognition that to address the industry challenges with new and impactful solutions, they needed to look across all customers and users: aircraft manufacturers, commercial airlines, airports, and, of course, passengers. Collins came to the conclusion that beyond the obvious and overriding need for safety, the biggest priorities for their customers were improved passenger experience, greater efficiency, sustainability, and increased on-time performance. Collins realized that there were data and tools available that could help address each of these developed priorities, but it required the available information to be gathered, combined, and interpreted appropriately.

The framework that Collins used to address this challenge was labeled the "connected aviation ecosystem," which they defined as the digitization of the aviation industry through connectivity, analytics, and value-centric solutions. For Collins, this ecosystem is industry-wide, and Collins's role is to accelerate the industry's ability to benefit from it. Making this vision a reality involved gathering several of Collin's existing businesses together into a new Connected Aviation Solutions (CAS) business unit. The first step—gathering information—continues today and includes deploying wireless sensors or using existing data sources on everything from galley equipment to wheels and brakes; using the company's FlightAware platform to understand the latest aircraft locations, traffic patterns, and delays; leveraging the company's ARINC networks, which manage air-ground connectivity to move aircraft data and messages; and gathering data from airport gates, check-in desks, and baggage operations. But gathering and combining are only the preliminaries. The real value add from the connected aviation ecosystem derives from using machine learning and advanced data analytics to predict future outcomes. This capability helps keep passengers better informed and helps operators get ahead of problems before they escalate into delays, cancellations, and costly operational issues.

Erin McCleave, vice president of strategy and transformation for the Collins Connected Aviation Solutions unit, describes getting the new concept off the ground:

> The critical ingredient was getting all the different parts of the solution to collaborate and work together. We knew we were breaking new ground and we believed in our ability to deliver something different than Boeing and Airbus were trying to do with their own integrated programs, because of our unique combination of aircraft systems knowledge and digital capabilities. We could not afford to have pieces with different reporting relationships scattered across the organization, so to be able to be focused and run fast we brought all the capabilities together into a single business under Collins with its own P&L, operating model, unique engineering skillsets, sales force, and service and support approach. We were a new business, but we also had strong capabilities and legacies; on day one we already had a team of two thousand people and over five thousand customers.[2]

Some elements of the connected aviation ecosystem, such as the maintenance reporting systems, were near-term adjacencies in the top left corner of

Figure 7.1, but others, including the flight profile optimization and linkages to airline passenger operations, represent new white space initiatives. They made sense because the value of the integrated system is greater than the sum of its parts.

Detect, Analyze, and Act

Collins provides a good example of the value of pursuing both close-in and longer-term digital opportunities. The company's strategy also illustrates what we call the *Detect-Analyze-Act value pyramid* for digital data and insights. See Figure 7.2.

In the most complex digital ecosystems we have looked at—including healthcare, aerospace, automotive, transport, entertainment, and others—there are typically billions of data points making up the base of the pyramid, and the value of any company **detecting** and adding to that base of information can be measured in pennies per data point. But if data can be combined and **analyzed** to create useful insights, those insights may be worth dollars, rather than pennies. Examples might include a warning on a hospital infusion pump that has detected a risk of dangerous drug interaction, a maintenance system that senses a high risk of an imminent failure, or a customer behavior that indicates a strong prospect for new services. **If you are at the *Analyze* level of the pyramid, the insights still require the user to make the ultimate judgment and take any required action.**

FIGURE 7.2. Detect-Analyze-Act Digital Framework

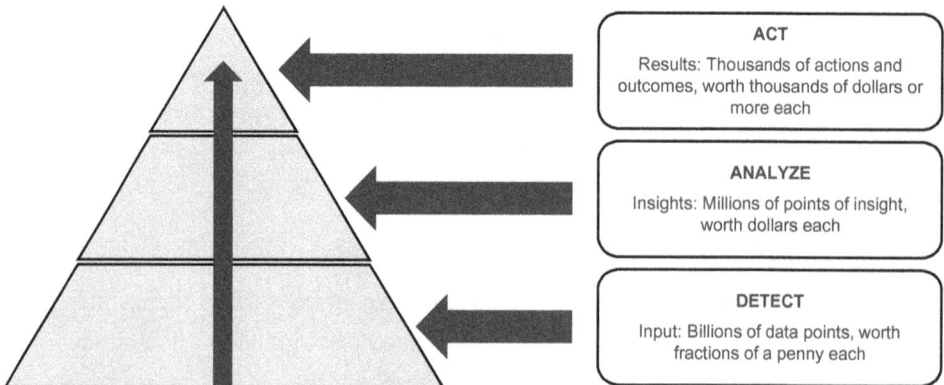

ACT
Results: Thousands of actions and outcomes, worth thousands of dollars or more each

ANALYZE
Insights: Millions of points of insight, worth dollars each

DETECT
Input: Billions of data points, worth fractions of a penny each

At the top of the pyramid, we have instances where the outcome from the system is *Action* **and results,** rather than just insight. Examples could be systems that reduce medication errors and result in fewer extended stays and improved patient outcomes, or removal of an aircraft component with a predicted failure before it has a maintenance issue that results in improved on-time performance for an airline. Again, if you can move up the pyramid from digital insights to action and results, then the value to each customer can easily be thousands of dollars—or sometimes much more than that.

Another illustration of the Detect-Analyze-Act value pyramid can be found in diabetes care. Diabetes is a chronic health condition that affects how the body turns food into energy. Insulin, naturally released by the pancreas, plays a critical role in letting blood sugars into the body's cells for use as energy. With diabetes, the body either doesn't make enough insulin or can't use it as well as it should, so patients need to find a different way to manage blood sugar and insulin.

There are essentially three technologies for managing diabetes, which roughly correspond to different levels of the value pyramid. The most basic is blood glucose monitoring (BGM), which requires a small finger stick to get a drop of blood. The glucose level is then measured in a simple analyzer. BGM is convenient but adversely affects the patient's quality of life over time. (Patients justifiably complain about being human pin cushions.) At the same time, it is a low-margin technology, with the main cost being the lancets for the finger sticks, which cost a few cents each.

Medtronic pioneered the next level of technology—continuous glucose monitoring (CGM)—which involves an implantable device that sends a signal to a small external monitor worn by the patient, which then analyzes the results. The main cost of CGM is the sensors, which need to be replaced every ten days or so, and the transmitters, which last about three months. Overall, the cost for CGM comes out to a few dollars a day compared to pennies for BGM, but it can help patients achieve better outcomes with fewer ongoing irritations and adverse events.

The latest and most advanced technology is closed-loop CGM. This technology doesn't just advise patients when they need to adjust their insulin; a connected pump provides the appropriate insulin dose as needed, without any action on the part of the patient. The closed-loop systems typically cost several thousand dollars per patient per year—a significant premium over older tech-nologies—but for the most serious diabetes patients, they have been shown to deliver substantially better patient outcomes with fewer adverse events. Not surprisingly, there is a long-term trend away from the simple BGM toward the more advanced CGM and closed-loop systems. In other words, moving up the pyramid results in both an enhanced customer experience and a higher value add.

Of course, not all businesses can benefit from adding data connectivity or big data insights to their product or service. But the fact is, almost every busi-ness has a website and some kind of digital connection to their customers. This begs an obvious question: How can businesses at least make that connection as effective as possible? Although this is a book about innovation and not market-ing, we should point out that sometimes just creating a better connection to the customer is sufficient to make the leap up to a new level of service or product experience. We've studied and worked with hundreds of companies that have transformed their connection to customers into a unique and differentiated platform—an important step toward the kind of improved customer experi-ence we're discussing in this chapter.

One company that stands out is Saga PLC, based in the UK. For the first thirty years of its existence, Saga was a travel company for people aged fifty and over. It developed a strong reputation for reliable service, and in the 1980s it launched *Saga* magazine and began offering home and motor insurance and financial ser-vices. Private pet and medical insurance followed. The advent of digital market-ing has helped the company cement its customer relationships even further. As the company describes: "Saga exists to create exceptional experiences every day, while being a driver of positive change in our markets and communities. . . . At the heart of our business model is our drive to know more about our customers' wants and needs so that we are best placed to serve them."[3]

Saga provides an interesting example of a company embracing the "upward imperative" of the Detect-Analyze-Act value pyramid:

> The size of our database, and the depth of information we hold on our cus-tomer group, is one of Saga's key assets. The continual expansion and devel-opment of this data, coupled with our unique insights, allows us to develop products and services that are tailored specifically for this group.[4]

On the business-to-business side, another company with a great track record of connecting with customers is McMaster-Carr. As an industrial distributor based in Chicago, McMaster-Carr sells MRO (maintenance, repair, and overhaul) products to help maintain factories and buildings. The company took a different approach from most of its competitors, deciding against the construction of a network of supply branches and instead relying exclusively on catalog—and now internet—sales. This put a premium on the company being able to deliver an exceptional customer experience, even though it was providing service remotely. In 2002, in a study by Stanford University, the company's website was ranked third in e-commerce websites behind only Amazon and Barnes & Noble. Since then (and unlike B&N), the company has continued to grow and expand, and it credits its customer-friendly e-commerce platform as a key component of its success.

Create Effective Digital Customer Connections

One of the most powerful applications of digital technologies is improving the speed and accuracy of customer communications. In that vein, we present **three rules for effective digital customer connections: 1. Be useful; 2. Be specific; 3. Be direct.**

The first rule is to make life easier for customers and, if possible, to **be useful** to them. Consider the first email to a new customer—the first "moment of truth" in starting to build a digital connection. "Welcome" and "thank you" are of course a good—even obligatory—start. Next, try to provide a nugget of useful information, such as "here's the tracking number for your order shipment," or, "here's the team who will be working with you." Avoid making demands of customers unless you can also point to a clear benefit for them.

Another way to be useful is by providing customers with valuable information. Companies love to know about their customers' and their competitors' trends and priorities. If you are a supplier to restaurants, chances are that your customers would love to know more about consumer trends. They would probably love to know what types of outlets and food styles are growing fastest or how different areas of the country compare. Being one step upstream in the value chain, as compared to your customers, should allow you to consolidate information to provide insights they cannot easily gather themselves. If you are selling to consumers, you can act as a hub for sharing ideas on useful apps and their applications.

Often the best way to be useful to your customers is to **be specific**. Let's imagine that you're a wine merchant who has created a beautiful new email campaign promoting select red wines. You have twenty thousand customers on your email list, and you're sorely tempted to send the new promotion to all of them. Why not? It won't cost you anything. The answer is because—as you well know—only two thousand of your customers are actually interested in reds from Bordeaux and Barolo. So why fill up the inboxes of those excellent customers who only ever buy Napa Valley Chardonnay and Sauvignon Blanc? By doing so, you're only creating what will be seen as spam by those customers and thereby teaching them to relegate your next communication—unread—to the trash folder.

Yes, it's tempting to communicate as often as possible—out of sight, out of mind, right?—but if you want to be useful to your customers, you have to listen to them, and you have to be specific—and that means being selective. In the early years of the internet, only a few companies such as Amazon or Netflix had the sophisticated algorithms to create targeted customer communications and recommendations, but with the recent ubiquitous availability of sophisticated marketing tools and AI, there is no excuse for not doing so.

Something that more and more companies are realizing is that it is hard to be useful and specific if you don't have a direct connection to customers. Distributors and intermediaries will always have a part to play with their readily assembled bundles of customers, but they are always at risk of being written out of the competitive script by customers who make the decision to **be direct**. You can benefit from this impulse on their part.

In 2023, nowhere is the switch to a direct model more pronounced than in pay TV streaming. Netflix was launched as an online streaming service in 2007. Rather than follow the model of other premium movie channels such as HBO, Netflix bypassed the cable and satellite TV operators who had previously acted as gatekeepers for different bundles of content. Customers loved the flexibility that Netflix offered, letting them choose from literally thousands of titles. Over time, other specialty content-owners saw that success and launched their own direct-to-consumer streaming services.

By 2016, the traditional TV channels were starting to fret, noting that millennial consumers were "cutting the cord" and switching away from traditional TV at an alarming rate. Their whistling-past-the-graveyard hope was that as these young consumers matured, they would revert to the same behavior as their parents and grandparents and embrace traditional media. But a pivotal 2016 study by our colleagues Martin Pilkington and Maria Palm showed that millennial and younger consumers were embracing new media even more strongly as they matured.

The writing was on the wall. By 2021, Netflix had exceeded 200 million subscribers across the world, while traditional TV had entered a slow but steady decline. Hundreds of millions of consumers are cutting the cord tying them to bundled pay TV services through cable and satellite operators and instead are embracing streaming services direct from content providers. The major content owners such as Disney have faced a difficult choice: either hold on to their highly profitable but slowly declining cable relationships, or launch their own direct streaming services. In the end, they have had no choice but to embrace the direct model—but Netflix, by being first to embrace that model, has had a huge head start.

This chapter has provided some initial perspectives on leveraging digital as part of new product initiatives. We will return to the topic again later in the book, where we (1) discuss the role that digital can play in defining the value proposition for a new product or service innovation, and (2) explore the costs and benefits of using different channels to bring your great product to market.

EXECUTIVE SUMMARY

Move up the Detect-Analyze-Act pyramid to enrich products using digital.

- Assess how digital technologies can improve the user experience and outcomes for your product or service (digital can benefit most businesses, but it needs to *genuinely* add value for customers).

- Use digital to defend existing franchises, disrupt and grow into adjacent areas, or unlock new opportunities in white space markets.

- Generate increased value from digital aspects of an innovation by moving up from *Detecting* data to *Analyzing* insights and ultimately to *Acting* on these insights to yield outcomes.

- Leverage digital tools to enhance customer connections and communications, keeping in mind three rules: 1. Be useful; 2. Be specific; 3. Be direct.

EIGHT

Use a Start-Up Mindset for Breakthrough Innovation in Large Companies

Many established and larger organizations develop successful models to nurture incremental innovation—but nevertheless still struggle with the kind of breakthrough innovation that's more often associated with independent start-up enterprises.

Obviously, the standalone start-up is a powerful platform for innovation and growth. At any given time, there are on the order of ten thousand emerging-growth businesses in California alone, with several hundred of those having already achieved "unicorn" status—that is, having achieved valuations above $1 billion before going public.

What explains this phenomenon? Whole bookshelves of volumes have been written on the topic, but very briefly, **start-ups tend to flourish when there is an established ecosystem of talented entrepreneurs and willing backers**. This creates a reinforcing cycle for exchanging and refining ideas; attracting, developing, and motivating talent; and recycling financial gains from successful exits into new opportunities.

But what if you are an established business trying to develop breakthrough innovation? One option is to simply outsource it, using your own financial heft to acquire businesses once they have proven a new concept that operates in the same general arena as your core business. Yes, there are obstacles inherent in this option, the most obvious being the acquisition cost and the need to integrate the new company's people and operations into your existing structures. Sometimes, however—for example, when the new company has developed a strong lead in a critical technology—acquisition may be your only option if you want to remain competitive. We will discuss acquisitions as a source of breakthrough innovation in Chapter 22.

But all too often, when a company completes a $500 million acquisition, you hear the internal teams saying, "Oh, well, *we* could have created that for $25 million!" In most situations, the internal team didn't get the funding because they didn't *ask* for it. In this chapter, we focus on how established businesses can build teams to target their own breakthrough innovations. A useful starting point is to **consider the challenges that internal teams face in comparison to their counterparts at well-funded independent start-ups** and **the ways companies attempt to mitigate those challenges**. Let's look at several key challenges and how companies respond to them.

We'll start with the *team*.

Build a Dedicated Team

In a sense, start-ups have it easy. Whether the innovation hinges on the work of a sole founder or that of a small team, the likelihood is that developing and launching the new product or service is the main or sole focus of the company and involves a relatively small core team.

At larger organizations, in contrast, we often see teams of ten, twenty, or thirty people involved in the development of a new concept. In theory, the inclusion of many people with a wide range of different backgrounds gives that team access to a broad suite of capabilities. In practice, though, many of those individuals are likely involved only on a part-time allocation, which means that their contributions—and by extension, the proposed breakthrough innovation—can easily be shoved aside by more urgent priorities. In effect, 10 percent of ten people's time is not the same as 100 percent of one person's time; it's much less. The best approach? The answer is generally to **start with two to four people who are devoted to the project full-time**.

Importantly, this team needs to consist of people with the right skills and outlook. As described in Chapter 3, breakthrough innovation requires different ways of thinking that can be at odds with the requirements for many corporate jobs, in which paying attention to detail and avoiding failures or omissions are critical attributes. When developing innovative concepts, however, people need to avoid cutting off ideas too early. At the outset, ideas should be judged on the opportunities and customer solutions they create. Yes, practical issues and roadblocks will have to be dealt with eventually—but that can happen later.

How to get there? How to make blue-sky thinking welcome? Many large organizations—including Disney, for example—have high-profile internal leaders whose role is to help spark creativity and innovation in their teams. Some companies rely on external speakers, coaches, and similar resources. Whichever tools you settle on, your organization needs to create an environment in which (1) naturally creative (but perhaps risk-averse) people are not just tolerated but are encouraged to *add value*, in roles that take full advantage of their abilities; and (2) those "liberated" individuals are balanced by others with more traditional skills in appropriate positions.

Balance Risks and Rewards for Team Members

Investments in the right kinds of innovative talent will be wasted if these people are not retained and motivated. Large organizations often tacitly present the prospect of punishments for product failures—with clear negative implications for subsequent careers—without presenting the prospect of extraordinary rewards for a breakthrough product success. This is ironic, because established organizations generally have the running room to do what they want. They can do any number of things to reward outsized successes—for example, making special stock grants if the new business line meets its goals and becomes established. At the same time, they can and should downplay the negative associations of product failure. Why shouldn't being part of a breakthrough new program—whether successful or not—be seen as a career requirement for those high-potential managers who want to rise rapidly through the ranks?

For most entrepreneurs pursuing breakthrough innovation, financial rewards are an important scorecard, but what *really* motivates most of them is the prospect of building and nurturing a team, seeing their product come to market, and building a business that has their name on the door. That kind of individual achievement and visibility are typical of standalone businesses, but they are easily obscured in the context of larger organizations. To offset this, **larger companies need to be proactive in celebrating innovation efforts and successes through company awards and public recognition**. This can take unexpected forms: For example, one company we worked with established a tradition of naming its meeting rooms after breakthrough innovators.

Celebrating the innovative role is particularly important as organizations look forward to the phases that come *after* concept development and ramp-up. As the new business matures, incremental innovation replaces breakthrough innovation, and vigilance and cost management become more important than creativity. Given that reality, it's often better for the successful leader to be moved into another early-innovation role, rather than encouraging them to grow with the business. Obviously, such a transfer needs to be managed delicately to avoid sending the wrong signal. It may be cast, for example, as a reflection of the company's determination to *hold on to* this rare talent by presenting them with a series of exciting new challenges. And this isn't just flattery; in a lot of cases, it *is* the best way to retain innovative talent.

Allow Accelerated Decision-Making with Guardrails

Entrepreneurs at standalone businesses have the authority to adjust priorities and reallocate resources according to changing circumstances. At the same time, they are subject to the discipline—sometimes the straitjacket—of limited available resources. Larger organizations have more flexibility. They can go some distance toward providing an environment of delegated decision-making. Of course, they do so within a defined budget and in keeping with ground rules that protect the parent company's larger interests—for example, on issues such as pricing or channel conflicts.

Compared to standalone start-ups, start-up teams within large organizations can and should have an important advantage because of their access to corporate infrastructure and capabilities. But sometimes those other corporate divisions see few incentives to supporting the start-up—and may even feel threatened by it, to the point that they actively withhold their support from the new venture. With this reality in mind, the company needs to take steps to encourage support, in part by providing fair incentives for cross-selling or sharing resources. It also helps to have a senior-level corporate sponsor who acts as a guardian angel for the start-up team. In the end, though, it's often best if the start-up retains the authority to go outside and find its own solutions, rather than being compelled to use reluctant in-house resources.

Define Clear Milestones and Tie Budgets to Achieving Them

For independent start-ups, the discipline of the fund-raising cycle provides important feedback on investors' satisfaction with progress toward goals. If the progress is there, more resources will generally be available; if not, the company will have to make do with the resources it already has or suffer the consequences of a down-round of funding, thereby creating unhappy investors and internal equity holders. This kind of "tough love" hurts, but it's generally beneficial.

Larger organizations should create a similar environment for their in-house start-ups, with clear milestones and expectations for the concept development and ramp-up phase. These could be financial metrics or—for longer lead-time innovation—could be related to product performance or market-testing outcomes. If performance exceeds expectations, you should consider accelerating the roll-out with increased funding. Conversely, if progress stalls and the project falls behind schedule, then you may need to impose the same discipline that venture capital investors rely on to avoid over-investing in a losing proposition.

Table 8.1 provides a summary of the key organizational challenges and potential solutions for early-stage development of breakthrough innovations in large organizations:

Example of Breakthrough Innovation Challenges at a Large Corporation

Let's take a deeper look at breakthrough new concept development in a large organization: this time in the context of Walmart—the world's biggest retailer (more than $600 billion in revenues in 2023) and also the world's largest private

TABLE 8.1. Solutions For Managing In-House Start-Ups

Challenges for In-house Start-ups	Solutions for Large Organizations
Lack of focused resources	Create small, dedicated teams
People lacking creativity and risk tolerance	Provide coaching; be a home for varied talent
Insufficient incentives given career risks	Increase rewards; make it a rite of passage
Lack of recognition and ownership stake	Create legacy-like recognition
Slow decision-making	Delegate decision-authority, within boundaries
Inconsistent support from divisions/functions	Encourage support, but allow go-arounds
Lack of feedback from fundraising cycle	Tie resources to progress against milestones

employer (2.1 million employees). As we'll see, sometimes things go according to plan, up to a certain point, and then go off the rails—but even then, there are still powerful lessons to be learned.

In September 2019, Walmart opened its first "Walmart Health" location in Dallas, Georgia. Located next door to a Walmart Supercenter—and with a separate door—the clinic's initial offerings included primary care, counseling, home care, eye and hearing exams, and dentistry.[1] The new facility aimed to offer basic medical services at prices between 30 and 50 percent lower than elsewhere. Pricing would be upfront and transparent. Care would be delivered by local medical professionals and offered during extended hours.

This initiative dated back to 2014, when Walmart created what became known as "Store No. 8." The name was borrowed from the chain's eighth store, opened years earlier in Morrilton, Arkansas, which was the location where company founder Sam Walton experimented with unorthodox retail ideas. In other words, the original Store No. 8 was a place dedicated to what might be called controlled risk-taking.

The new "Store No. 8" would try to find or grow three types of companies: those developed from scratch internally, those acquired to gain control of novel concepts, and those acquired because they had special capabilities that could be imported into the retail sector and scaled. In all cases, leaders of these companies had to have led a start-up, had to have experience in team-building, and had to relate to Walmart culturally. All Store No. 8 ventures would have their own boards, executive leadership, and business metrics—including things like repeat business, successful demonstrations of technology, and a continued positive read on the unit's strategy and economic potential.

Store No. 8 hit the ground running, starting two companies in its first year, three in its second, and two in its third. Almost inevitably, the Store No. 8 team became increasingly focused on healthcare delivery: an industry worth more than $2 trillion in 2022. Competitors like Target, Walgreens, CVS Health, and Rite Aid were already jumping into the healthcare pool. Walgreens, the second-largest pharmacy chain in the United States, had health clinics in four hundred of its stores and was about to experiment with standalone "Partners in Primary Care" clinics in Kansas City. Ominously—from Walmart's point of view—Amazon spent $1 billion in 2018 purchasing PillPack, an online pharmacy.[2]

In several important ways, Walmart too was already deep into the healthcare pool. By 2019, for example, the company was running a $40 billion business that provided in-store pharmacy and optical services. In addition, Walmart previously had experimented with in-store clinics in Georgia, South Carolina, and Texas. Those facilities, however, didn't include on-site doctors and only took up 1,500 square feet, as opposed to the 10,000-square-foot model now being planned for introduction in Dallas, Georgia. Sean Slovenski, Walmart's president of health and wellness, underscored that the 2019 push into Georgia was a top priority for the company's senior leadership. "We finally got to the point this past year with the right strategy, the right team, and the right timing," Slovenski said. "We recognized that Dallas, like so many communities across the country, was struggling to meet all the community's healthcare needs. And with the size and strength of Walmart, we knew we could make a difference by providing quality, preventive health services at affordable, transparent prices for all who need it—regardless of insurance status."[3]

By late 2020, there were five Walmart Health locations in Georgia and one in Arkansas, and the division was planning an expansion into Chicago, Jacksonville, and other parts of Georgia. Walmart Health also went into a partnership with BLOX, a modular builder of healthcare buildings. This partnership meant that local medical service centers could be fabricated at a central man-ufacturing plant and then erected quickly and cheaply in local settings. And beginning in spring 2022, Walmart Health's Florida locations adopted Epic health technology—the most widely used and comprehensive electronic health records system in the United States—allowing the growing Walmart Health network to share information among patients, health care professionals, insur-ance carriers, and other stakeholders.[4]

By 2022, there were thirty-two Walmart Health centers in operation. In March 2023, Walmart announced plans to open an additional forty-five facil-ities by 2024, a total that at that time represented a doubling of its footprint. The parent company continued to leverage its existing resources and by all accounts continued to think big: "With 90% of the U.S. population located within 10 miles of a Walmart," the company announced in a press release, "Walmart Health is in a unique position to provide quality, affordable health and wellness services where our neighbors already live and shop."[5]

But as we foreshadowed above, things don't always work out according to plan. Even with the best of intentions and efforts, entering an entirely new business through organic development can be extremely difficult. Ironically, this may be all the more true when the innovating company is a finely tuned and demanding organization like Walmart. Just over a year after its March 2023 expansion announcement, the company announced that—because its health care and virtual health care economics were not meeting expectations—it was shutting down all fifty-one Walmart Health Centers. Specifically, the company pointed to a "challenging reimbursement environment and escalating operat-ing costs" as key factors contributing to the decision.

We'll give the last word to Walmart. "While we will no longer operate health centers," a corporate press release summarized, pointing to a silver lining, "we will take what we learned as we provide trusted health and wellness services across the country throughout nearly 4,600 Pharmacies and more than 3,000 Vision Centers."[6]

Be Aware of the Challenges of Corporate Venture Capital

One way for large organizations to bring start-up company discipline to invest-ments in breakthrough innovation is through the **corporate venture capital**

(CVC) model. The CVC model sits about halfway along the spectrum between completely in-house development and arm's-length investing in external businesses. Simply stated, the parent company creates an in-house venture capital fund with a professional investment team that is measured on investment returns as maturing businesses are acquired into the parent's P&L at a fair price or spun off to operate independently or as part of an acquiring organization.

Of course, corporate venture capital is not a new model, having been pioneered by companies such as Xerox and DuPont more than forty years ago. But it has recently enjoyed a resurgence, fueled by the success of many venture-backed businesses; it has recently been taken up by such respected companies as Microsoft, Alphabet, and Amazon.

Figure 8.1 shows the recent growth in CVC investing, which spiked in 2021 and returned to what appears to be a more sustainable growth rate the following year.

GV, formerly Google Ventures, stands out as one of the more high-profile corporate venture capital arms. Established in 2009 as the venture capital subsidiary of what is now Alphabet, GV focuses primarily on early-stage start-ups, actively participating in Series A and Series B funding rounds.

FIGURE 8.1. Corporate Venture Capital (CVC) Funding Chart

Global CVC-backed Funding
(2018–22)
Billions of dollars

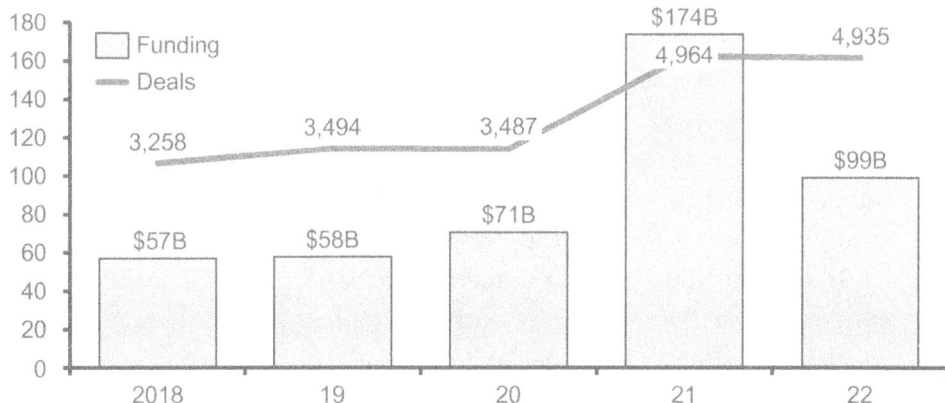

According to the Google website, GV operates on long time horizons, think-ing in terms of decades. At launch, it had a $60 million capital commitment and the "desire to partner with founders moving the world forward."[7] Today, GV has more than $8 billion in assets under management, claims some four hundred active portfolio companies across North America and Europe, and boasts of notable investment outcomes, including Uber, Nest, Slack, GitLab, Duo Security, Flatiron Health, Verve Therapeutics, and One Medical.

According to GV's website, success hinges on its experienced team, which includes seasoned venture capitalists, entrepreneurs, and industry experts. Beyond traditional financial support, the GV team offers invaluable hands-on guidance and strategic mentorship to start-ups. And, of course, being part of the Alphabet family provides GV with access to Google's vast resources and networks. From the outside, it's not clear what kinds of support GV-backed businesses actually receive. It's safe to say, though, that these investments have given Alphabet an insider's look into, and what amounts to a call option on, a wide range of emerging (and possibly breakthrough) technologies.

While the likes of high-flying Alphabet, Amazon, and Microsoft have no problem attracting top venture industry talent for their CVC investing, this has historically been a challenge for more traditional companies that have ex-perimented with the model. One reason is that many of the traditional cor-porations that experiment with CVC struggle with the idea of *letting go* and learning to live with effectively independent businesses—and they therefore end up experiencing all the challenges associated with in-house start-ups that we described earlier in this chapter.

But even at forward-looking companies, things can go bad in the CVC space. Take for example Intel's New Device Group, launched in 2015. The team had ambitions to break into the wearable-technology space and other new growth markets to complement Intel's commanding lead in the semiconductor business. Intel sank hundreds of millions into investing in new technologies and development, including investments in Basis Science, a smartwatch busi-ness, and Recon, a maker of wearable displays for active users.

Theoretically, these emerging technologies would be amplified inside of the Intel engine, which would help fast-track them to success. In reality, though, the group struggled to produce results. Product wins kept going to competitors like Fitbit and the Apple Watch, and while a few devices did make it to market, none of them achieved the hoped-for commercial success. The group had to deal with layoffs beginning in 2016, and eventually the plug was pulled in 2018.[8]

So while the rationale underlying CVC—that it's potentially safer than direct in-house development—seems solid, remember that the risks of investing in unproven technology are always present.

Alignment and Investment

One of the primary challenges that can arise with CVC—as those involved at Intel certainly learned—is that **corporate strategic goals frequently fail to align with the ambitions of start-ups.** The need to generate profits and satisfy shareholders can cause corporations to unintentionally sabotage their CVC endeavors. Start-ups need time to develop and reach their full potential; corporations prioritize short-term gains. Managing these conflicting imperatives is a delicate balancing act. In addition, the importance of *autonomy* to start-ups can't be overstated. Their ability to make independent decisions often forms the foundation of their success, and excessive corporate intervention can stifle creativity and take away growth options or attractive exit pathways that might conflict with the corporate parent.

Additional factors—including the inherent volatility of the start-up environment, inadequate due diligence, evolving corporate priorities, financial limitations, and fierce competition—all play a part in shaping the demanding CVC landscape.

So what's the right response? For companies that don't have the scale of Alphabet or Amazon (and the associated ability to absorb start-up losses over extended periods), the better model for CVC may be to **take a minority stake in an independent fund, with professional management, incentives, and long-term return metrics.** This can give companies a window into new start-up technologies and business models, with the potential for more favorable accounting treatment than would pertain to a wholly-owned fund.

Another alternative is to sidestep CVC altogether and simply **make direct minority investments in emerging businesses that compete with the parent's core business** but are not yet big enough to justify the expense and upheaval associated with a full acquisition. If the emerging model reaches a certain scale, then the parent company will be well positioned—and may in fact feel compelled—to bring that emerging model into the core business and deal with any resulting conflicts.

This is what happened at Disney, which in 2009 acquired a 27 percent stake in the streaming service Hulu, even though Hulu's strategy conflicted with Disney's own preferred model of working through bundled cable providers. Eight years later, after Hulu and other streaming services had grown enormously, Disney increased its position to gain control of Hulu through the acquisition of 21st Century Fox's Hulu stake and an agreement with Comcast. In 2019, Disney launched its own streaming service, Disney+, into which it folded Hulu.[9]

The upshot? On balance, while CVC or minority investing can play a useful role at some corporations, our experience is that **most companies are better off finding ways to support breakthrough innovation as part of their mainstream operations**—using all the tools described at the beginning of this chapter—or **sourcing early-stage breakthrough innovation through acquisition**, as described in Chapter 22.

EXECUTIVE SUMMARY
Use a start-up mindset for breakthrough innovation in large companies.

- Be aware of the seven organizational barriers that can make breakthrough innovation harder *inside* established organizations.

- Take advantage of proven approaches to mitigating these barriers through innovation-friendly team structures, coaching, incentives, recognition, and resourcing.

- Understand the benefits and potential pitfalls associated with corporate venture capital (CVC) and other investment models designed to nurture breakthrough innovation *outside* existing business structures.

Part 2: Developing Product and Service Concepts Checklist

Configuring for Success
- ☐ Use a systematic approach to reduce failures at every step of the innovation journey
- ☐ Manage risks by evaluating multiple indicators of success
- ☐ Avoid the seven behaviors that reduce the odds for many innovators

Developing Product and Service Concepts
- ✓ Look for what's broken, who's not being served, and how to leverage your strengths
- ✓ Take advantage of direct market feedback and rapid prototypes
- ✓ Embrace continuous upgrades and lean development for digital-led businesses
- ✓ Move up the Detect-Analyze-Act pyramid to enrich products using digital
- ✓ Use a start-up mindset for breakthrough innovation in large companies

Forecasting Revenue
- ☐ Build a business case to avoid the product graveyard
- ☐ Size the prize and identify the customers you will win
- ☐ Gather customer insights, not "voice of customer"
- ☐ Never take market research at face value
- ☐ Assume competitors are at least as smart as you
- ☐ Price to unlock the full value of your innovation
- ☐ Build a high-confidence revenue forecast
- ☐ Create a bulletproof business case

Ensuring Commercial Success
- ☐ Identify and lower the biggest barriers to adoption
- ☐ Plan enough but not too much, creating a "living" launch plan to ensure smooth execution
- ☐ Take the shortest path to value by optimizing launch scale and picking the right channels
- ☐ Prime the organization for a successful launch by tailoring capabilities and nurturing alliances

Creating Long-Term Value
- ☐ Turn a single success into an enduring franchise
- ☐ Make use of acquisitions and partnerships to accelerate innovation value
- ☐ Embrace proven pathways for long lead-time innovation
- ☐ Use incremental developments to complement breakthrough innovation
- ☐ Turn gaps into strengths for start-ups and entrepreneurs

PART III

Forecasting Revenue

A compelling revenue forecast and business case for a new product or service concept are critical to winning support from investors and other stakeholders. A rigorous research and forecast development process covering opportunity size, target customers, realistic adoption expectations, competitive threats, and pricing will generate conviction in a revenue forecast and lay the groundwork for a successful commercial launch.

NINE

Build a Business Case to Avoid the Product Graveyard

In the preceding chapters, we explained the process of identifying and refining good ideas that can turn into successful products and services. Now we turn our focus to the next critical task facing anyone with a great product idea: persuading investors, senior leaders, and other stakeholders that this idea is worth their support—and their investment.

Of course, this process of persuasion tends to unfold very differently depending on the context. Are you an entrepreneur at a start-up or an innovator in a large corporation with well-established ways of doing business? Does your industry expect and welcome innovation or not? But no matter where you locate yourself across this wide spectrum of contexts, you're going to have to make the case for your proposed business.

The Five Elements of a Robust Business Case

Regardless of context, there are five key elements of a business case that are almost always the same:

- A clear articulation of the market need and why your product or service uniquely meets that need

- An explanation of which groups of customers will be served, both initially and eventually

- A projection of the size of the market opportunity and the growth you expect

- A defendable revenue forecast that encompasses customer-adoption expectations, pricing, and competitive dynamics

- A clear and specific view on the resources and investments required to enable the opportunity

In the next seven chapters, we'll consider each of these elements in turn, identifying best practices, tools, and techniques. We'll also discuss the traps that innovators commonly fall into, such as being misled by adoption-overstatement biases, focusing too much on early adopters, and underestimating competitors. Finally, in Chapter 16, we will discuss the approach for pulling all of these elements together into a compelling narrative that delivers the "ask" to investors, senior leaders, and/or partners.

We're well aware that, at least in some circles, the "business case" has gotten a bad reputation as a theoretical and impractical tool that, at best, unnecessarily slows innovation and, at worst, prematurely kills novel products (especially digital ones) that can't easily be evaluated by the same metrics as more traditional products. There's certainly some truth to these criticisms. But at the same time, there can be immense value in a business case that is put together correctly and that is at the right scale for the organization and context. Yes, the needs of a tech entrepreneur for a Series B fundraise are different from those of a young general manager trying to secure funding for a new product concept at a large consumer packaged goods company. But both need a compelling pitch to convince their audiences to invest in their product—and in them.

Avoid the Product Graveyard

First things first: **Going through the process of building a rigorous business case—in and of itself—increases your odds of success**. This is because innovators are forced to really think through all the critical aspects of their product or service opportunity, at a sufficiently thorough level to defend it to external audiences. Implicitly, this process helps you understand the road to take so that you can avoid the product graveyard and not serve as a cautionary tale to others.

The starting point for any great product is finding customers who will buy it. The product graveyard is full of great ideas that became great products that—as it turned out—no one actually wanted to buy. We provided one example in Chapter 3: the SaaS solution for hiring senior managers, which flopped in the marketplace. In subsequent chapters, we discussed at length the approaches that can be taken not only to come up with great ideas but also to vet and refine them so you can be sure there's someone out there who's willing to pay for your offering. And as noted, the business literature over the last two decades is rich with guidance about using lean principles—like validated learning—to stay out of the product graveyard. In our view, **an optimal "product/market fit" is a *necessary* but not a *sufficient* prerequisite for success.**

What else is needed? **Commercial success with a product or service requires finding not just a group of early adopters but also the next wave of adopters.** Otherwise, the innovation risks being relegated to a niche, only relevant to a small segment of the market, which usually isn't sufficient for building a viable long-term business. "Crossing the chasm" from early adopters to mainstream customers—a notion popularized by Geoffrey Moore—is the next necessary step.[1] You have to segment your customers effectively to go beyond early adopters and get to a broader customer runway. Imagine you're flying a plane: You surely don't want to run out of runway before you take off.

But a long customer runway by itself is still insufficient for success. Even if you manage to cross the chasm to a broader customer base, there's one more key challenge that needs to be met, and it can be the difference between the product Hall of Fame and the product graveyard: Are you positioned to win vis-à-vis competitors? **Just because you develop and sell a great product doesn't mean that you'll be the one to prevail in the market and capture the value you've created.**

Take the example of the Pebble smartwatch.[2] Pebble was an early innovator in the category, gaining initial traction via its 2012 Kickstarter crowdfunding campaign, which—at $10.3 million raised from sixty-eight thousand people—was the most successful Kickstarter up to that point. The company scaled rapidly, selling four hundred thousand watches by 2014 and more than 2 million by 2016.[3] But it soon ran into a host of challenges scaling the business (many of them tied to poor sales forecasting, which we'll discuss later), and it ultimately was surpassed by multiple fast followers, including the Apple Watch and Samsung Galaxy Watch. Simply stated, Pebble just couldn't innovate quickly enough in the fast-paced consumer electronics market, especially compared to the deep R&D pockets and captive ecosystem user bases of Apple and Samsung. The lesson? **Picking a market segment in which *you* can win is as critical as building the right product and finding customers who will buy it.**

In Chapters 10–16, we will focus on collecting the market, customer, and competitor insights needed to avoid the product graveyard and, ultimately, to build a compelling business case.

EXECUTIVE SUMMARY

Build a business case to avoid the product graveyard.

- Plan your business case process to collect the insights and data needed for the five key elements of a robust business case.
- Avoid the product graveyard by achieving product/market fit, finding early adopters *and* the next wave of adopters, and picking a market where *you* can win.

TEN

Size the Prize and Identify the Customers You Will Win

The most fundamental starting points for a business case are a thorough understanding of (1) the market opportunity and (2) the customers you are planning to serve. We will consider these two separate but interrelated topics in this chapter.

The size and potential growth of the opportunity are basic building blocks that all innovators assess. Is there enough to get excited about? Is the "juice worth the squeeze"? As we will discuss shortly, there are different ways to estimate and articulate the size of the prize that you are pursuing.

Related to this is identifying the customer segments you will pursue and in what order. This often links directly to the opportunity, given the size (and willingness to pay) of different customer segments. As discussed in Chapter 9 in the context of the product graveyard, defining a customer runway beyond your early adopters is critically important. In this chapter, we'll consider how to use "strategic" segmentation to identify your options and build this runway.

Define a "Big Enough" Market Opportunity

First things first: if the market you're planning to launch into (or create) is not big enough or does not have the potential to be big enough, it will be difficult to convince anyone to spend time and money on it. Of course, the definition

FIGURE 10.1. Market Sizing Framework

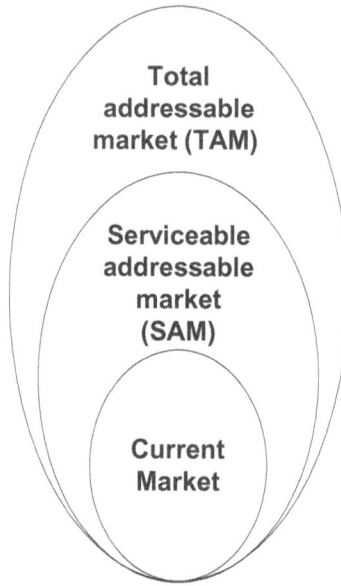

of "big enough" ranges quite widely across different industries and therefore is typically a reflection of your audience's frame of reference. In general, though, it's good to know the typical magnitude of markets being considered by your audience—whether it's hundreds of millions, billions, or tens of billions of dollars. **This market sizing is critical for setting the context for an innovation's opportunity**.

There are typically three different "sizing" exercises that can be useful for a business case. They can be most easily expressed as a series of concentric circles, as shown in Figure 10.1.

The innermost circle is the **current market** size. This is how much is spent on the relevant products or services by customers today—in other words, the aggregate revenue of all the current competitors in the market. The biggest circle is the **total addressable market (TAM)**, which is commonly thought of as the theoretical potential market. If all customers were spending as much as they could spend on the relevant products or services, how big would that market be?

Finally, the middle circle is the **serviceable addressable market (SAM)**. This is often the trickiest to quantify, but it's a helpful measure to consider. Why? Because the current market is usually insufficient for a new product or service, given that innovations typically expand the current market rather than just take share from existing competitors. Although many innovators expend significant effort defining their TAM, it's a measure that's ultimately too theoretical to be useful, other than as a ceiling against which to compare your SAM. This means that **in most cases, your focus should be your SAM**.

To bring this to life, we provide an example in Figure 10.2 with the U.S. market for outpatient mental health therapy. In this case, we've defined the SAM based on two drivers: increasing the proportion of diagnosed patients who get treated and increasing the frequency with which patients who are treated see their healthcare provider (i.e., optimal treatment beyond the standard of care, or SoC). These are both tangible dimensions that can be impacted

FIGURE 10.2. Market Sizing Waterfall Example

U.S. market for outpatient mental health therapy, 2019
$, Billions

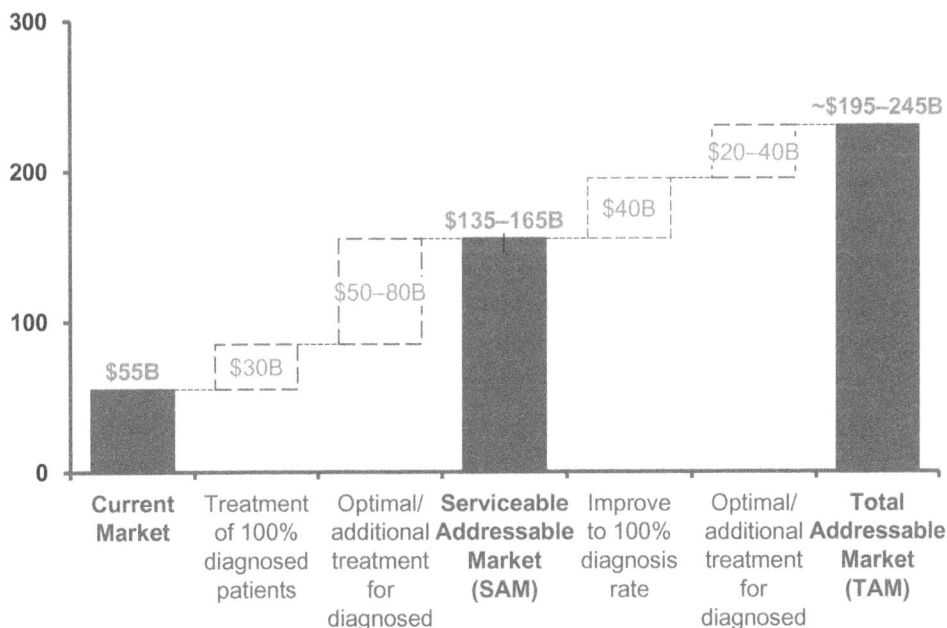

by an organization trying to expand the market. Assuming a 100 percent di-agnosis and treatment rate in the entire population and optimal treatment for each of those patients brings us to a TAM, but it's highly theoretical and cer-tainly not as actionable.

SAMs can be defined by addressable customer segments (e.g., fully pene-trated vs. completely unpenetrated), geographies (e.g., currently covered vs. not), and features/revenue streams (e.g., offered vs. not offered), among other possible dimensions. A SAM can also be defined differently for two players in the same market. For example, Whole Foods, a leading grocery retailer, operates in for-ty-five U.S. states, whereas Winn-Dixie, a regional grocery chain in the south-eastern United States, operates in five states. The two participate in the same broad market, but their SAMs are vastly different, being driven by their respec-tive geographic coverage of serviceable addressable households—or stomachs![1] A SAM can also expand over time as a product or business matures, accounting for an increasing proportion of the TAM (which can also grow, especially with population growth). The takeaway: **Your SAM is usually the key number that you want to showcase to potential investors, managers, and other stakehold-ers.** It's your definition of an aspirational but still achievable opportunity.

Identify Growth Tailwinds

Once a "big enough" market opportunity is established as context, the obvious next question concerns the potential growth of that market. As you'd expect, most investors and managers want to see both healthy historical growth in a market and the prospect of continuing growth. Again, *expectations matter.* If average growth in the markets your audience typically looks at is mid-single digits (e.g., something like 4–5 percent for the global medical device market), the people you're trying to pitch to may be excited by high single digits or just above 10 percent growth (which would be the case, for example, for continu-ous glucose monitors like Abbott's Libre), but a tech investor accustomed to growth rates at multiples of this would be disappointed by a "mere" 10 percent growth rate. While estimating the current growth rate is important, perhaps most important is being able to tell a story about how your product is aligned with the macro trends in the market and is expected to be buoyed by growth tailwinds, as opposed to hindered by growth headwinds.

So *your narrative matters*, too. How do you develop it? In some situations, good market growth data is readily available, or proxies—the number of subscribers to streaming services or the number of users for ridesharing apps—can serve your purposes. But if a more robust approach to quantification is needed, **it may be helpful to break market growth into its component parts: volume and price growth**. Let's look at these in turn.

Volume is usually the most critical and most challenging aspect of growth to estimate. There are multiple variables that may contribute to both murkiness and volatility in the metric: the underlying growth in the number of potential customers or users, the *propensity* of product use (in other words, the percentage of potential customers using), and the *intensity* of product use (that is, the number of units per customer).

Price may seem self-explanatory, but it can get tricky when—for example—you seek to account for inflation. (Unless absolutely necessary, we recommend avoiding inflation forecasts, which are best left to the economists.) In most cases, there are established industry norms and expectations for price growth or declines that you can build into your pricing assumptions.

One important aspect of price that is often missed, though, is *product mix*. In many markets, there is an ongoing shift to higher-value, more premium products, which impacts the average sales price (ASP) of products in the market. This overlooked but important dynamic is particularly evident in product markets in which technologies are becoming smarter via digital and IoT capability additions. The automotive industry, for example, has experienced this dynamic, and ASPs for new vehicles have grown 1 to 2 percent above inflation historically.[2]

Finally, remember that when you bring volume and price growth together to calculate a total market growth rate, they do not technically sum to the total, because they compound one another (e.g., 10 percent volume growth and 10 percent price growth together will yield 21 percent market growth in five years). In most situations, though, adding volume and price growth gets you close.[3]

Now, with a reasonable estimate of growth and its key "drivers" (e.g., underlying volume, trends in propensity of use, trends in intensity of use, price growth from product mix shifts), you can begin to craft a narrative on how your innovation is impacted by these drivers. Are you offering a service that benefits from greater interest in outsourcing due to regulation, making in-house options more difficult and expensive? Are you providing a digitally enabled product that creates efficiencies for customers who are struggling with labor shortages? Are you catering to shifts in consumer tastes toward a new way of consuming a product? You can see how this plays out. **You need a narrative for your innovation that recognizes the changes in the relevant market and, optimally, links your innovation to these changes in a positive way.**

Segment the Universe of Potential Customers

Once you have contextualized the opportunity for your product with market size and growth estimates, it is time to define your universe of potential customers.

That universe, which can be very broad, is commonly reflected in your TAM (again, your total addressable market): the universe of customers to whom you could potentially sell. This usually includes both the *number* and *key types* of potential customers, which can often be derived from industry and market research sources. For example, W.W. Grainger, a leading U.S. distributor of maintenance and repair products (and competitor to the aforementioned McMaster-Carr), defines its universe of customers as every nonresidential building in the United States and is able to use data from sources like the U.S. Census Bureau to get an estimate of the number of facilities by type (e.g., factories, warehouses, schools, offices). Less patient business leaders—which, let's admit, is most of us—often skip this step and instead focus immediately on identifying target customers.

But impatience here is often a mistake. Why? Because in most cases, it's valuable to be familiar with your full set of customer options, both currently and in the future. And it's as important to **understand which customers you will *not* target (or at least not yet) as which ones you *will* target**.

Once the universe of potential customers is defined, *segmentation* becomes critical to the process of customer targeting. Plenty of books exist on the topic of segmentation, so we won't cover this rich field of marketing theory in detail, but we will comment on different approaches and tools and when they are useful.

Let's begin by clarifying what we mean by "segmentation," which is one of the most overused words in business. On the face of it, the principle of

segmentation is quite clear: splitting customers into groups reflecting simi-
larities that matter for selling or servicing them. But there are different types
of segmentation that can be put to different uses. In a prior book, we artic-
ulated the difference between a *marketing* segmentation and a *strategic* segmentation.[4] A marketing segmentation, used commonly by marketers and
advertisers, seeks to define customer groups useful for differentiating marketing channels, messages, and engagement approaches. By contrast, **a strategic
segmentation—used by general managers and product managers—seeks to
define customer groups where you can create and sustain competitive advantage to win.**

For the purposes of product innovation and launch, we focus on the latter:
strategic customer segmentation. In practice, we find that a useful strategic
segmentation creates customer groups that

- can be distinguished from one another via observable attributes (i.e.,
  who they are);
- seek meaningfully different value propositions as related to your product
  (i.e., why they buy);
- exhibit different willingness to pay for these value propositions; and
- demonstrate differences in how they buy the product.

In our experience, customer segmentation is as much an art as it is a science.
**Judgment is required to decide which dimensions matter to make a segmen-
tation not only accurate but also useful for selling.** We find that **the optimal number of customer segments is usually three to five.** Fewer than three
doesn't create enough separation between customer groups, and more than five
is too burdensome for commercial efforts. Of course, this can vary, and certain
types of businesses may require more segments (e.g., the Grainger example
above). Again, experience and judgment should come into play.

You are likely to find that there are multiple dimensions that you can consider in strategic customer segmentation. These can include, for example, demographic (B2C attributes such as age, gender, and income level), "firmographic"
(B2B demographics such as industry, company size, and financial standing),
psychographic (attitudes, values, interests, and beliefs), behavioral (actions and
behaviors in usage and purchase decision-making such as occasions, loyalty,

and buying habits), technographic (technology usage and online behaviors), and user status (active, lapsed, and prospective product users).

For strategic segmentation, we often find that at least two of these dimensions are necessary, but more than three are rarely helpful. Typically, either demographics (B2C) or firmographics (B2B) is required to create observable customer segments. The second dimension is usually the trickier one. For consumer products, for example, the psychographic dimension can be very powerful. It can draw out unique insights for targeting that enable much more thoughtful differentiation compared to competitors and therefore have a host of downstream implications for marketing (e.g., positioning, messaging). For many other types of product and service categories, behavioral and user status can be more powerful dimensions, since they directly help determine the best way to sell to a segment.

Regardless of the dimensions you end up using, our experience suggests that less is more. In other words, **use the smallest number of segmentation variables that still enables you to meet the requirements for a useful segmentation.**

In many ways, this approach is a practical application of the jobs-to-be-done or circumstances-based segmentation popularized by Clayton Christensen. Christensen pointed out that marketers often develop attribute-based segmentations that show correlations between behaviors and attributes of customers but don't capture the cause of the behavior. By focusing on the "job" that the product or service is being "hired" to do, you can understand why they are buying and therefore develop much more useful insights. This is closely linked to our second criterion for a strategic segmentation, which focuses on distinguishing different segments based on why customers buy.

Developing a strategic segmentation requires market insights and datasets on which to exercise your judgment. We will discuss gathering market insights, especially the methods for determining differences in why customers buy and distinct value propositions that matter, in Chapter 11. In the meantime, let's discuss how you might use data that you gather from various sources to analytically derive a strategic segmentation.

In cases where quantitative data is available—whether through online customer surveys, specialized industry datasets (e.g., point-of-sale data for consumer goods or prescription data for pharmaceuticals), or proprietary datasets (e.g., a company's customer sales data)—a variety of techniques and tools can be used to analytically derive customer segments. But we'll underscore again that **regardless of the sophistication and rigor behind segmentation analytics, it is still critical to *exercise judgment* to ensure that the segments derived are useful for finding and selling to distinct groups of customers.** For example, a "stressed homemaker" segment may emerge from your analysis. Fine—but if you can't identify and quantify who the customers in this segment are, it isn't a very practical differentiation.

To ground this discussion of segmentation in the real world, let's look at the example of lululemon athletica, inc. Founded in Vancouver, Canada, in the late 1990s with the intention of creating technical athletic apparel suitable for yoga, the company has grown at an astounding rate, achieving more than $8 billion in revenue in 2022. Lulu, as its loyal customers call it, innovated and popularized the yoga pant and has driven significant growth in the athleisure apparel category. Lulu's initial customer insight was tapping into a macrotrend emerging in the early 2000s focused on health and wellness, a trend embodied by the growing popularity of yoga in the United States and Canada. This was particularly evident among health- and style-conscious, affluent Gen X women, who became the company's initial primary customer target. By 2016, lululemon described its customer targeting strategy as follows:

> Our primary target customer is a sophisticated and educated woman who understands the importance of an active, healthy lifestyle. She is increasingly tasked with the dual responsibilities of career and family and is constantly challenged to balance her work, life and health. We believe she pursues exercise to achieve physical fitness and inner peace.[5]

Clearly, lululemon employed both demographic and psychographic attributes in determining which customer segments to target. It didn't just focus on women aged 18 to 35, for example, but on those with a specific mindset and set of motivations (seeking a specific set of use cases and benefits from athletic clothes). The company's later expansion of focus to include men with a similar demographic and psychographic profile (often married to and influenced by the primary customer), as well as teenage girls "growing into" the primary target customer segment, was quite logical. While highly effective segmentation was certainly not the only driver of lululemon's remarkable success, it has been an important contributor.

Lululemon had the advantage of relatively good and accessible data. But keep in mind that **segmentation does not always require the unearthing and analysis of massive datasets.** This is a common misconception. The truth is, there are many situations in which data just doesn't exist or is impractical to gather. In those cases, qualitative interviews with customers and other market stakeholders can (and must!) be used to arrive at a viable segmentation in a practical way. These are necessarily context-specific.

Take the pharmaceutical contract research market as an example. Pharma and biotech companies outsource a variety of research activities to specialized contract research organizations (CROs). Given that there are relatively few buyers of these services in each company, it is not practical to conduct a large-scale quantitative segmentation. But interviews can quickly make it clear that established pharma and early-stage biotechs have different decision-making processes and seek different support from CROs, given the differences in in-house research capabilities. Furthermore, needs also vary based on the therapeutic areas in which the company participates. Combining these two dimensions—company maturity and therapeutic area of focus—can yield a meaningful and useful segmentation.

Before we wrap up our discussion of segmentation, let's return to a central idea expressed at the beginning of the chapter: **Your approach to strategic customer segmentation should be the right size for the need.** An early-stage company may not need or have the resources to invest in a robust quantitative segmentation, even if that kind of segmentation is feasible. Early discussions with potential customers can often yield enough insight to develop a preliminary segmentation that can be vetted and refined as product development progresses. That said, the importance of a thoughtful and actionable segmentation can't be overstated.

Build a Customer Runway

We talked previously about customer runways and "crossing the chasm": that is, building upon your early adopters by adding more mainstream customers. Armed with a useful customer segmentation, skilled business leaders can approach and leap across that chasm by prioritizing the segments they want to target.

Where do you start? Finding your early adopters is usually not that diffi-cult. In fact, in the initial market-testing phase, it often happens organically. Which customers seem most excited and passionate about the product? Who is clamoring for the opportunity to try it? Many innovators find that early adopters can "just happen to you," meaning that they are often *not* the group initially hypothesized to be early adopters. Yes, anyone can sell a handful of products to friends, family, and tech junkies, but these are not what we call "early adopters." **Early adopters are not just customers willing to buy your product before anyone else; they are the customers who love your product.** Their passion and loyalty help you build a sustainable base of customers (and revenue) who serve as a reference and unlock network effects for later adopters. In other words, early adopters need to disproportionately care about your value proposition. Often, they are a subset or micro-segment within a broader group you have identified through your segmentation process (i.e., the "bullseye" of that customer segment, such as women yoga teachers for lululemon).

As you build your customer runway, then, early adopters come first. But who do you target next, and then who after that? Logically, one could just pursue the customer segment that loves your value proposition "next most" after the early adopters—that is, the second-most-passionate crowd. But here's where you have to factor in the size and accessibility of the opportunity. Should you prioritize a bigger, less passionate segment over one that is smaller but with whom your value proposition resonates more? (Sometimes the answer is clearly "yes.") And what about the feasibility of accessing those customers? Some customer segments may be difficult to reach because you don't have channel access, or it's prohibitively expensive. In addition, there could be in-terdependencies between customer segments (e.g., selling to one may make it easier to sell to another) and competitive considerations (e.g., an imminent new competitor may alter customer segment priority, or you may even focus on a segment to proactively discourage a competitive entry).

So determining the customer runway can involve a mind-boggling series of tradeoffs. The bad news is that there's no straightforward rule-of-thumb answer. You have to do the homework. You need to weigh the options and care-fully consider the tradeoffs of pursuing each customer segment in turn. The good news is there's rarely an overwhelming menu of options. Some options are clearly not viable, and if you typically only have five customer segments to choose from—see the relevant discussion above—it is usually a choice among the two or three that you are choosing to sequence. In our experience, **the most important determinants of customer sequencing are the relative strength of the value proposition and the feasibility of reaching the customer.** Other considerations may prove more important in one-off situations, but these two factors will always be high on the list.

Again, to bring this discussion to life, let's look at a real-world example, in this case the story of Intuitive Surgical. Intuitive is the pioneer and market leader in the rapidly growing field of robotic-assisted surgery (RAS), featuring its innovative line of da Vinci surgical systems. RAS enables minimally invasive procedures for patients across a variety of surgical specialties (e.g., urology, gynecology, general surgery, bariatrics), which can offer improved clinical outcomes (e.g., fewer complications, quicker recovery). It also helps physicians in their effort to reduce variability in the outcomes of their surgeries, improves their precision and vision, and provides better ergonomics—by allowing the surgeon to sit at a console with a monitor as opposed to standing hunched over a patient holding foot-long laparoscopic instruments (for hours on end, in the case of complex procedures). The major drawback to RAS is its cost (at least as an upfront cost for a procedure). As a rule, it's less expensive (sometimes *much* less) to perform many surgeries with traditional minimally invasive (i.e., laparoscopic) or open (i.e., with a scalpel) techniques.

Intuitive originally believed that cardiac surgery would be the most likely area for success with RAS, and there were what might be called "early adopters" who bought and used the product. These were often key opinion-leader surgeons at academic medical centers, interested in publishing and being the first to perform a certain type of procedure robotically. But referring back to our definitions of early adopters above, these academic pioneers did not constitute Intuitive's *true* early-adopter segment. The real early adopters—those who *really* loved Intuitive's value proposition—were urologists. Why? Because the urologist community discovered an ideal use for the system: radical prostatectomies (the removal of the prostate for patients with prostate cancer). Previously, given the hard-to-reach anatomy involved, most urologists couldn't perform this procedure with traditional minimally invasive techniques. But the da Vinci system made it possible. This shift from an open to a minimally invasive RAS procedure could meaningfully improve clinical outcomes for patients (e.g., less pain, faster recovery, lower risk of infection) as well as economic outcomes for hospitals and insurers (e.g., shorter hospital stays).

No, not all urologists were early adopters. For Intuitive, the micro-segment (or "bullseye") was urologists performing high volumes of prostatectomies at large community and academic hospitals that (crucially) could afford to make the initial capital investment in RAS. But as RAS increasingly became the standard of care (i.e., the preferred technique) and as access to RAS became an important tool for hospitals to differentiate themselves to patients, Intuitive was able to move quickly along to the broader population of urologists. By 2022, as much as 90 percent of radical prostatectomies in the United States were performed robotically.

As the da Vinci system began to demonstrate its value in the urology field in the large-hospital context, Intuitive continued to build a broader and longer customer runway. After urologists, the next customer targets were gynecologists, colorectal surgeons, bariatric surgeons, and general surgeons—and at an increasingly broader set of institutions beyond large community hospitals and academic centers. The company has driven maturation of each specialty along the S-curve of adoption by continuing to methodically build clinical evidence and support for additional regulatory approvals, while continuously developing the advanced instrumentation that surgeons require to perform a broader set of procedures. Intuitive has also proactively focused on addressing cost concerns by enabling (and proving with data) that high efficiency and utilization combined with reducing costly clinical outcomes can deliver economic benefits.

To summarize: In the case of Intuitive, the customer runway was dictated primarily by the relative strength of the RAS clinical value proposition but also by considerations such as the economics of hospital customers (e.g., minimum volume of procedures, the given institution's access to capital budgets), physician decision-making influence (e.g., urologists have greater influence than many other specialties), and technical complexity (e.g., adding advanced instruments to the da Vinci was difficult but important for general surgery). Success in urology soon opened the door to adoption across a range of other specialties, overcoming barriers to the initial investment that RAS required. Enhanced patient outcomes—and yes, to some extent, bragging rights—brought more and more hospitals on board. It is also worth noting that while Intuitive entered the market with well-informed hypotheses on which customer segments to target, its ultimate customer runway was shaped by real-world experimentation and results.

In short: Define your customers, find your markets, build your runway—and you're on you way to creating a predictable winner!

EXECUTIVE SUMMARY

Define the customers and markets where you can win.

- Define a "big enough" market opportunity. Focus on a serviceable addressable market (SAM) with a target that is aspirational but realistic.

- Identify growth tailwinds. Build a narrative that links market tailwinds to the opportunity for your innovation.

- Segment the universe of potential customers, focusing on a strategic segmentation that defines customer groups where you can create and sustain competitive advantage.

- Build a customer runway. Find early adopters who love your product, followed by segments based on the strength of your value proposition and the feasibility of reaching your customer.

ELEVEN

Gather Customer Insights, Not "Voice of Customer"

In Chapter 10, we discussed the importance of developing a strategic customer segmentation to identify segments in which you can win.

Of course, to do this well, you need to understand your customers. Early market feedback—as described in Chapter 5—is a good starting point. But while this can yield valuable insights, it doesn't usually provide enough information about your customers to segment them or plan for launch. This is when we turn to market research. The old adage from Marketing 101 is to *never assume your customers are at all like you*, and in practice we have certainly found this to be true. We therefore always advocate for sufficiently robust market research that can help put you in the customers' shoes.

Let's begin by underscoring the distinction made in this chapter's title: between what's typically termed "voice of customer" and what we consider meaningful customer insights. The challenge is that simply speaking to customers does not necessarily yield insights. For example, looking at the life insurance industry in the 1990s, some of our colleagues came to a dramatic conclusion. At that time, the large majority of whole life insurance was sold by in-person salespeople working through friends and family contacts, visiting potential customers in their homes and offices. The theory was that in-person selling was needed to "push" a product that had no immediate benefit. Our qualitative interviews showed that most customers bought life insurance as a result of a change in personal circumstances such as marriage or a new child. The reason why insurance agents had such low productivity (and needed to be paid huge commissions on each sale to compensate) was that most of the time, they were trying to sell to customers who were not ready to buy. Our client challenged the findings but admitted that most of their voice of customer research had covered what insurance features people were looking for, rather than when and why they chose to buy. We repeated the research with a larger sample, and the same findings came back. As a result, the client shifted to an entirely different model, adding consumer advertising (so people were aware of the product when they needed it) and replacing the field sales force with branch-based salespeople, often in banks or other convenient locations. The branch-based salespeople ended up achieving sales productivity five times greater than their field sales predecessors. Today, the model of door-to-door life insurance sales is almost completely gone.

As this example demonstrates, voice of customer work—that is, gathering feedback directly from customers—all too often goes through the research motions without delivering the insights that are so critical to a company's success as an innovator.

Whom you collect feedback from, how you collect that feedback, and how you analyze and synthesize it all have significant implications for its usefulness. Remember that **without in-depth customer insights, the entire innovation journey is in jeopardy**. In this chapter, we discuss how you can ensure that your research translates into *insights*, rather than just a set of interesting but not particularly helpful data points. In particular, we share some of our observed best practices as well as what practitioners commonly miss when it comes to the two most common forms of market research: qualitative interviews and quantitative surveys.

Know Your Tools for Market Insights

Market research looks different, and plays a different role, depending on whether your product or service innovation is truly novel or is an incremental innovation for an existing customer base. In the latter case, your focus may be on head-to-head comparative testing against existing products. For example, many consumer food companies ask consumers to rate new products on attributes such as taste, appearance, health, and the customers' willingness to buy and benchmark the scores against other products in their portfolio.

But our focus in this chapter is on breakthrough innovations and on the kinds of research that can help you better understand the potential from customers in different strategic segments.

Market research can take many forms, including interviews, quantitative surveys, focus groups, site visits/field studies, usability tests, and product demonstrations, to name just a few. Which ones should you use, and when? Are all of them relevant and applicable to strategic segmentation? Do you always need explicit market research, or can other data suffice? Table 11.1 summarizes a selection of commonly used market research tools along with their respective pros and cons. As quickly becomes evident, there are various use cases and tradeoffs among market research tools—and there are many others we didn't include in this brief summary. Consequently, it's not surprising to find them being used in combination or in sequence. **For strategic segmentation (and building a business case more broadly), interviews are typically the most valuable market research tool, regardless of the product or context, followed by quantitative surveys, and the two methods are often more powerful when used together.**

Occasionally, we're asked if market research is always needed. The question usually comes up either when the company's own customer data is available or when there is a significant amount of customer data available from secondary sources. The short answer is *yes*.

It's a rare circumstance when existing datasets can yield the insights needed to create a tailored, useful strategic segmentation and enable the definition of both early adopters and a broader customer runway. That said, market research can and should often be complemented with real-world data. While such data is not always available, it is becoming increasingly accessible as more of the world goes digital. In the appendix of this book, we share some further thoughts on data sources and how you can even create your own real-world, empirical data through various online and other tools.

But to underscore the point more broadly: **Market insights are always required when developing and launching a new product or service, and market research is nearly always a key source of these insights.**

TABLE 11.1. Market Research Tools Summary Table

Selected market research tools	Pros/cons	When to use it
Qualitative interviews *(Synchronous discussions with customers and other market participants)*	✓ Critical for understanding the "why" behind customer behaviors and perceptions ✓ Flexible (able to adjust questions in real time, especially helpful in formulating hypotheses and testing early product concepts) ✗ Suboptimal for collecting significant quantitative data ✗ Inefficient and costly for gathering large sample	**Always** • *Just about every product or service innovation benefits from customer interviews*
Quantitative survey *(Questionnaire completed by customers themselves, typically online)*	✓ Efficient for collecting large sample quickly and at relatively low cost ✓ Effective for gathering custom quantitative data (e.g., brand awareness and perception, price sensitivity) ✓ Helpful for quantitative customer segmentation ✗ Inflexible (difficult to change questions in field) ✗ Time-consuming upfront to "dummy-proof" (clear questions, sound logic) and analyze on back end ✗ Impractical when targeted respondents are few or difficult to reach ✗ At risk of incorrect responses (e.g., inclusion of non- target respondents, "respondent fatigue")	**Most of the time** • *Highly complementary to qualitative interviews* • *Valuable for large majority of product and service innovation situations* • *Best when hypotheses or product concepts are reasonably well developed*
Focus groups *(Small group discussion led synchronously by professional moderator, in-person or virtual)*	✓ Effective for live feedback on products to test features, messages, and advertising prompts ✓ Uniquely valuable for capturing nonverbal customer reactions ✗ Susceptible to groupthink ✗ Views of quieter participants can be crowded out ✗ Moderators can inadvertently inject biases ✗ Relatively time-consuming and costly to set up	**Selectively** • *Best for consumer products that can be experienced and incremental innovations* • *Rarely useful for strategic segmentation*

Selected market research tools	Pros/cons	When to use it
Field studies/site visits *(Direct "ethnographic" observation of customers in their context)*	✓ Excellent for identifying things "broken" in the customer experience but to which customers have become accustomed ✓ Effective way to gather rich insights into workflows, customer journeys, and day-to-day experiences ✗ Time-consuming, complex to organize, and difficult to conduct at scale ✗ At risk of incorrectly extrapolating conclusions from narrow set of customer observations	**Selectively** • *Best for upfront concept development (commonly used for design thinking)* • *Valuable complement to customer interviews*

Without hearing directly from customers, there's no reliable path toward strategic segmentation and no way to reduce risk in the innovation and commercialization process.

Get Full Value from Market Interviews

The first key step in preparing for research is to **understand the specific goals you are trying to achieve with your interviews.** Typically, this might cover insights into customers' unmet needs, their satisfaction with current solutions and competitors, customers' purchasing processes and decision-making criteria for adoption of a new product, and feedback on potential innovation concepts. There can be multiple agendas that reflect where you are in the innovation process and what key issues or hypotheses you are trying to evaluate. Getting alignment with internal stakeholders on these issues is critical. This may involve a fair amount of consensus-building, especially if the effort is taking place within a larger, established organization. But it's well worth making that upfront effort. You need to **develop a clear view on the goals of the research, how it will inform decisions for your business, and how it will tie to any further (or prior) market insight gathering effort.**

We often recommend starting with a research blueprint—that is, a high-level outline of your target issues, grouped hierarchically by topic and in a logical sequence. This blueprint will be the foundation for creating an interview guide, which is the research tool with your questions for interviewees. Most likely, the blueprint will need to vary if you'll be speaking with multiple distinct groups of interviewees (e.g., homeowners vs. remodeling contractors). By extension, you're likely to need separate interview guides for each group.

The next step in preparing for your research is to determine whom you want to interview. Who is best positioned to answer the specific questions required? Who are the key stakeholders? The first and most obvious answers are not always the correct ones. For example, a digital AI solution for analyzing medical images might be targeted for hospitals, but *which* hospitals and *which* stakeholders within those institutions can matter a lot. Should you focus on academic medical centers or community hospitals? How much time do you need to spend with physicians, as opposed to department heads, procurement, and the IT department?

You may not know the answers right away, but in most cases, you can start with some reasonable hypotheses and sharpen your focus as you learn. Usually, we find that targeting a mix of stakeholders is appropriate, on the assumption that different constituencies are better positioned to answer different kinds of questions. **The key is to recognize what the information limitations might be among the stakeholders with whom you are speaking.** In other words, as you consider the range of possible stakeholders, think systematically about your different candidate groups and what they may offer both in terms of potential insights and information limitations. Think about customer decision-makers vs. influencers, current customers vs. prospective customers, types of customers, industry thought leaders, suppliers, competitors, channel partners, and so on and so on. What are they in a position to know, and what *aren't* they in a position to know?

Thought leaders, competitors, and channel partners can be important for answering industry questions about the size of the market opportunity and the state of competition—obviously, questions to which customers will have less helpful answers. On the other hand, competitors may be well positioned to articulate customers' unmet needs—but remember that this is no substitute for hearing directly from customers!

To sum up: If you ask questions of the wrong stakeholders or don't understand their information limitations, you will end up with less useful, potentially misleading, or just flat-out wrong answers. So it's critical to invest the time needed upfront to determine with whom you need to speak and what you need to ask them. And you may want to consider this an open question as your research progresses. If during your interviews you're getting answers you didn't expect—or you're not getting the information you hoped for—it may well be an issue with whom you are speaking, not the questions you are asking.

Once you have determined who is likely best positioned to answer your questions, you can decide how many individuals to speak with, how to distribute your sample, and how best to identify and recruit them. If you have an existing customer base to target, that can be a powerful starting point and accelerator for the project (as can any early product testers). You can also use third-party panels that provide access to readily available interviewees, as well as support in finding individuals with specific expertise; or you can source your own interviewees using available online resources like LinkedIn, conference attendee/presenter lists, and trade association leadership/member lists.

Finally, it's time to turn to the interview guide itself. Table 11.2 lays out the component parts of a typical interview guide and suggests how the allotted time should typically be spread across those components. (There is additional detail on how to develop the interview guide and best practices for question-writing in the relevant appendix in the back of the book.) Once you have a completed draft of your interview guide in hand, it is critical to test it and refine it through a series of early interviews. Do you need to rework its flow to make it more logical, reword questions that confused interviewees, shorten it? Even after any initial refinements are incorporated, you should **treat the interview guide as a dynamic document that will keep evolving as you conduct your interview campaign**. New questions may emerge and existing ones may fall away, and you should view this as progress.

TABLE 11.2. Interview Guide Structure

Interview guide sections	Key components	Percent of interview time
Introduction	• Welcoming background statement (who you are, goals of call) • Estimate of interview length (time) • Assurance of confidentiality and anonymity (if required) • Thank you for participation	5%
Qualifying/ warm-up	• Critical questions used to qualify for participation (screener) • Only questions essential for eligibility • Avoid asking sensitive questions if possible	10%
Main guide	• Follows the interview guide blueprint • Starts with easy, less threatening questions and builds to more challenging and sensitive questions • "Nice-to-have"/secondary questions at the end	80%
Closing	• Reinforcement of value of participation/ thank you • Permission to follow-up (if wanted) • Referrals (if wanted/needed) • Honorarium (if needed)	5%

When conducting the interviews themselves, pay attention to good listening! This is an undervalued skill, especially if—like many of us—you're not accustomed to thinking much about it. Here are some useful habits that may help you keep your listening focused:

■ Always ask "why" or "what's your thought process behind that?" for key questions.

■ Play back key points to the interviewee to make sure you understood correctly.

■ Think of the discussion more as a conversation and less as an interview . . . but don't be afraid to redirect.

■ If you think your interviewee misunderstood your question, go back and clarify.

▪ Use language to demonstrate sincere interest in the subject matter and your interviewee's perspective (e.g., "I'm curious, can you tell me why you think . . . ?")

It's important to listen to the word choices, the interviewee's tone and level of confidence, even what *isn't* being said. Listening "between the lines" is an extremely valuable learned skill for generating insights, rather than simply eliciting "voice of customer" commentaries.

Some final thoughts about interview guides and interviews: First, **an interview guide is exactly that: a *guide*, not a script. One of the most common missteps made by interviewers is following the guide too closely.** Yes, keep your guidelines in mind—but at the same time, don't be afraid to go off-guide when circumstances warrant. If an interviewee says something strikingly different, surprising, or interesting, don't just move on to the next question on your list—ask him or her to elaborate! **The most meaningful customer insights are often discovered when you veer off-guide and pull on a new, unexpected thread.** To do this effectively, the interviewer needs to truly understand the goal of the interview and to stay focused on "the why"—that is, *discerning the reason behind behaviors and perceptions.*

Know How and When to Use Surveys

In Figure 11.1, we discussed the pros and cons of using quantitative surveys. To reiterate, surveys—which are largely administered online—are an efficient tool for capturing a large amount of data points quickly and cost-effectively. They provide the quantitative backbone for difficult-to-gather customer insights. On the other hand, they don't provide much visibility into *why* respondents answer questions the way they do. For this reason, we often see them as complementary to interviews.

An advantage of this complementarity is that interviews can dramatically accelerate survey research. In many cases, you can use your interview guide as the initial basis for your questionnaire, convert it into a survey format, and add or subtract questions. A survey can be structured similarly to an interview guide (as in Table 11.2) with the primary difference being the use of a screener instead of a "qualifying/warm up" section. There are of course some important differences between an interview guide and a survey questionnaire, but taking advantage of the overlaps can be an effective and expedient approach.

In that vein, we always recommend conducting some interviews before launching a survey in order to ensure that the phrasing and logic of your questions make sense. One of the inherent challenges of a survey is that it's hard to go back and change it once it's out in the field, which means that you have to do your best ahead of time to think through—for example—the possible ways a question can be misinterpreted by a respondent.

Surveys can vary significantly in their length and complexity. A quick, focused survey—using an easy-to-use tool like SurveyMonkey or Qualtrics—can be a good solution, especially if you have limited budget or are looking for a rapid initial view on a narrow, specific set of questions. This approach can be particularly helpful in earlier-stage research, when you may be testing the hypotheses that underpin your innovation efforts. These types of surveys are simple enough to program yourself, meaning that in many cases, they can be written, designed, and fielded in a few days. They tend to follow a simplified version of the same structure as a longer survey and can benefit from the same best practices for question-writing.

If you're seeking deeper insights about a product or service concept or want to enable a robust segmentation, you'll probably need a much more in-depth survey. We will focus our discussion on these more substantial surveys because (1) they are more challenging; and (2) they are all too easy to get wrong. Furthermore, many of the same best practices that apply to a long survey also apply to a short one.

An in-depth survey tends to consist of forty to sixty questions, intended to be answered by a respondent over about twenty minutes. In most end markets, it generally takes a minimum of two weeks to write, program, and field a survey like this, and in some geographies it can take substantially longer. It can also involve complex programming logic that takes a respondent from one question to the next or customizes questions to individuals. In such cases, a third-party programmer can be a valuable resource.

As with interviews, determining the right audience for the survey is a critical first step—done wrong, it can be the root cause of what may turn out to be inaccurate or misleading findings. You should consider whether there are any potential audience issues with which you will need to deal. For example, is this a high- or low-involvement category (i.e., do people care and have strong opinions)? Are people available and willing to participate in a survey? How much time might they have for a survey? Is the information you're seeking in any way sensitive? All these considerations may help refine your audience or inform how you structure or design the survey.

In addition, as you build your survey blueprint or questionnaire, you will likely determine that specific subgroups will be of interest. **Determining hypothesized subgroups that matter is a key driver of insight generation** as well as a requirement for developing the "screener" portion of the survey: the set of questions that are used to qualify respondents for participating in the survey.

When fielding a survey, you need to determine the total number of responses you are seeking (i.e., sample size) and how many you need from different groups of respondents. Determining the sample size requires balancing tradeoffs: A small sample may lead to low confidence in your results, while a large sample may be impractical due to cost and time.

In the appendix at the back of the book—which we suggest you scan at this point to get familiar with the relevant vocabulary—we provide additional detail and considerations on how to determine the right sample size, but some basic rules of thumb can help. **Most B2C surveys are effective with sample sizes in the hundreds and low thousands, while most B2B surveys are effective in the 100- to 200-respondent range.**

As you think through your survey instrument, you'll probably find yourself grappling with the concept of "quotas." These are pretty much what they sound like: targets for a specific number of respondents from different groups within your sample. A quota can be a specific number or can be set as a minimum or maximum. For example, if you're evaluating a new enterprise software, you may want to include decision-makers from businesses of different sizes in your survey and set quotas to split up your sample across them. In this case, you might base your quotas on estimates of the number of businesses by size, or you might over-index toward a specific group based on your hypotheses of where your product will resonate most.

Now let's turn to the "screener" portion of the questionnaire. The screener is the set of questions that determine if the respondent qualifies for the survey and, if so, into which quota group they fall. Here's something to keep in mind: While everyone likes to focus on the main questions in the survey, **the screener is actually the single most impactful portion of the survey on the quality of your results.** So take the time needed to craft it carefully.

Screeners are (naturally) at the beginning of the survey, and they need to be fairly short—fewer than ten questions, if possible. If you fail to screen adequately or include qualifying questions later in your survey, you can end up paying for respondents who should not have been included in the survey. The screener must be carefully worded so that it's not immediately obvious to respondents what qualifies or disqualifies someone. If the question is too obvious, respondents can game the system and "qualify" for the survey even if they are not the target audience. For this reason, more sophisticated survey writers tend to mask qualification by including other categories or products that are not of interest—sometimes going so far as to include made-up brands.

A relevant sidebar: On one occasion, the made-up brand scored higher than our client's brand, revealing some sobering realities about our client's brand appeal!

One less well-known characteristic of screeners is their potential to provide "free" insights. You don't pay for respondents who do not qualify for the survey, but you are still able to discern insights from their screener-question responses. For example, if looking at a novel snack food for kids, we might only allow parents who currently buy some type of snack for their kids to qualify for the survey, but we could still estimate what percentage of parents do not buy snacks based on the portion of respondents who drop out as a result of this question.

Now let's turn to the main questionnaire. First, it's worth highlighting the key differences between a survey questionnaire and an interview guide. Surveys tend to focus on closed-ended, structured questions (e.g., yes/no, multiple choice, rankings), while interviews tend to focus on open-ended, unstructured questions (e.g., "why," "to what extent," "how"). As a rule, you should try to minimize the number of open-ended questions in your survey, as they tend to consume too much respondent time and are more difficult and time-consuming to analyze on the back end. Surveys are also specifically designed to enable more quantitative question designs, which can be used to capture robust quantitative responses to questions that are asked more qualitatively in interviews. Again, this is why they are very much complementary to interviews.

Another important point: **A good survey demonstrates an awareness of the respondent experience**. This means, among other things, that you need to keep the length of the survey under control. More is not necessarily better. Most of the time, respondents are answering voluntarily (and perhaps to earn an honorarium). If you bore them or tire them out, you're likely to compromise the quality of responses and increase dropouts. You also need to be careful not to make your survey too complex and thereby place an interpretative burden on the respondent. **In a survey, simple is almost always better**. The respondent experience can also be enhanced by using appropriate language and simple terms, avoiding jargon, explaining acronyms, being mindful when asking for difficult or socially unacceptable information, and remembering the age, education level, and experience level of your respondents. **Ultimately, your best litmus test is how *you* would react to the survey.** Would you complete it or bail? Obviously, you're aiming for the former. We have provided additional best practices on survey question writing and programming logic in the appendix at the back of the book.

Once your questionnaire is written and programmed, you need to take several additional steps before fielding it to respondents. First, you need to test the survey thoroughly. This means taking the survey yourself to make sure the questions are clear and the logic makes sense (and again: would *you* bother to complete it?). This is your opportunity to check that the questionnaire was properly translated into the programmed version of the survey and to make any final adjustments. Testing the survey also entails trying to "dummy-proof" it. To do this, you need to make every attempt to "break" the survey, by entering responses that should not be acceptable to the programming logic (e.g., testing that you can't select two options on a single select, or that only numerical values within a specified range can be entered).

After testing, you're ready to launch the survey—but it's always a good idea to "soft launch" first. This means you send the survey out to a subset of respondents (e.g., typically less than 10 percent of your respondent list). You then sense-check these responses to ensure that the results look as expected (e.g., respondents didn't misinterpret a question) and that there aren't any logic errors (e.g., skips that shouldn't be there).

Finally, you're ready to field the survey! While the survey is in the field, you should be monitoring the quotas and tracking that the survey is being filled out as planned, including by the right people. Meanwhile, you can (and should) be thinking about useful data cuts based on initial responses.

As the preceding pages illustrate, writing, programming, and fielding a survey is an involved process—but these are the necessary steps you need to take to ensure that you have good inputs for the final step: your analyses. First, before any meaningful analyses can be done, the raw survey data needs to cleaned up. This is when you need to review the data to remove bad respondents like "speeders" (who fly through the survey to earn an honorarium) or "gamers" (who try to fill the survey out more than once) and identify any outliers who will likely skew results on certain questions. Outliers are tricky, as they may be a real data point, so this assessment requires nuanced judgment. When the data is ready for analysis, you can slice and dice them (often iteratively) to derive insights.

Derive Insights, Not Data

Now, let's look at the challenge of synthesizing your research, beginning with interviews. When you speak with dozens—or even hundreds—of market stakeholders, it can be challenging to identify your most important insights and develop a clear narrative out of them. How do you separate the wheat from the chaff?

Simply speaking, you need to look for patterns among the responses— rather than just summarizing the responses—and identify linkages among seemingly disparate data points to explain the patterns you are observing. Are certain interviewees responding more positively to your product concept than others? Did they also respond similarly on a key purchasing criterion? Why might the responses between groups of potential customers vary—for example, what's the relationship between current satisfaction with an available market solution and interest in your product concept?

This is the phase in which we see the most market-research missteps. Business leaders, marketers, and market research practitioners often fail to hold up the right lens to the data, which makes it impossible to connect the dots between data points to surface the all-important patterns. To do this effectively,

you need to keep asking *why* **and find creative ways within the limitations of your data to answer as many** *whys* **as you can.** You also need to have a thorough understanding of the people you interviewed, their background and experiences, and what might drive differences in responses—hence our emphasis on this necessity earlier in the chapter.

Turning to surveys, **the art of generating insights from a survey lies in thinking through the right crosstabs among variables.** This is driven by hypotheses but also by experimentation. What happens when you cut the data along one dimension rather than another? Do you need to weight the responses in any way (e.g., by their representation in the market, which may not be in line with your sample)? You can often arrive at surprising answers, depending on what you include in your data cuts. With the benefit of having conducted interviews, you can usually determine if you are onto something or if your data is wrong in some way. One key piece of guidance: **Be hypothesis-driven**. Don't just boil the ocean with every data cut you can do. With any luck, by the time you're analyzing your survey, you have well-informed hypotheses from any research or interviews you have done.

Which leads to our concluding observation: **The most important insights derived from both your interviews and your surveys often arise when you succeed in connecting patterns of responses that—on first glance—may not be obviously linked**. And if you have conducted both interviews and a survey, then this can be enhanced by bringing together data from the two complementary techniques. Your interviews can be used to explain your survey data, and the survey data can provide quantitative robustness to lend greater credence to findings from interviewees. At its best, this is like striking gold.

EXECUTIVE SUMMARY

Gather customer insights, not "voice of customer."

- Take advantage of the full range of market insight tools for understanding your customers.

- Get full value from interviews by selecting the right stakeholders and understanding the limitations of the information they can provide.

- Create a flexible but rigorous interview guide, and don't be afraid to go "off-guide."

- Always ask "why"—seek to understand not just behaviors and responses but motivations.

- Deploy a questionnaire that screens out the wrong respondents and makes it as easy as possible to accurately and quickly complete the survey.

- Minimize research biases with interviewing and survey writing best practices.

TWELVE

Never Take Market Research at Face Value

The preceding chapters have emphasized the value of market research for col-lecting customer insights. In the context of new product and service innova-tion, one of the most important uses of market research is gauging adoption potential among different customer segments. Your strategic segmentation—discussed in Chapter 10 —should reflect your differential expectations for adoption among customers. But how do you effectively capture feedback on potential adoption? And once you do, can you trust that feedback?

Customers are notoriously bad at estimating their true future behaviors, especially when it comes to considering new products and services that they have never experienced. Steve Jobs once famously observed that customers don't know what they want beyond what they already have experience with, which obviously limits their ability to provide meaningful feedback on any-thing but incremental innovations. And while Jobs could rely on his uncanny intuition for designing radical-departure products that customers would wind up loving, most of us can't do that. So while we need to recognize the limits to what market research can do in this respect, it can still serve as a barometer for an innovation's potential. And through iterative approaches to develop-ment and market testing, we can develop a reasonable level of confidence in an opportunity.

That said, estimating adoption too early in concept development is usually a waste of resources. This is why many of the best practitioners set reasonable stage gates or thresholds for the level of concept development (using the tools described in Chapters 4–8) *before* they spend time and money on customer research.

Getting Adoption Estimates Right

Quantitative surveys and interviews are important tools for determining likely adoption of new products and services. But they are usually insufficient on their own. Just as early navigators would estimate their position using several "fixes" based on land or celestial observations, **to accurately forecast likely adoption, you need to combine stated intentions with factual observations and behaviors.** Essentially, instead of just asking one question about the intended adoption of an innovation, you are asking three questions:

1. Among potential customers, how many are stating that they *intend* to adopt the innovation?

2. Based on customer priorities and situations, for whom does it *make sense* to adopt?

3. Given how many customers are *actually using* any analogous products or services today, what can we infer about the likely adoption for the innovation (taking account of how it compares to existing offerings)?

Let's bring this to life with an example. Several years ago, we assisted in the planning and forecasting for a new international high-speed rail service between two European cities. It was expected to cost billions of dollars to build the upgraded track and rolling stock, so it was important to get an accurate assessment of likely ridership.

If we had just used market research to gauge customer intentions, it would have been a straightforward endeavor: Start by surveying ten thousand people who live in either of the two cities, asking questions about how often people travel to the other city and their likely use of a high-speed rail link versus other modes of transport. Then segment the data—e.g., by travel frequency and income—so that the findings can be extrapolated to the full population, consistent with the proportion of each demographic. Then make corrections for overstatement bias and aggregate findings.

Instead, the team decided at the outset to use a combination of observed behavior and research. They started by looking at data sources from cellphone and GPS vehicle tracking data to identify the travel frequencies for 2,500 origin-destination pairs located in and around the two cities. This helped answer a range of questions: How many journeys start and end near city centers and so are likely to be quicker by train? How many journeys start and end near the airport, so air travel is advantaged? How many journeys are in locations and at times of day when car travel would be badly impacted by traffic? For different origin-destination pairs, what is the current mix of travel modes and cost of travel, including fuel, parking, taxi at the far end, and so on?

With this data in hand, the team developed some hypotheses around which types of journey fit best for the new service. The next step was to conduct customer research with two objectives. The first was to understand the importance of different factors in customers' choice of travel: speed, risk of delays, access to phone/Wi-Fi on journey, seat comfort, access to one's own car at the far end, and cost. Responses were grouped according to different categories of origin-destination location and customer priorities. This allowed the team to determine which customers were "better off" with the train service, according to their stated priorities and travel patterns.

The second objective of the survey was to gather the stated intentions for use of the new service. This was done at different price points and service levels to allow for fine-tuning of the usage model, according to attributes that were still being finalized: ticket prices, seating, service frequency, and so on. As part of this, the team "calibrated" the findings by asking about intended usage of current travel options (standard rail, air, automobile) and comparing this against actual observed usage for different origin-destination pairs. The final step was to develop an accurate "integrated forecast" of likely usage by reconciling the findings on who would be "better off" using the service, who said they intended to use the service, and who was actually using different travel modes.

Had the team just used market research, the results would have been overstated and the level of confidence—especially critical when billions of investment dollars were on the line—would have been much lower.

As part of their research, the team used illustrations of the train carriages and seating to gauge customer interest. The right prompt—what market research experts call the "stimulus"—is critical to eliciting the most accurate response. This is the tool you use to convey your product or service concept to potential customers. In the life sciences, this is often called a target product profile (TPP), while in other sectors it is more commonly called a concept profile. Regardless of what it winds up being called, this stimulus needs to have the following components: a brief overview of the product or service concept (what it does, when you use it), articulation of the benefits, description of the features, and any relevant visualizations—for example, a picture or flow diagram, if applicable.

Sometimes it's helpful to show a comparison of specifications to a technology that's already in the market, especially when that will be the primary frame of reference for the customer. Sometimes drawbacks to the concept need to be included (e.g., a safety profile in a drug TPP). Pricing can be included as well, but it is often excluded, as it may be something you plan to test (i.e., ask about adoption at multiple price points).

The stimulus can take the form of a PowerPoint slide (optimally, only one or at most two slides), a paragraph description (if sufficiently simple), a visual mockup with a description, a video, or even a short interactive demo. You can decide on the format of your stimulus based on the type of concept, how novel the concept is, how difficult it may be to articulate, or how savvy the target customers/respondents are (e.g., physicians are very accustomed to responding to TPPs, so they can handle much more detail than ordinary consumers). **Ultimately, the more realistic and specific you make your stimulus, the more accurate your responses are likely to be.** Best practice is to use as few words as possible, be as specific as possible in language, minimize room for interpretation, and create a logical flow to the benefits and features. You typically use the same stimulus in both interviews and survey, and you should use the interviews to refine the stimulus before employing it in the survey.

Once you have a high-quality stimulus, you can ask prospective customers about potential adoption of your product or service innovation. In the relevant appendix in the back of this book, you will find more detail on best approaches for asking about purchase intent and, perhaps even more important, **adjusting for overstatement bias.** For all sorts of reasons, respondents tend to be overly optimistic about their future adoption of a new product or service. This is yet another reason why we advocate using multiple approaches to validate findings, whenever possible.

Pressure Test with Analogs and Triangulations

How can you be sure that your adoption estimates are neither too rosy nor too conservative?

There are several answers. First, what's your company's experience base? If you've evaluated many innovations over the years using the same method consistently, you're in a good position to compare your current results. In fact, this is exactly what many specialized marketing firms do.

While experience can be helpful, real-world evidence tends to be far more reliable. **Analogs—in other words, lessons from apples-to-apples comparisons—are the best way to pressure-test your estimated adoption.** They may not always be available, but often, there are reasonable proxies.

For example, several years ago we assisted a leading sports entertainment company with developing and launching a direct-to-consumer (DTC) streaming service. In the vein of the strategic segmentation discussed in Chapter 10, we created a segmentation that defined early adopters and the customer runway by assessing the company's audience on (1) level of engagement with streaming services (e.g., weekly hours of streaming and number of paid streaming subscriptions), and (2) their fan "avidity" (gauged by showing a picture of an athlete and asking the respondent to name the athlete correctly). Using these two dimensions, we were able to define segments such as "Hardcore, Streaming Engaged Fans" and "Casual, Streaming Engaged Fans," among others. Segmenting on meaningful dimensions—and in this case, developing a tailored metric for avidity—ensured that when we tested adoption potential, we were truly asking the right customers.

This was also a good example of using observed behaviors (e.g., existing use of and spend on streaming, attendance at relevant sporting events, etc.) to inform research and to identify which segments were likely to buy the new service (because they were already spending money on streaming services and were highly engaged fans).

We also tested stated purchase intent. We created a concept profile for testing, collected data on purchase intent, and adjusted for overstatement bias by asking about adoption of another streaming service that was already available and comparing to actual usage. While these steps helped ensure we had as accurate a view on adoption as possible, what really gave the executive team confidence in market expectations was several analogs. We were able to contextualize adoption relative to several streaming services, ranging from other sports to Netflix and Amazon Prime.

Sometimes you also have to balance adoption based on rational behavior versus "intuition" about how consumers are likely to react to an entirely new product. When Apple launched the iPhone, they projected that sales of their smartphone handsets would overtake market leader BlackBerry in the fourth quarter after launch. It was a bold forecast. As noted earlier, BlackBerry had built a strong army of users who were fans. But the iPhone was so . . . *cool.* There were powerful analogs for the importance of personal devices as a fashion statement and not just a functional device, starting with the original "brick" cell phones, the iconic Motorola Razr flip phone, and of course, Black-Berry itself, which originally used prominent influencers to stoke its appeal.[1] Ultimately, in many cases, the best way to validate "intuition" is with some convincing analogs.

When no analogs are available, triangulation can be a helpful way to pressure-test adoption. Triangulations are exactly what the name implies: a back-of-the-envelope sense check reflecting "what you have to believe" for your estimated adoption to be true. For example, if we are looking at the adoption expected for our Hardcore, Streaming Engaged fans, we could ask if the amount of implied spending on the new service as a share of their total annual spend on streaming services is believable. Similarly, we might wonder whether the projected adoption among casual fans vs. hardcore fans tracked when you set it alongside their current relative consumption of relevant sports content. Triangulations require you to be resourceful in using available and reliable data points, and they often benefit from your having collected some relevant secondary market data—for example, competitors' sales or market-sizing estimates.

To summarize, market research can help you estimate potential adoption of your innovation, but you can't rely on this feedback at face value. **Make sure you gather purchase-intent insights the right way but then appropriately adjust for biases and—most important—contextualize with observed behaviors and analogs to build confidence in the results.**

EXECUTIVE SUMMARY

Never take market research at face value.

- Combine factual observations and behaviors with customers' stated intentions to forecast adoption of your innovation.

- Capture stated purchase intent as accurately as possible with a realistic stimulus.

- Adjust purchase intent appropriately for overstatement bias.

- Use analogs to pressure test adoption estimates and use triangulations where analogs are not available.

THIRTEEN

Assume Your Competitors Are at Least as Smart as You Are

We began Chapter 9 by introducing the premise that avoiding the product graveyard requires a few things: developing the right product/market fit, defining a customer runway, and ensuring that you are configured to succeed against competitors. Our last several chapters focused on gathering the insights and making the right decisions to meet the first two of these requirements. In this chapter, we dig into the competitive dynamics you need to evaluate to meet that last precondition: ensuring that you can win in the market against competitors. This is, of course, critical to improving the odds of success for your innovation.

Competition is a thoroughly studied and well understood topic, in both economics texts and in business literature. Seminal works in strategy—like Michael Porter's 1980s classic *Competitive Strategy*—increased the acuity with which business leaders began to think about this topic. The technology disruptions of the 1990s and 2000s further heightened interest in what determines a sustainable competitive position, leading to works like Jim Collins's *Good to Great*. Your authors, too, have contributed to the literature of competition by introducing concepts like Strategic Market Position (SMP) in *Where Value Hides*, which highlighted the importance of defining market segments appropriately to accrue competitive advantage.

So in a sense, this is already a crowded space—and our goal here is *not* to introduce yet another framework for thinking about competition and competitive advantage. Instead, we focus on bringing some of these good ideas into the marketplace. Why is this important? We've seen in our practice that **innovators, and business leaders more broadly, struggle to operationalize the many insights available on the topic of competition**. Our observations from real world practice of strategy are that business leaders

- systematically define their competitive sets incorrectly;
- consistently underestimate their competitors; and
- underinvest in understanding competitive responses.

Let's turn that list around into a positive assertion: **If you can successfully address these missteps, you will be well positioned to understand how and why your competitors go to market, and you will be able to predict their behavior.** This, in turn, will enable you to pursue the right strategy to win in the market.

Define Your Current and Future Competitive Set

Starting with the first of our three observations above, most innovators think too myopically—or, ironically, too broadly—about their competitive sets.

To explore this point, let's look at the coffee market and the story of Nespresso. Nespresso, part of the Nestlé Group, sells machines that brew espresso-based coffee drinks rapidly from single-use pods.

The story began in the mid-1970s, when a young Nestlé engineer named Eric Favre was tasked with finding a product that could sit somewhere on the spectrum between tasty/laborious (ground coffee from an espresso machine) and less tasty/effortless (instant coffee). Inspired by the espresso machines he had seen in Rome, Favre came up with a technology that used sealed coffee pods (to ensure freshness) injected with hot water at high pressure.[1] It was far from an overnight success story, but for the sake of brevity, let's jump to the punchline: in 2020, the Nespresso division was selling 14 billion coffee capsules a year, which amounts to something like 400 Nespresso pods consumed *every second*, in more than eighty countries around the world. By 2022, Nespresso's revenues were approaching $6.5 billion.[2]

Going back to the outset of that story, one could assume that Nespresso's competitive set was, and is, coffee makers and instant coffee—but that would be an overly narrow definition. What if on this particular morning, instead of drinking your coffee at home, you grab it on the way to the office? That would make coffee shops and other food service venues also "competitors" to your Nespresso machine, in a sense. Or what if today, you decide to drink tea instead of coffee or maybe a Coke or a Red Bull later in the morning or as an afternoon pick-me-up? Well, those too could be considered competitors. But wait—are we starting to think a bit too broadly? Arguably, we are.

So how do you define your set of competitors correctly?

First, let's recognize that there are different types of competitors that can be characterized as being most similar or least similar to your product or service. In the first group are your **direct competitors**: those market players that are most closely aligned with your value proposition and set of use cases. In the case of Nespresso, in-home machines would be considered direct competitors, as they seek to provide the taste of coffee-shop drinks at home.[3] In the second group—least-similar competitors—are your **indirect competitors**. In Nespresso's case, instant coffee and bulk drip coffee—as well as the local coffee shop or the corner Starbucks—are **indirect competitors**.

Finally, something like tea (and, to a lesser extent, Coke and Red Bull) would be considered **substitutes**, which—although they can compete for some of the same demand—should be assigned to a different category. But "different" doesn't necessarily mean "less important." **Substitutes are often entirely omitted when defining competitive sets—and that omission can be a serious mistake.** Substitutes can include technologies that create a new competitive category (e.g., portable CD players like Sony's Discman being challenged, and ultimately replaced, by mp3 players like Apple's iPod) or that chip away at or even negate the need for a product (e.g., electric vehicles reducing market demand for gas stations). Sometimes the substitute is not using the product at all. This is particularly true when creating a new market.

When you're undertaking incremental innovations in a well-understood market, it isn't difficult to define your competitive set. **It is much more difficult to define a competitive set for breakthrough innovations,** since—by definition—you're creating something novel that rarely has much direct competition. **Ultimately, the right way to define your competitors is by determining who is in the consideration set when the customer is making a buying decision.** By extension, this also means that, even for the same customer, your competitive set may not always be the same but may vary by use case (e.g., your morning cup of coffee may always be Nespresso, but your afternoon cup may depend on whether or not you are at home). Determining which use case or cases you are competing for can therefore be critical.

More often than not, innovators are surprised to learn that their true competitive set is so narrow for any given customer and use case pairing. **In our experience, irrespective of industry, the true competitive set for a buying decision is usually fewer than five competitors.**

This is true even in highly competitive industries, in part because customers typically use a variety of purchasing criteria (e.g., price, quality, reputation) to narrow down the consideration set to a manageable number of options. For example, there are dozens of car brands, but once you specify your preferred body type (e.g., sedan vs. SUV), size, motor type (e.g., gas vs. electric vs. hybrid), and price range, the list gets surprisingly narrow. The same is true in our own industry: consulting. While there are many thousands of consulting firms, clients rarely look at more than three or four for a specific type of service in a specific sector.

One last thing to add on defining the competitive set: Don't forget to look ahead! **Innovators need to be particularly wary of future competition.** For many, this doesn't come naturally: People are often too focused on the static state of the competition they are trying to beat right now, *today*. But just because you are the disruptor today doesn't mean you won't be the disrupted tomorrow. Your competitive set will almost certainly evolve. Therefore, you need to have a view on who you will be competing with at various milestones on the timeline: one year post-launch, three years, five years, and possibly beyond.

At the risk of stating the obvious, this can have substantial implications for your financial forecast (e.g., share loss to new branded or generic drugs in pharma) and for your value proposition and messaging, your customer runway (e.g., priority of customer segments), your launch planning (e.g., limited vs. full-scale launch), and your continuing product development (your R&D

priorities going forward). This may require you to consider different competitive scenarios, which we'll discuss shortly (in the context of wargaming) as well as in Chapter 16, where we look at revenue forecasting.

Understand Your Competitors and Their Advantages and Disadvantages

Once you have appropriately defined the competitors for your innovation, you need to ensure that you have a sufficient understanding of them. Competitive intelligence-gathering is well understood in the business world, so we won't go into detail here, but we do recommend being thorough as well as creative. **You can't know your competitors too well. The more you understand them, the better you can predict how they will behave, and the more likely you are to pursue a winning strategy.** You are also far less likely to underestimate them.

Your market-insight gathering efforts (e.g., interviews, surveys) should help you understand not only who your competitors are but also their positioning in the market, key strengths and weaknesses (real and perceived), go-to-market approaches, and so on. Many of the same datasets and techniques for gathering customer insights described in Chapter 11 and the supporting appendix can also be used for gathering data on your competitors in a systematic and cost-effective manner. This can include financial filings (if the competing company is publicly held), web-scraped data on portfolios and pricing, web traffic measures, customer reviews, employee reviews, job postings, regulatory filings, patent filings, fundraising data, press releases, news articles, and more. You can also use market datasets to estimate current share and share trends, often at high levels of granularity and accuracy, depending on the country and end market. In short, **there is almost always an immense amount of data that can be gathered—and this is homework that many innovators do incompletely**.

All this data gathering about your competitors will help you understand their true competitive advantages. As mentioned, there are many, many books—and probably too many business frameworks—devoted to defining and assessing "competitive advantage." Even so, we've attended all too many corporate workshops during which the management team articulates their competitive advantages in such vague terms as "quality," "people," "service." While these attributes may well be in place and may be contributing to the company's success, we argue that *much greater specificity* is needed. What's special about your organization that every other competitor wouldn't also say?

Let's keep it simple: **A competitive advantage is the reason a competitor wins**. Often, there aren't that many entries on that list, and they're not necessarily the most inspiring attributes. They may be strong relationships with hard-to-reach customers, control of a channel, expertise with manipulating a raw material, brand longevity, size of an installed base, and so on. These are all examples of real, tangible competitive advantages, which are both hard to replicate *and* contribute significantly to a winning strategy. Again, your competitive homework needs to help you to understand what's on the short list for each of your key competitors.

Sometimes, your competitive advantage may simply be the flexibility to do things your competitors can't. Among U.K. supermarkets in the early 1990s, Tesco was always a little behind the market leader, Sainsbury: lower share, lower margins, and a more down-market positioning. Ten years later, Tesco was twice the size of Sainsbury. How did this role reversal unfold? Yes, there were some innovations that Tesco brought in, such as its loyalty program, but the big reason they were able to gain share was simply that they built more stores. Sainsbury—with the founding family still owning a significant stake— targeted a hefty 21 percent return on equity. Tesco, by contrast, was happy with 18 percent, so a greater number of proposed store openings leapt over their investment hurdles, and they had more freedom to respond to low-price discounters. Investors were happy, too, because they could see the company was growing and gaining share.

One less well-covered aspect of competitive intelligence gathering in business is understanding the people in the competing organization. Let's call this the Machiavellian side of competitive intelligence. On a fundamental level, **competition is never truly between organizations; it is between people**. Just as you are contemplating how to successfully win with your innovation, there is someone (or several such people) at each of your competitors plotting how to thwart you and all other competitive threats. In our experience, many innovators don't even bother to identify the individual leaders who hold key positions in competing companies. But this can be critical. Getting a read on these individuals—their motivations, their experiences, and their track record—is critical to understanding how they may behave when you enter the market.

How aggressively will they respond? How have they responded to competitive challenges in the past? What levers might they pull to protect their business interests, meet their P&L goals, and ensure their own career success?

Certainly, some of this data is much harder to uncover than publicly disclosed information. But speaking with former employees ("former" tends to be safer in a legal sense) and reading between the lines of your accumulated competitive data can provide a decent picture. And while this is generally hard work, it's well worth the effort. Again: **Identifying a competitor's advantages goes beyond understanding the constraints within which an organization operates; it also comprises learning about the characters and personalities with whom you are competing—and how they might act within those constraints.**

Use Wargaming to Predict and Prepare for Competitive Responses

Having developed a thorough understanding of your competitors, you're now ready to play chess. It's an overused metaphor, but in this case, it's apt. You need to be thinking several moves ahead: "If I do this, what will each competitor do, and how will I respond?" Great chess players not only see the moves ahead and prepare; they make moves that force their opponent to respond in a specific way because there are no viable alternatives. So how to do this in the realm of business? A good place to start is to **stop playing chess with yourself**.

Most business leaders approach the task of determining their competitors' actions as if they were playing chess with themselves. What do we mean by this? When you play chess with yourself, you're always tempted to have "your opponent" play the game you *want* them to play. This is just human nature, right? You subconsciously bias your moves based on what you want the other side to do. In the business realm, **competitive responses are usually assessed far too optimistically, and the range of possible actions assigned to competitors is far too narrow.**

So how do you get out of your own way? One answer is *wargaming*. Borrowed from the military and adapted for business, wargaming is a technique whereby participants roleplay as different competitors. Participants are provided the background needed to "get into character"—that is, to simulate the mindset and perspective of the role to the extent that it is possible. This background material can often be created by leveraging the competitive intelligence gathered (e.g., a two- to five-page company profile). Next, one or more scenarios to be roleplayed are defined. A very basic example would be, "Company A launches product X to customer segment Y in year Z." Finally, participants act out the scenario, determining their responses to that scenario *from the perspective of the role they are playing.*

The key to success with this technique is to give participants enough time to really get into their roles and put themselves in that competitor's shoes. A robust wargaming exercise can take from a few hours to a full day, depending on the number of competitors, scenarios, and participants. As an aside: Wargaming can be used to play out scenarios not only with competitors but also with other stakeholders like channel partners and key customers, especially in the context of negotiations or strategic moves that can create conflicts.

Wargaming can be a very engaging experience, in part because it draws on the imagination of the players. More importantly, **wargaming can be surprisingly effective in both broadening the range of potential competitive responses and bounding the likely outcomes.** In effective wargaming, many ideas for possible actions can come up, but in most cases only a few paths will appear to be rational and likely.

This juncture is when it's likely to prove helpful that you've done your homework on the individual stakeholders and not just the company with which you are competing. To boost creativity in your potential responses, it also can be helpful to acquaint yourself with the kinds of legal competitive responses that can be deployed by companies.[4] In our experience, we have seen "aha" moments arise when previously hypothesized actions or scenarios are proven to be off-base and are replaced by more likely and more nuanced expectations for competitive responses.

Although wargaming can be highly useful, it's very much underutilized in the business world. Why? Partly because of the time investment and thought required to do it right and partly because of general unfamiliarity with the technique. But the truth is, we have yet to see a wargaming exercise that "wasn't worth it." If it seems unlikely that your company will do the kind of deep dive described above, consider a less intense version of wargaming. You may get much of the benefit without as big an investment.

No matter how you proceed, keep in mind that the spirit of wargaming—and indeed, of most steps along the path of innovation—is to **never assume that you are smarter than your competitors. Don't underestimate your competitors. It's almost always better to overestimate them and then be pleasantly surprised when they play into *your* chess game.**

EXECUTIVE SUMMARY

Assume that your competitors are at least as smart as you are.

- Define your competitors by those actually considered at the time of a customer buying decision, including direct and indirect competitors and substitutes.
- Remain wary not just of current competitors but also of future competitors.
- Invest in deeply understanding your competitors (both the organizations and key leaders).
- Identify real competitive advantages (reasons why someone wins) both for competitors and for yourself.
- Predict realistic competitor responses by putting yourself in their shoes through wargaming (i.e., don't play chess with yourself).

FOURTEEN

Price to Unlock the Full Value of Your Innovation

Customers want to pay less and get more. Breakthrough innovation is the pathway to delivering that—while still generating an attractive return for innovators and investors.

Consider the Apple iPhone, mentioned in earlier chapters, and which many consider one of the greatest innovations of the past twenty years. Yes, it sells for twenty times the price of a basic mobile phone. But if you think about all the devices it replaces—phone, GPS navigator, calculator, pager, email, internet browser, camera, video camera, gaming console, audio recorder, emergency rescue beacon, mirror, magnifier, compass, word processor, flashlight, music player, and so on—you realize that the iPhone delivers fantastic value to consumers, especially given the seamless and more or less integrated delivery of all those functions. The result? In 2023, Apple—once thought of as a relic destined for the scrapheap of business history—was the highest-valued company on the planet.[1]

Of course, not all products can be as revolutionary as the iPhone. But every breakthrough product needs to

- **Give customers more:** more disease-free years for cancer patients, more economy and comfort for car drivers, better experiences for cat owners and their pets, more on-time arrivals for airlines, more efficient operations for businesses, and so on.

- **Cost customers less:** not necessarily less in absolute terms but less considering the full range of perceived benefits, less over the life of the product, less when reduced waste and pollution are factored in, less considering the value of improved safety and lives saved, and the like.

In this chapter, we discuss how to apply these basic principles to how products are priced, in a range of contexts, and the pricing decisions you need to make as an innovator. We also cover some of the common pricing missteps innovators make and best practices they should employ to improve the odds of commercial success with their innovation.

Price to Win the War, Not the Battle

When it comes to breakthrough innovations, the innovator has to make several critical pricing decisions:

- What price should be set?
- How should customers pay (i.e., what is the pricing model)?
- What pricing strategy should be used (i.e., how do you price to different customer segments and at different stages of launch)?

Innovators often fall into the trap of thinking myopically about these decisions. They tend to focus more on winning the upcoming battle *at launch* and less on winning the war—that is, transforming their new product or service into an enduring franchise in the long term. Consequently, close engagement with pricing decisions and tradeoffs is not just a "nice to have" but a prerequisite for the commercial success of an innovation. **Pricing decisions need to anticipate evolution of your product and of the market as it matures.** The pricing decisions you make at the outset will be important for the whole future of the innovation—and possibly for the new market you may be creating.

Furthermore, innovators cannot think about these decisions in a vacuum. Pricing needs to be intimately aligned with all the broader go-to-market activities of the organization and with launch priorities, such as the sequencing of customer segments, mix of channels, and sustainability of sales rep incentives and economics, among others. We'll look at all of this in more depth in Part 4.

One additional observation: The order in which you tackle these pricing decisions may vary depending on your market. For example, choosing the pricing model can often be a more critical early decision than setting the price, especially for digital products where the model will drive how you communicate value to customers.

Always Start with Value

In the not-too-distant past, it was standard operating procedure for companies to price their products and services on a cost-plus basis. Using this approach, the innovating company predetermined an acceptable target profit margin and calculated a price based on a markup to the cost of the product.

While this pricing strategy still prevails in some industries and companies, it is now more often the exception rather than the norm, because most companies understand the strategy's built-in disadvantages. Remember: Profit margin depends on volume (i.e., costs typically decrease with volume) and volume depends on price (i.e., higher price lowers volume). With cost-plus pricing, this creates a circular logic problem, because you're setting price based on assumed volume at the same time that the volume is a reflection of the price. In practice, cost-plus pricing causes companies to change prices, often in the wrong direction (e.g., when demand is low, costs increase, so prices increase and lower demand even further).

A more attractive and now common best practice is *value-based pricing*. In this approach, **price reflects both value created and customer willingness to pay (WTP) for that value.** Notably, this can vary meaningfully among customer segments—a subject we'll come back to when we discuss pricing strategy. The upside resulting from this approach can be much more significant and completely untethered from the cost. Consider the example of Keytruda—the cancer immunotherapy drug we referred to in Chapter 1—which has a list price of nearly $11,000 per infusion, or roughly $100,000 for the average treatment duration of a non–small cell lung cancer patient. Expensive? Yes, when considered in a vacuum. But less so when other treatments have failed or are arriving too late.

So in many cases, *perception* **is critical and should serve as the jumping-off point in the process of price setting.**

Economics teaches us that price should be set to maximize profitability—but this requires understanding how price will affect customer demand (elasticity) and your marginal cost of production. For most novel products or services, both of these data points are elusive. In fact, the traditional economics-based approach is only useful in mature markets—and even then it's not often reliable. **The price-setting approach that works best for breakthrough innovations is triangulating estimates of what customers** *state* **they are willing to pay with estimates of the lower and upper bounds of what they** *should* **be willing to pay, based on the value created by the innovation.**

The lower bound on your price should be the price of the next-best alternative. This assumes that you indeed do have a product or service that is superior to the alternative (which throughout this book we assume to be the case!). The next-best alternative is a product or service that your prospective customer could fall back on to address their need. In the language of Chapter 13, this could be a directly or indirectly competitive product, a substitute, or no product at all (i.e., nonconsumption). Notably, more than one alternative may exist, and alternatives may vary by customer segment. Many of the sources of market and competitive data, as well as the primary market research techniques discussed in prior chapters, can provide benchmark prices for the next best alternative(s). Quite possibly you don't perceive some of these competitive alternatives to be benchmarks—but if your prospective customers do, you need to know that!

To estimate the upper bound, we use the concept of "exchange value." Stated simply, the exchange value equals the price of the next best alternative plus the value of incremental benefits (net of any drawbacks). In theory, **the exchange value is the most a rational customer should be willing to pay for the benefits your innovation delivers**. For exchange value, we will focus on the monetary benefits (which can be direct or indirect) but not on psychological perceptions of value. Customers' perceived value of the innovation can be either above or below the exchange value, which will be reflected in our estimates of their willingness to pay (again, WTP). More on this later; for now, exchange value is particularly important for B2B customers (although also commonly relevant for B2C) and can often be quantified quite effectively through a combination of customer interviews and market data points.

To estimate exchange value, we need to catalog a customer's financial impacts from buying your product or service. As discussed, these can be both positive (e.g., increased revenue, reduced costs) and negative (e.g., increased costs) and necessitate a detailed understanding of the current situation for a prospective customer. A simple B2C example is the car cost calculator on Tesla's website. Tesla sells premium electric vehicles and therefore takes care to justify its relatively high price point by helping customers calculate the estimated savings from using electricity instead of gasoline as well as accounting for any relevant government incentives, which will vary with geography. In theory, a more complete calculator could also include items like reduced maintenance costs (e.g., no oil changes, less frequent brake pad changes) and the added cost of installing a home charger—but this is a sales tool, after all, and the company has limited it to include just the biggest and most positive drivers of monetary value.

B2B calculations tend to be more complex. A B2B estimate is usually critical for articulating value to customers and can feed data into an ROI calculator that can be used as marketing collateral (more on this in Part 4). To illustrate the concept of exchange value in a B2B setting, let's look at a medical device that reduces the risk of patient hospitalization from a chronic disease. In Table 14.1, we've catalogued the costs that are displaced by using this device on relevant patients. We have dramatically simplified this real-life example, but the basic principles remain: What are all the costs avoided, and what is the likelihood of avoiding these costs? This then helps set the exchange value (or upper bound) on what hospitals should be willing to pay for the product.

With a lower and an upper bound in hand, we are well on our way to understanding what value we are creating and therefore what price we can set. Now it's time to look at customer willingness to pay (WTP) again. Having the exchange value makes assessing WTP easier, because you have some

TABLE 14.1. Exchange Value/Cost Displacement Example

Cost displacement category	Description	Cost	% of patients who incur these costs	Expected costs
Hospitalization	• Cost of hospital stay including any treatments received	~$10,000-15,000	100%	~$10,000-15,000
Drug treatments	• Prescription medications provided	~$5,000-7,000	5-10%	~$350-700
Non-drug treatments	• Rehabilitation required • Additional medical interventions	~$4,000-6,000	10-15%	~$450-800

Total cost displaced	~$10,800-16,500
% risk reduction of incurring costs	~60%
Avg. cost displaced per patient	~$6,500-10,000

foundation on which to base your hypothesized price points, and you have something to which you can compare responses. For meaningfully innovative products (and breakthrough innovations in particular), WTP can be difficult to measure and can yield results that require overstatement adjustments (as discussed in Chapter 12)—again, because customers have limited to no experience with the category and an inadequate frame of reference with which to accurately judge their WTP. For these reasons, in the case of a true breakthrough product or service, innovators sometimes decide not to bother assessing WTP. This is short-sighted. **Using the right methods, a meaningful WTP signal from customers can be discerned—and that signal is almost always a useful input to setting price.**

For an example of a product launch that missed the mark on WTP, consider Disney's streaming service Disney+. It was launched in 2019 at a price of $6.99 per month, about half of Netflix's standard $12.99 plan. The launch was successful in attracting millions of subscribers, but the company faced severe profitability headwinds with a low price and no advertising revenue. This was likely an intentional penetration pricing strategy (more on this below) for quickly attracting subscribers but may not have been necessary given the premium content the service was offering relative to others. In the four years after launch, the company implemented a series of price increases with the standard (ad-free) service increased to $14 per month at the end of 2023 and a new service with ads priced at $8 per month.[2]

There are several methods available for testing WTP, and you can choose to use one or several of these approaches. But in all cases, in order to conduct a meaningful WTP assessment, you need a thoughtfully developed target product profile (TPP) or concept profile to share. If you're promoting a truly novel innovation—especially if it is a category-maker—you need to be sure to make your stimulus specific and understandable (e.g., with visuals or demos) and potentially share a useful frame of reference (e.g., "this offering is like the Uber of service X").

The simplest way to assess WTP is the **price sensitivity method**: asking directly how much a customer would expect to pay and what they would consider to be expensive or inexpensive.[3] (You can refer to the relevant appendix in the back of the book for more detail on scales and adjustments for purchase intent questions.) This method is particularly useful when your innovation is truly novel and the potential price range is not clear. It also helps you develop anchor points on the potential price—information that can be leveraged for subsequent testing with other methods.

Another common approach is the **purchase probability method**.[4] Using this method, you simply ask customers whether they would buy your innovation at the stated price, on a five-point scale. You can either start with a low price and keep increasing it until they score 3 or below (won't buy at that price) or start with a high price and keep decreasing until they score a 4 or 5 (will buy at that price). This provides an initial view on pricing elasticity and potential key inflections at psychological price points (for example, a common inflection point occurs in consumer WTP when the hypothetical price point increases from $99 to $100).

The purchase probability method is more useful when the attributes of the product or service are reasonably well defined (based on where you are with your product development), if the category is not entirely new to the world, or if you already have defined a reasonable price range with the price sensitivity method.

The third common approach to assess WTP is the **simulation method**, also known as "conjoint analysis."[5] This is a complex analytical approach in which participants are presented several "buying simulations" in which they consider multiple concept profiles with different attribute combinations—such as price, features, or brand—and are asked to select which option they prefer. This is an effective approach for arriving at specific price points, identifying optimal price/feature packages, and understanding different WTP across customer segments; however, it may be less useful for breakthrough innovations, where the participants may have trouble understanding the attributes of the product or service well enough to give an accurate opinion of their preferences.

In the case of the sports entertainment DTC streaming service mentioned in Chapter 12, we were able to use a conjoint analysis to measure WTP because consumers understood the concept of a streaming service well enough, even if the category and programming itself was very different from what was available on the market. But in many cases this is not true, which means that the other two methods are likely to be more useful, even if they are less precise.

The research methods available for testing WTP are summarized in Table 14.2. It is worth mentioning, though, that WTP often changes over time with the maturity of the market and entry of alternatives/competitors. This translates into different price level choices over time and adjustments to pricing strategy (to be discussed shortly).

So how do you ultimately set a price? **For B2C products, WTP most likely will inform your choice of price point**, especially if value is more driven by psychological perceptions than exchange value (e.g., luxury goods, convenience-driven innovations). In those situations, an exchange value calculation may be impractical and unnecessary. Occasionally, though, B2C innovations have an important monetary story to tell (e.g., Nest's smart thermostats generating cost savings by lowering utility bills), which makes an exchange value calculation useful.

In B2B products and services, exchange value is usually critical, as the financial impact on the organization is an important consideration for decision-makers. If WTP is above the exchange value, this can indicate that the

TABLE 14.2. Pricing Methods Overview

	How it works	When to use it

Price sensitivity method	• First ask (open-ended):
	  – What price do you think is too inexpensive (or too cheap) that you would have doubts about its quality and reliability and would not consider purchasing it?
	  – What price do you think is inexpensive enough to be considered a good bargain?
	  – What price do you think is beginning to get expensive but you would still consider purchasing it?
	  – What price do you think is too expensive and you would not consider purchasing it?
	• Then ask purchase intent on a five-point scale:
	  – How likely would you be to purchase it at [insert "inexpensive" price point]?
	  – How likely would you be to purchase it at [insert "expensive" price point]?
		• Useful for novel products with limited pricing references
		• Helps set possible price range early in research

Purchase probability method	• Ask purchase intent on a five-point scale: – How likely would you be to purchase this product/service at [insert price]? • Repeat up to five times with price points in ascending or descending order	• Useful when reasonably well-defined or known concept for customers • Helps refine prices within a range
Simulation (conjoint)	• Present respondents with a set of concept profiles varying one or more attributes (typically up to eight) including price • Respondents asked to select their preferred concept profile • Purchasing simulation repeated with different set of options • Possible to have respondents "build their own" optimal product and then vary attributes around it	• Useful when concept attributes are well understood • Helps clarify importance of price vs. other attributes and set specific price points (especially if paired with purchase probability)

perceived value of nonmonetary benefits is meaningful. Conversely, if WTP is below the exchange value, this can be an indication that customers are not fully informed about the benefits and that market education is needed. **In practice, it's generally best to price slightly below the exchange value, unless WTP is much higher.**

In Figure 14.1, you can see how we can illustratively use exchange value, the price of the next best alternative, and WTP to bound and set price for the medical device referenced earlier. Consistent with the goal we outlined at the start of this chapter, the optimal price offers great value to customers, even though it is at a 40 percent premium to analog products.

The price-setting approaches described above cover many situations, but some circumstances exist in which other methods may be relevant. For many digital products in particular, it can be practicable to engage in price experimentation and real-world testing to gauge WTP far more accurately—and less theoretically—than would be true with traditional research techniques. This of

FIGURE 14.1. Triangulated Pricing Zone Example

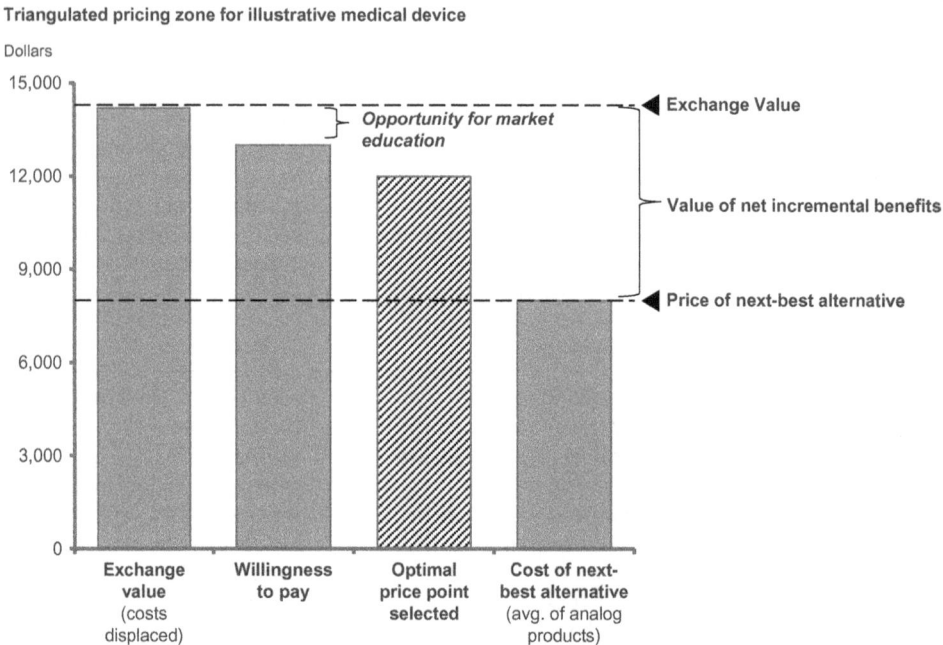

Triangulated pricing zone for illustrative medical device

course is limited to certain types of products and services but can be a powerful and preferred method to research-based WTP.

One such alternative approach is **auction-based pricing**. In this approach, the market value of your product or service is defined by the customer through competitive bidding. This is a highly efficient mechanism (no need for WTP research!) and works well in situations when supply is constrained and there's plenty of demand. This model has been deployed quite notably by Google AdWords and in marketplace settings like eBay.

Another alternative approach is **dynamic pricing**. This sounds simple enough—you reset your price frequently—but often turns out to be very complicated on the back end. Dynamic pricing works well in fixed or constrained capacity businesses (e.g., airlines, hotels) with perishable inventory and in which WTP and the level of demand can vary meaningfully as a function of changing conditions (e.g., season, time of day, weather, etc.). This is the logic behind surge pricing for rideshare apps like Uber and Lyft when localized demand jumps on a rainy day or right after a large sporting event. But it's best to be careful: While dynamic pricing can be an attractive model, it can also frustrate customers (e.g., when your airline ticket price changes significantly in a short span of time).

Select the Right Pricing Model

One revelation in the world of business over the last several decades has been the importance of the *pricing model*. What's a pricing model? It's simply *how* customers pay the price you set. There is obviously a linkage between selecting the pricing model and setting the price, as the model may impact willingness to pay (e.g., customers may be willing to pay more in total over time than upfront). Selecting the right pricing model for the near term as well as the long term and determining if you expect it to change along the way—these are all crucial decisions. In fact, **getting the pricing model right is usually at least as important to commercial success as getting the price right.**

There are many pricing-model options, but they all involve some combination of four basic models—see Table 14.3—which vary payment on timing, product or service usage, and achieving benefits (outcomes). Ultimately, **the**

TABLE 14.3. Pricing Model Summary

Pricing Model	Model dimensions			Considerations
	Timing	Usage	Outcome	
Transactional	Pay now	Pay regardless of usage	Pay regardless of benefits	• Simple to understand and communicate • More difficult to align price with value (as value may not be known upfront)
Subscription	Pay over time	Pay regardless of usage	Pay regardless of benefits	• Simple to understand and communicate • Lower upfront cost • Predictable
Consumption based	Pay over time	Pay based on how much product is used (optionally with thresholds)	Pay regardless of benefits	• Lower upfront cost • Cost linked to value accrual • Less predictable
Performance based	Pay later (optionally with milestones)	Pay regardless of usage	Pay based on benefits derived	• Cost linked directly to benefits derived (particularly valuable if benefits are unproven) • Requires agreement on clear and observable outcome metrics • Relatively complex to execute • May be risky for supplier

right pricing model should align how customers accrue value with how they pay for it.

The most common and simplest pricing model is **transactional**: Pay now to receive a set amount of the product or service, regardless of whether or not it achieves all of its promised or expected benefits. A common variation of the simple transactional model is a tiered transactional model based on volume (i.e., volume-based discounts). Transactional models have the advantage of simplicity. Not surprisingly, they are particularly effective with products or services that are consumed immediately or only purchased once.

While transactional models make sense for many innovations, it is **subscription** pricing models that have really transformed the economy in the last twenty years.[6] A subscription simply spreads payment and access to a product or service over time. Of course, subscriptions are not a novel concept—in the context of newspapers and other print publications, dating back decades or even centuries—but they have grown dramatically in line with the expansion of digital businesses, for which they are a great fit. They've become the basis of innovation for many new entrants in a wide range of traditional product categories: Dollar Shave Club for shaving needs, beauty boxes for cosmetics, Spotify for music, and so on. In fact, SaaS, originating as a subscription model in the software industry, has now been popularized and translated into many other contexts as "XaaS" (anything as a service).

There are many advantages to subscriptions, which explains why they have become so common. For customers, they lower the cost of adoption and spread cost over time, which is financially attractive. For companies, they boost the lifetime value of a customer by reducing transaction frictions with fewer buying decisions (especially with automatic renewals), increase the average consumption level of the product or service, create greater customer stickiness and loyalty, and provide opportunities for upselling and cross-selling. They also smooth revenue flows over time, providing businesses with financial predictability—which can be enormously valuable—and reduce the direct and administrative costs associated with having to make the sale repeatedly. (If you only have to sell your product or service once, you're ahead of the game.) These benefits can accrue differently across product and service categories. For example, for "box moving" businesses (like Dollar Shave Club) minimizing customer churn is often the key benefit, while maximizing consumption and value perception is more relevant for digital offerings.

Despite the many positives of subscription models, they're not for every type of business. They tend to work best when the marginal cost of the product or service is relatively low (e.g., digital products, low-COGS (cost of goods sold) products, and unit cost subsidized by advertisements).

Another increasingly common model is **consumption-based** pricing, which links payment to usage. Customers pay over time proportionate to their use of the product or service. This is particularly beneficial when usage can vary substantially among customers and when customer willingness to pay may change with usage (especially if greater usage drives greater cumulative value). This can work well for innovations where lowering the cost of entry is important—for example, with customers who may not yet know how much they'll use a novel product or service and don't want to risk (1) overpaying up-front with a transactional model or (2) assuming a potentially inaccurate usage level in a subscription.

The key to this model is defining the right unit metric by which to mea-sure usage—in other words, one that accurately measures usage, is easy to track, and is aligned with the value being generated. Sometimes this can be tricky. For example, many software businesses that have historically offered consumption-based pricing using "per data" metrics have realized that the value is generated from querying the data and therefore have begun to shift to "per query" consumption-based models. While such models have also been around a long time (e.g., electric and gas utilities), they are becoming much more common in a wide variety of applications, ranging from cloud storage (pay per GB used) to car insurance (pay per mile) and robotic surgery (pay per procedure). Consumption-based models also can include elements of other pricing models, such as an initial upfront payment or tiered pricing at different levels of usage. Price tiers are, in fact, often critical for maximizing WTP with a consumption-based model, but they require a nuanced understanding of cus-tomer usage patterns and expectations to ensure that customers are satisfied with their tier options.

The final and least common of these models—although it is also growing in popularity—is **performance-based** pricing. This model links payment to the outcomes or benefits delivered. It truly requires sellers to put their money where their mouths are by risking nonpayment or lower payment if the product or service doesn't deliver the promised benefits. This model presumes advance agreement on clear and observable metrics for measuring the hoped-for outcome—a prerequisite that in many circumstances can be impractical or difficult to achieve.

Performance-based models generally come in two flavors: *risk-sharing* and *gainsharing.* In a risk-sharing agreement, the customer pays (or pays a higher amount) only if the product or service delivers the agreed-upon and measured outcome. In a gainsharing agreement, the customer pays more as a function of benefits delivered and often "splits" value that is mutually created. Given the inherent risks and complexities, this is not the preferred pricing model for most companies.

That said, there *are* some situations where it makes sense—for example, if the innovation promises to deliver high value but the willingness to pay doesn't reflect the value without proving the benefits. In the real world, we have seen performance-based risk-sharing agreements put in place for expensive pharma-ceuticals (especially in oncology), whereby the government pays retroactively for patients whom the drug helps but not for those it doesn't. Gainsharing agree-ments are commonly used by attorneys in contingency cases (e.g., win the case, get a portion of the payout) and consultants in cost-reduction projects (e.g., share the savings). Despite their inherent complexity, these models are growing in practice, particularly because customers like the fact that the incentives of buyer and seller are aligned. And at the risk of stating the obvious, most perfor-mance-based models are not *purely* performance-based, as most companies try to capture a baseline level of payment to manage their risks and cover their costs.

The software industry provides a fascinating longitudinal portrait of the evolution of pricing models in recent history. In the 1980s and 1990s, software was primarily sold through a transactional model. This evolved fairly quickly to pricing based on the number of users (i.e., a tiered transactional model) and to SaaS, a subscription model, in the 2000s. (The SaaS industry grew by some 500 percent between 2016 and 2023.)[7] This worked well because customers didn't want to be left behind with constantly having to upgrade to new versions of products, and companies didn't want to lose out on the value of upgrades. The next step in the evolution has been consumption-based models, which are now becoming more common as some customers value the added flexibility over traditional SaaS models and prefer to pay based on their consumption (e.g., Amazon Web Services in a range of cloud services).

So which model is right for your innovation? The answer typically depends on several key considerations:

- **Customer preference:** What do your customers prefer? Customer preference will almost always be the primary determinant of a pricing model, especially if customers are used to paying a certain way for a relevant category of products or services. In the case of software and IT services, customers are clearly signaling that they prefer the simplicity of the SaaS model. That said, keep in mind that some of the most successful innovators, including Uber, have flipped the pricing model in their industry on its head to differentiate and drive success. Remember that **innovations can redefine how they communicate value!**

- **Near-term viability:** Can your organization manage the near-term requirements of implementing the pricing model? For example, if you're selling a product with a meaningful upfront capital outlay, you need to determine if you can handle the upfront cash outflows but more gradual cash inflows of a subscription or consumption-based model.

- **Long-term viability:** Will the pricing model fit the needs of the market as it changes? Will the pricing model fit your organization's needs over time (including delivering growth with more customers, greater usage, more features, etc.)? If the market into which you are entering is shifting toward use of a different pricing model (e.g., from SaaS subscriptions to consumption-based), you may not want to align with the outgoing paradigm. Your R&D pipeline may also inform the durability of a pricing model for your needs as an organization. If you can anticipate a subsequent product or service that will require a different pricing model, you may want to consider whether that scenario comes to bear on your model choice for *this* product or service.

- **Feasibility:** Practically speaking, how difficult is it to implement the model? It's important to understand the operational requirements and customer readiness for a pricing model. If your anticipated operations will require access to data or investment in technology that you don't have, this could be a substantial barrier (although one that may still be worth overcoming). If customers require education on the pricing model, you may need to consider the implications of that fact for the commercial launch (e.g., possible delays in adoption, possible investment in marketing/communication, and so on).

Clearly, **to inform the pricing-model decision, you need to test customer preferences on pricing models.** Interviews and quantitative surveys work well, and pricing models should be tested in tandem with WTP. An effective way to determine these preferences is to present customers with multiple pricing model options with the same total price and see which one they choose (and who chooses which one). This works well because if the potential cost of one model or another to the prospective customers is the same, the importance of nonfinancial considerations and preferences becomes apparent. A good example of this is in airline ticket pricing: Even if the total price of the ticket ends up the same, leisure travelers typically prefer a lower base ticket fare even if it means paying extra for baggage fees and other add-ons.

As you weigh these considerations, you need to also determine if your pricing model will remain the same over the life cycle of your product or service. Usually, companies prefer to keep the same model, as it can be difficult to change. But just as we've seen in the software industry, your circumstances may well evolve as the market changes. Another good question is whether the same pricing model should be used for all customer segments. To answer it, you'll need to make choices on how much segmented pricing you have—in other words, different pricing for different customers—to which we'll return shortly. But in the interest of managing complexity, most companies prefer to stick with one pricing model for one product or service.

Finally, it's worth noting that **sometimes the right answer is to offer multiple pricing models with equivalent value to you**, both to be responsive to varying customer preferences and to maximize adoption. This is one reason why the car industry offers both outright purchase and lease arrangements. It would be nice if "one size fits all" pertained, but often that's not the case.

Determine Your Pricing Strategy

When you have assessed your likely range for setting prices and determined the right pricing model, you still need to address the question of *pricing strategy*. Pricing strategy really means two things: (1) how, if at all, prices will differ across customer segments, and (2) how, if at all, you plan to change your price after launch. **Setting pricing strategy requires you to step back and evaluate your objectives, especially in the near term at launch: Are you trying to maximize adoption or profitability?** This can vary dramatically depending on the innovation and the competitive context.

Regarding **segmented pricing**: the simple reality is that different customer segments will have different WTP. Consequently, the profit-optimizing way to set prices is to charge each segment the highest price they would be willing to pay—in economics parlance, "price discrimination." In practice it's not always possible to charge different prices to customers. It may be difficult to control which customer receives which price, it may be difficult to determine which customer falls into which price segment; in some circumstances, it may even be illegal.

That said, there are many (legal) tools in the pricing toolkit for successfully deploying segmented pricing, and companies use "segmentation hedges" all the time. Does your favorite bar charge less for drinks during happy hour, or does your favorite movie theater offer lower prices to seniors? These are common segmentation hedges. Most important for a successful segmentation hedge: It needs to efficiently sort customers based on their WTP. It also should be explainable, fair, and unambiguous to customers. Some common hedges include demographics for B2C (e.g., age, income level) or firmographics for B2B (e.g., organizational scale), time of purchase, volume or frequency of purchases, and location of purchase. There's significant research out there on different approaches for segmented pricing, and it's a topic that's worth exploring further if your customer segments have meaningfully different WTP.

As for changing your price after launch—should you choose to do so—you have three basic options. You either charge the long-term target price, charge a lower price to drive faster adoption (penetration pricing), or charge a higher price to maximize near-term profitability (price skimming). Pricing at the long-term target from the outset is more relevant for products and services entering established categories where there are multiple competitors already with different price-to-value positioning. **Penetration pricing is attractive when your innovation benefits substantially from network effects, and/or the competitive environment is such that a "land grab" is necessary.**

So-called "freemium pricing" for apps is a good example of penetration pricing: Customers can access a free version of the product with limited functionality, which drives adoption; over time, the company hopes to convert these users into paying customers. Of course, *all* innovators expect to capture customers and then raise prices up to a long-term target—but in real life, this can often be tricky, which makes this strategy risky. Sometimes it works very well (e.g., LinkedIn, Facebook), but more often it does not (only 1 to 2 percent of freemium users typically convert to paid versions) and significant profit is left on the table or forever forgone.[8]

For most breakthrough innovations, it makes sense to use a price-skimming approach but in such a way that you sequentially bring the price down to hit the next tier of customers by WTP over time. Early adopters tend to inherently perceive more value and have a higher WTP, which makes this approach particularly viable with a meaningfully differentiated breakthrough innovation. Further, for many products and services, capacity of supply may be a challenge at time of launch, so setting a higher price helps maximize profit early on. And higher profitability in the early stages yields many benefits, including enabling further investment in capabilities and providing stronger incentives to channel partners to carry and advantageously place or support your innovation.

We offer one final thought on pricing: **It's not a one-and-done set of decisions.** Almost certainly, you will need to constantly monitor and manage pricing after you launch your product or service. Throughout that period and afterward, assessing customer reactions and competitor responses will be critical. To support this, best-in-class innovators institutionalize pricing into a strategic capability for their organization with dedicated resources, systems, processes, and requisite governance structures.

EXECUTIVE SUMMARY

Price to unlock the full value of the innovation.

- Ensure that pricing decisions anticipate future evolution of your product/service and of the market.

- Set the price correctly by reflecting value created and customer willingness to pay (WTP) using customer insights, real-world experimentation, and pricing benchmarks.

- Align the pricing model to how customers accrue value—getting the model right is at least as important as getting the price right.

- Follow a pricing strategy at launch to reflect financial goals and competitive context—pricing higher at the outset is usually preferred for breakthrough innovations.

FIFTEEN

Build a High-Confidence Revenue Forecast

In the past several chapters, we walked through all the major inputs you need to develop a revenue forecast for your innovation—sizing your SAM, defining and prioritizing target customer segments, estimating adoption by customer segment, understanding your competitive set, and determining price point and pricing model.

In this chapter, we'll pull it all together. But first, a word about revenue forecasts. At face value, revenue forecasts are very simple—take your expected number of customers each year, multiply by price, and voilà! So why bother dedicating an entire chapter to this seemingly simple and formulaic exercise? Because although anyone can create a revenue forecast, **the real challenge is to create a forecast that has a high probability of coming true when the product is launched. If done right, this is also likely to be a forecast that can withstand the scrutiny of discerning, sophisticated investors and senior leaders.**

As described in Chapter 1, our consulting work often involves developing revenue forecasts for breakthrough new products. (If more straightforward incremental innovations are involved, clients generally don't go to the expense of hiring us.) Even with all the uncertainties involved in creating new customers and revenue streams, we generally aim to deliver forecasts that on average are within 10 to 20 percent of what is ultimately achieved, assuming there are no technical failures in product performance or time to market.

So how do you create reliable revenue forecasts? First, by **breaking down your assumptions to the simplest level possible,** and second, by **selecting justifiable inputs.** While there may be many assumptions underpinning a revenue forecast, there are only a few assumptions that are both impactful and have the potential to be proven way off the mark, as things unfold. Typically, for a radical innovation, **the most critical and contentious assumptions are the level and rate of adoption** (that is, the adoption "ramp curve" and peak adoption, which we discussed in Chapter 12). This means that you must **identify the key contentious assumptions and disproportionately direct your efforts to rigorously validate them.**

In addition to having clear and rigorously supported assumptions, **you need the forecast to be internally consistent, to sync with your broader narrative, and to sense-check with other data points.** "Internally consistent" means simply that your assumptions—as well as any outputs such as revenues and implied market share—make sense relative to each other, with no contradictions. At the same time, that forecast needs to sense-check with other data points in the market. This often includes analogs, triangulations, and other market data points, such as competitive revenues.

What if your revenue forecast comes in below where you had hoped? Better to know about this problem before the launch, rather than after! Can pricing or features be adjusted to drive faster adoption? Do you need to plan for a broader market launch or additional distribution partners? Maybe the world has moved on, and you need to live with a different reality than you had originally hoped for (as in the Iridium example from Chapter 1). If so, you need to go back and revisit some of your original assumptions and plans. Remember, the first step in solving a problem is knowing that you have one.

Remember, too, that **the *process* you take to get to a high confidence revenue forecast is as important as the forecast itself.** By "process" we mean all the steps described in the prior chapters—market-testing your value proposition, market sizing, customer segmentation, and so on. Collectively, these efforts ensure that you are armed with the data and insights needed to create a forecast that has anticipated and planned for the obstacles you will need to overcome.

As we delve into the science (and art) of creating a revenue forecast, it is worth underscoring up front that your approach and the level of creativity you need to deploy may vary depending on the end market and type of product or service you are forecasting. If you're developing a novel drug, for example, pharma revenue-forecasting methodologies are well established and data availability is superb (which is one reason why we make numerous references to best practices used in that market throughout this chapter). But if you're working on a new kind of digital AI tool for agricultural applications—a promising niche that as of this writing has only begun to emerge—you might have relatively little to go on. In most cases, though, the approaches and best practices we share here should be generally applicable and can be tailored to your specific situation.

The Fundamentals of Building Revenue Forecasts

A revenue forecast is generated from a model—an analytical tool, usually in Excel—comprised of three core components: inputs, calculations, and outputs. (A fourth component, a control panel, is often included to allow assumptions to be "flexed" for the assessment of scenarios and sensitivities.) How do these three core components interrelate? Simply stated, **inputs are the assumptions that are manipulated via calculations to generate outputs** (for example, number of customers, predicted revenue, implied share of current market).

Many kinds of models can be used to generate revenue forecasts, and you need to determine which is best for your needs. Let's look at several of the most common:

A **"top-down" model** starts with a topline number and cuts it down to the revenue forecast for your product or service. The simplest form of this involves taking a current market size or SAM estimate from a market or analyst report and multiplying by your expected share, thereby yielding revenue. Of course, these models can certainly be more complex than this, but the truth is that **top-down models are always limited in their defensibility**. For example, top-down models often include non-addressable or non-target customer segments in the topline number, which can make your adoption estimates difficult to apply directly. Furthermore, because you have only a limited ability to adjust the assumptions that drive the topline number, it's challenging to create meaningful scenarios. For these reasons, top-down modeling is usually most useful as a tool for triangulation.

A **"bottom-up" model**, not surprisingly, starts from the ground up to estimate the addressable market and, hence, revenue. In a bottom-up model, you typically begin with an estimate of the underlying volume of customers (e.g., population) and progressively whittle this down until you arrive at the number of addressable customers (by segment), from which you can then (1) derive the number of adopting customers, (2) multiply by price, and (3) estimate revenue.

Here's the good news: All the limitations of the top-down model are addressed by the bottom-up model. You can apply adoption rates specifically to the appropriate customer segments and flex a variety of assumptions that can impact the addressable market (e.g., population shifts, utilization rates). The only drawback to the bottom-up model is that it is much more time- and effort-intensive than a top-down model. But the truth is, this effort is usually worthwhile if you really want to be able to defend your forecast. **Ultimately, because the bottom-up model allows for substantial rigor, it is the recommended basis for most revenue forecasts.**

Figure 15.1, below, depicts the bottom-up model in its most basic form.

FIGURE 15.1. Bottom-Up Model Structure

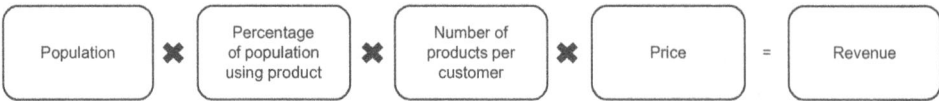

There are several varieties of bottom-up models. The simplest is what we'll call a **linear-flow model**, whereby you calculate your volume of customers in each year independently. (Figure 15.1 could be considered Year One of such a sequence.) This contrasts with a **stock-flow model**, in which the number of customers in the current year impacts the number of customers in the next year. This is often most relevant when you are modeling markets with installed bases—things like capital equipment, other durable goods, and subscription businesses—and allows for complex kinds of calculations over time. For example, customers acquired in each year create cohorts that contribute to an existing installed base and thereafter have different timelines of revenue impact (including, for example, replacement demand after your product hits the end of its useful life, customer retention/churn, changes in product utilization with customer maturity, and so on).

FIGURE 15.2. Stock-Flow Model Example

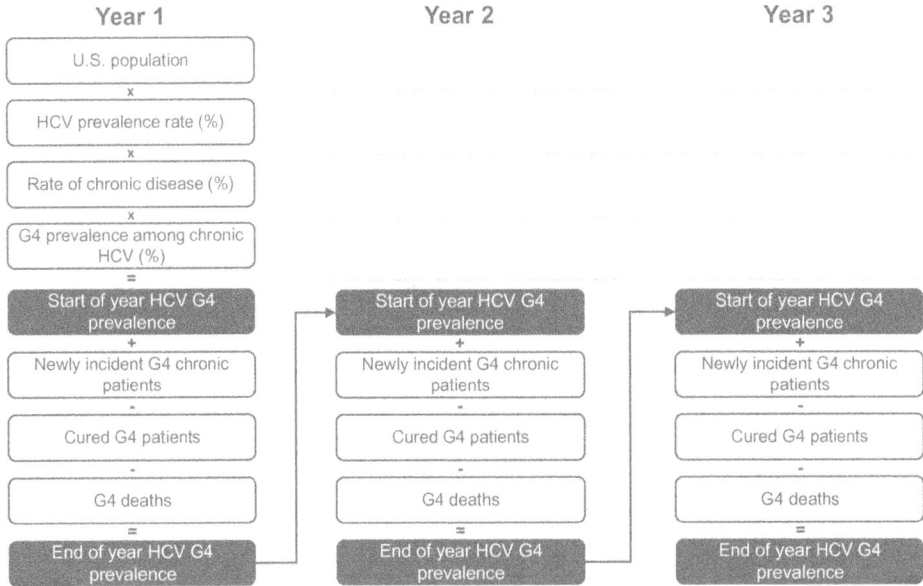

Another common application of stock-flow models is incidence-based patient flow forecasting in the life sciences. The addressable pool of patients changes from year to year due to factors like cures (at one end of the spectrum) and deaths (at the other). Obviously, then, the number of patients in Year 2 needs to be linked to the number of patients in Year 1.

See Figure 15.2, which is an illustrative stock-flow model applied to the life sciences context (specifically, HCV G4/Genotype 4 Hepatitis C).

Stock-flow models typically require more assumptions than linear flow models and therefore can be much more complicated to build. For this reason, you may choose to simplify your stock-flow model "down" into a linear-flow model by simplifying one or more of your assumptions (e.g., assuming an average installed base age across cohorts, and thereby an average replacement cycle). When should you consider this? There's no easy answer. The choice depends on the level of detail required from your model, your available time, and the available granularity of your assumptions.

Throughout the rest of this chapter, we'll assume that you're using a bottom-up model for developing your revenue forecast (whether linear-flow or stock-flow). In general, though, **you should use more than one approach, if possible, which typically means complementing your bottom-up model with a top-down one for triangulation**—a subject to which we'll return shortly.

Develop Your Model Methodology

Once you've decided upon the modeling approach that is most relevant for your innovation, you need to develop a model methodology. Think of this as a summary flow-diagram of the entire model on one PowerPoint slide. This serves as a useful tool for communication as well as a critical reference for planning. The methodology not only includes the calculation steps but also identifies the likely sources of inputs. Put in the time needed for this exercise. If your methodology can't be summarized in a simple flow-diagram, it's too complicated!

Your model methodology should be designed before, and refined in parallel with, key research workstreams like interviews and surveys, to ensure that you can collect the right inputs in the right format. Again: *Invest the required time in advance.* If you design the methodology after you've completed the bulk of any research, you may be severely constrained by insufficient or imperfect assumption inputs.

Figure 15.3 is a typical (but slightly simplified) model methodology for a new drug product. Drug revenue forecast models have many of their own nuances and complexities, but they tend to follow the same generalized flow as other models.

Let's revisit the sports entertainment company that we discussed back in Chapters 12 and 14. As you'll recall, that company was preparing to launch a DTC streaming service. As you can see in Figure 15.4, this revenue forecast model was quite detailed and had the benefit of a tight linkage between the survey and the methodology. All the research workstreams tied together to define and estimate the size of different customer segments, apply adoption expectations to them, and then quantify the revenue generated from each.

FIGURE 15.3. Example Model Methodology—Life Sciences

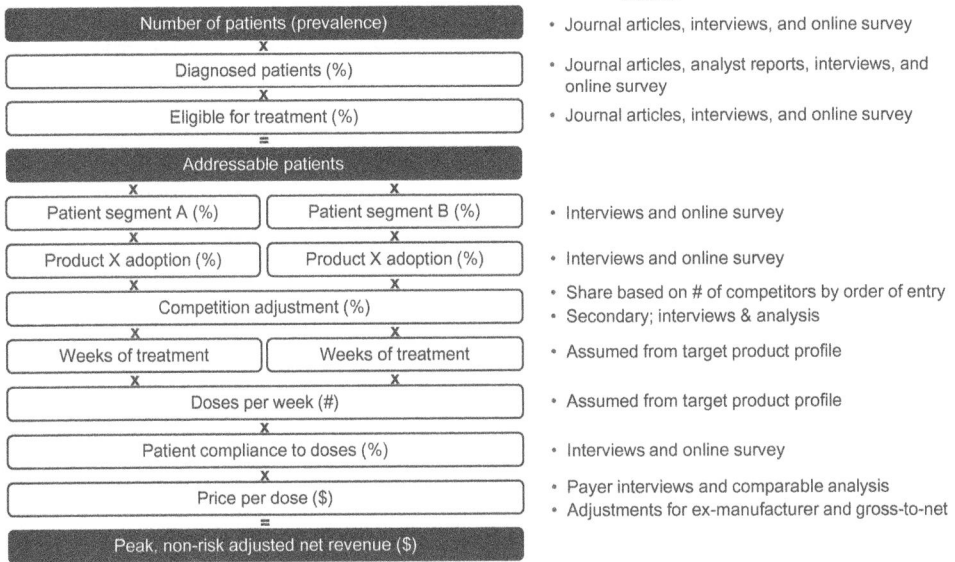

Model	Source
Number of patients (prevalence)	• Journal articles, interviews, and online survey
x	
Diagnosed patients (%)	• Journal articles, analyst reports, interviews, and online survey
x	
Eligible for treatment (%)	• Journal articles, interviews, and online survey
=	
Addressable patients	
x ... x	
Patient segment A (%) / Patient segment B (%)	• Interviews and online survey
x ... x	
Product X adoption (%) / Product X adoption (%)	• Interviews and online survey
x ... x	
Competition adjustment (%)	• Share based on # of competitors by order of entry • Secondary; interviews & analysis
x ... x	
Weeks of treatment / Weeks of treatment	• Assumed from target product profile
x ... x	
Doses per week (#)	• Assumed from target product profile
x	
Patient compliance to doses (%)	• Interviews and online survey
x	
Price per dose ($)	• Payer interviews and comparable analysis • Adjustments for ex-manufacturer and gross-to-net
=	
Peak, non-risk adjusted net revenue ($)	

FIGURE 15.4. Example Model Methodology—Consumer

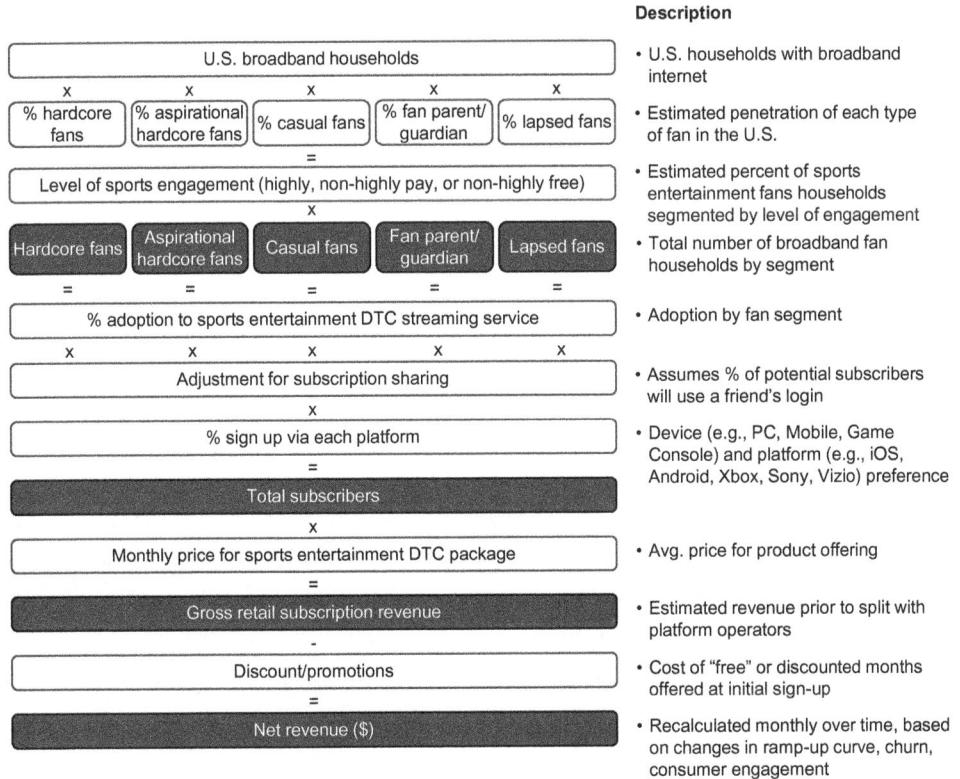

Model	Description
U.S. broadband households	• U.S. households with broadband internet
x x x x x	
% hardcore fans / % aspirational hardcore fans / % casual fans / % fan parent/guardian / % lapsed fans	• Estimated penetration of each type of fan in the U.S.
=	
Level of sports engagement (highly, non-highly pay, or non-highly free)	• Estimated percent of sports entertainment fans households segmented by level of engagement
x	
Hardcore fans / Aspirational hardcore fans / Casual fans / Fan parent/guardian / Lapsed fans	• Total number of broadband fan households by segment
= = = = =	
% adoption to sports entertainment DTC streaming service	• Adoption by fan segment
x x x x x	
Adjustment for subscription sharing	• Assumes % of potential subscribers will use a friend's login
x	
% sign up via each platform	• Device (e.g., PC, Mobile, Game Console) and platform (e.g., iOS, Android, Xbox, Sony, Vizio) preference
=	
Total subscribers	
x	
Monthly price for sports entertainment DTC package	• Avg. price for product offering
=	
Gross retail subscription revenue	• Estimated revenue prior to split with platform operators
-	
Discount/promotions	• Cost of "free" or discounted months offered at initial sign-up
=	
Net revenue ($)	• Recalculated monthly over time, based on changes in ramp-up curve, churn, consumer engagement

Creating a revenue-forecast model methodology that's right for your innovation requires you to think through and answer several questions. For example:

- What output is required (e.g., revenue, volume of units, volume of customers, market share)?

- What level of output detail is required (e.g., in total, by segment, by product, by geography)?

- How does the nature of your innovation and its expected pricing model impact potential logic flow (e.g., linear-flow vs. stock-flow)?

- What time frame needs to be modeled (i.e., number of years) and at what periodicity (e.g., annual vs. quarterly vs. monthly)?

- What are the data requirements, the likely data availability, and the likely data fidelity for your key inputs? What will the sources of this data be?

Defining Adoption Curves

With a functional model and key inputs from any research you may have conducted, you are nearly ready to start outputting a revenue forecast. But one area we haven't yet discussed is how to model adoption over time. In Chapter 12, we primarily focused on estimating peak adoption adjusted for overstatement bias (i.e., what percent of potential customers will adopt at $X?). But how do you think about the length of time it might take for you to "ramp" adoption? Will you achieve full penetration in your target customer segment(s) in three years? In five years? Will it vary by customer segment?

The most defensible way to model your "adoption curve" is with analogs. For example, in the case of the DTC sports streaming service, we were able to use analogs like Netflix, HBO, and others where public data was available on the number of subscribers over time. These analogs can be directly used for your adoption curve if they are perceived to be relevant enough for your innovation. Alternatively, several analogs can be averaged, or you can use them as bounds (e.g., faster than analog 1 but slower than analog 2). You do need to be careful to contextualize your analogs to ensure applicability—for example, given the level of marketing spend that Netflix deployed, would this still be a reasonable analog for the sports streaming service? In general, the *functionality of the offering, competitive context,* and *marketing tactics* need to be considered to determine how to use the analog—whether as a direct comparator, an upper or lower bound, an input into an average, or not at all.

The pharmaceuticals market is a special case, in part because the analogs are particularly well established and available. Data on sales of just about any drug is available, and you can typically collect at least a handful of analogs that are in the same drug class and/or targeting comparable patient groups. That said, even here, analogs can sometimes be difficult to select when a product is a first-of-its-kind, as was the case with several cell and gene therapy products that entered the market recently.

But what if your innovation just doesn't have any good analogs, or data isn't available on those that exist? Don't worry—there are options! The concept of an adoption curve came out of work in the 1960s by Everett Rogers and Frank Bass. Rogers's "diffusion of innovations" theory introduced the idea that innovations spread in a society in stages via uptake by different categories of adopters (i.e., innovators, early adopters, early majority, late majority, and laggards); he also hypothesized that these adopters are distributed along a normal distribution (i.e., a bell curve). The cumulative adoption by each of these groups looks like an S-curve.

Bass, for his part, famously formalized technology diffusion into a mathematical formula—today known as the Bass diffusion model—that estimates adoption over time. Bass's model categorizes adopters into innovators (those who adopt independently of others in the social system) and imitators (those who adopt through the influence of prior adopters). The rate and timing of adoption is therefore a function of each group's respective degree of innovation and imitation. The mathematical model is not overly complex and has been studied extensively, and it has demonstrated its usefulness in providing reasonably accurate estimates of technology diffusion across a wide range of product categories. While other technology diffusion models can at times be more accurate, **the Bass diffusion model can be applied in many situations as an alternative to analogs.**[1] If the Bass model appears to be overkill for your situation, then the standard S-curve (cumulative normal distribution) is a simple but still viable option.

There is also a pragmatic lens that you should use to scrutinize your adoption curve. Yes, you can estimate adoption unconstrained by investment, but that is often unrealistic, especially if accessing your customers is not easy or cheap or if education or training is required. Will you need to make marketing investments? Pay for channel access through distributors? Hire sales reps and deploy them to educate and convert customers? If so, there are several ways to handle this issue.

In some situations, it can be as simple as adding an assumption on the percent of your customers you will be reaching (i.e., "commercial reach"). This basically reduces the total number of adopting customers by the proportion that will not be reached. For example, in a new drug revenue forecast, it is common to use data on physician prescription volumes to decide what proportion of the physicians will likely be worth targeting by your sales team (for example, "We'll only target the top 40 percent of physicians who account for 80 percent of total prescriptions").

You can also consider a different kind of practical calculus. What level of commercial investment is your forecast implying? For example, to achieve the forecast, how many sales reps would you need to hire in each year? How many customers could each rep reach, and how many could they convert? You can perform some rough math based on the number of customers a rep can cover, the ramp-up time for a rep, and the duration of a sales cycle. A similar exercise can be performed for a digital product, where you might use search engine marketing (SEM), affiliates, and other sources for finding new customers and then estimate the percentage of those customers that your expected level of marketing investment is likely to convert. This analysis is a useful sense check for ensuring that your forecast isn't implying an unrealistic level of commercial investment.

Adjusting for Competitive Impacts

Your adoption curve and peak adoption can also be affected by changes to the competitive context. The farther out you forecast, the less certain you are of your competition. This is why in Chapter 13 we emphasized the importance of carefully defining your competitive set and evaluating how it is expected to evolve. A breakthrough innovation usually enters a market with few true competitors. But while this may be the case today, the market may be much more crowded tomorrow—especially if you are successful. As a result, you can expect that your level of adoption will be curtailed by competitive share losses. This will be impacted by both the number of competitors that enter and how successfully they are able to capture share.

Let's start with the number of competitors. Based on the competitive land-scape identified in your research, who is likely to become a competitor? Are there specific companies of which you are already aware? Or do you just expect that someone else will likely enter down the road, in what is a more hypo-thetical scenario? And when will they likely enter the market? If you do have some specifics—based on market information such as press releases, hiring behaviors, market interviews, and so on—then you can make some assump-tions on which competitor(s) will enter when. There is usually greater visibility regarding the entry of specific competitors in more regulated markets, such as aerospace, mining, power generation, and pharmaceuticals, where approval processes are part of the market-entry process. In these cases, you can be quite specific about your assumptions.

Now let's turn to share capture. In some markets, the first-mover advan-tage can be massive (e.g., Uber in ridesharing, Facebook in social networks), while in others, fast followers can become market leaders (e.g., Apple in smart-watches). We won't dig deeply into this fairly complex topic, but for our pur-poses of modeling a revenue forecast, we need to appropriately account for future competition. How do you estimate the share that a competitor might take? Again, the best resource here is usually analogs from public data, analyst reports, market reports, or even possibly your own primary research (for ex-ample, by means of a survey). Sometimes it's possible to use analogs to derive reasonable estimates of competitor share as a function of their order of entry.

For example, in some markets, first-to-market products on average will retain 35 to 45 percent of market share even after multiple new entrants, whereas second-to-market products will generally only achieve 25 to 35 per-cent of market share; this drops further for each subsequent player. While the values vary depending on the number of competitors you assume, the first en-trant consistently holds an advantage in share captured over all others. This is not true for all markets, but it is common.

Finally, it's time to bring these assumptions on competition—number of competitors, timing of entry, expected share—together in our model. Actually, this is quite simple. You will need to model the number of customers that you and each of your assumed competitors are able to attain in each time period. For your own innovation, you will use estimated peak adoption and the adop-tion curve you have selected or derived. For your competitors, you will use their expected peak share of market and, most likely, the same adoption curve. This will essentially reduce the number of addressable customers for your innovation.

Assessing Risk with the 3S's: Sensitivities, Scenarios, and Simulation

Once you have built a base-case revenue forecast, it's important to assess how this forecast can vary with different assumptions. How significantly does it change? What are possible outcomes you can expect? What's the likelihood of these different outcomes? These are all different ways to think about the level of risk implied in your forecast. There are three common tools used to evaluate risk in a forecast: *sensitivities, scenarios,* and *simulation*—the 3S's. They all have merit and can often be complementary. We will discuss each in turn, with a focus on their respective tradeoffs.

Sensitivity analysis evaluates how the base case forecast is impacted by independently varying one assumption. This is accomplished by defining a range of possible values for an assumption (i.e., low and high) and plugging in the numbers to see what happens to the forecast (e.g., Year 5 revenue). This determines which assumptions are most impactful and, therefore, to which your forecast is most *sensitive*. See Figure 15.5:

FIGURE 15.5. Sensitivity Analysis Example

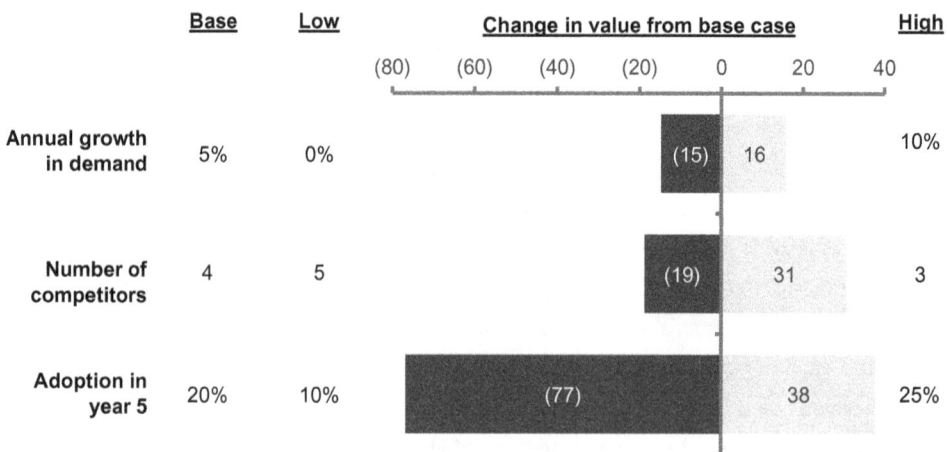

	Base	Low	Change in value from base case		High
			(80) (60) (40) (20) 0 20 40		
Annual growth in demand	5%	0%	(15) 16		10%
Number of competitors	4	5	(19) 31		3
Adoption in year 5	20%	10%	(77) 38		25%

An assumption to which the forecast is highly sensitive and which has substantial potential to vary is one of those critical, contentious assumptions you *must* get right. Notably, there are plenty of assumptions that may have high impact but low expected variability (e.g., population growth), so in most cases, not all that many assumptions fit this characterization. Sensitivity analysis is also useful for testing specific assumptions (e.g., what is the impact if a competitor enters the market one year earlier than expected?) and alleviating concerns (e.g., even if we change assumption X dramatically, the impact on the forecast is <$YM).

That said, there are several downsides to sensitivity analysis. For instance, the ranges tested for variables are often subjective and may not be used consistently across assumptions; there is no information on the likelihood of the values you select; and it may not account for interdependencies between assumptions (e.g., one may not change without another also changing). But **while sensitivity analysis alone may not address all the risk considerations you may want to understand, it is a foundational tool that's useful for just about all forecasts.**

The second type of risk assessment is **scenario analysis**. Scenario analysis enables you to examine the impact of varying multiple key assumptions at the same time. This is useful not only for assessing the combined impact of potentially related assumptions (as opposed to sensitivity analysis) but also for testing hypothesized "future worlds" (your product becomes the new gold standard) and what-ifs (e.g., what if one more competitor enters the market *and* adoption is slower than expected?). These analyses are usually presented as the base, low, and high cases, as in Table 15.1, below. In the low case, the values for key assumptions are set to the low end of each range; in the high case, they are set to the high end of each range. Of course, additional cases can be created that combine different assumptions.

TABLE 15.1. Scenario Analysis Example

Scenario	Annual growth in demand	# of competitors	Year 5 adoption	Year 5 revenue
Base case	5%	4	20%	145
High case	10%	3	25%	251
Low case	0%	5	10%	58

Like sensitivity analysis, scenario analysis has its shortcomings. It doesn't provide information regarding the *likelihood* of any of the scenarios, the selection of scenarios can be subjective or even arbitrary, downside risk and upside potential may be overstated, and a risk-adjusted expected outcome cannot be calculated. It can also raise some difficult questions, such as whether all the relevant scenarios have been modeled, whether the base case should be thought of as the "average" outcome to be expected, and whether assumption ranges should be increased or decreased. All that being said, scenario analysis is almost always valuable, as it provides an indication of the range of expected outcomes of your forecast and tests specific "future worlds" about which stakeholders (and particularly investors) may be concerned.

Finally, we turn to simulation—and specifically, **Monte Carlo simulation**, which is a computerized mathematical technique for estimating the range and likelihood of outcomes based on the uncertainty of the inputs. A Monte Carlo simulation models the outcomes of hundreds or thousands of different combinations of assumptions and plots all those outcomes in a distribution, as illustrated in Figure 15.6.

This is like running many, many different scenarios varying the values of the key assumptions instead of selecting just a few scenarios. The output can be interpreted as the probability that your forecast will fall within a certain range (e.g., 90 percent confidence it will be $99 million to $186 million, as in Figure 15.6).

FIGURE 15.6. Simulation Analysis Example

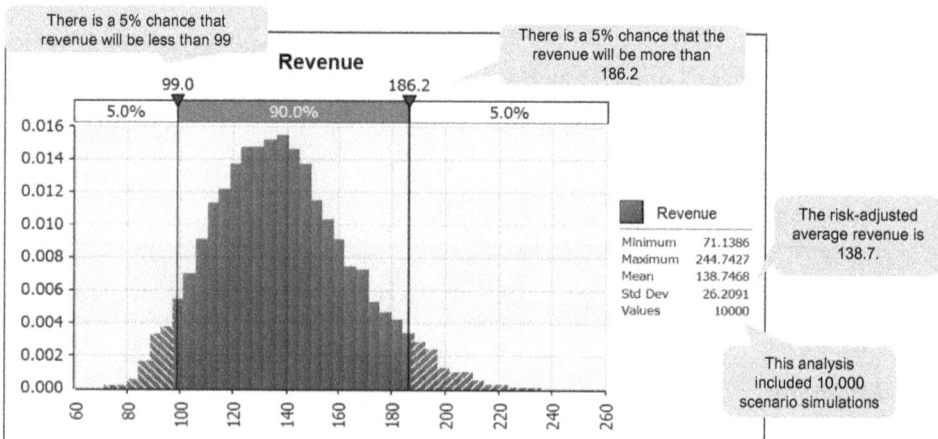

This technique provides some improvement over scenario analysis: You gain a perspective not only on the level of risk but also on the *likelihood* of that risk. A Monte Carlo simulation also helps address some of the unresolved questions that sensitivity and scenario analyses leave us with, such as:

- How do we know what ranges to select when we test assumptions that have a high degree of uncertainty? Can we make the process less subjective?
- How likely are different ranges of the uncertain variables?
- Which scenarios should we examine? How many?
- How likely is each of the scenarios?
- How likely are different ranges of outcomes?
- How do we calculate a risk-adjusted expected outcome (if that's different from the base case)?

This all sounds great, but there are drawbacks to Monte Carlo simulations. They are only as good as their underlying assumptions and the relationships among those assumptions. **Simulations typically assume that assumptions vary independently from one another, but that's rarely the case.** If simulation is applied using erroneous assumptions, it can lead to a false sense of confidence and precision. Simulations also require more time to prepare and run and may be more difficult to explain to your audience than less sophisticated risk assessment techniques. Still, simulation can be a powerful tool, and the process has been sufficiently automated that it can be learned and used fairly readily by most business practitioners. In our experience, **simulations are a useful part of the toolkit but should be reserved for special situations where these drawbacks can be mitigated and the benefits are particularly valuable.**

When should you use each of our 3S's? Table 15.2 provides a summary. Note that as a general rule, because these risk assessment techniques complement each other and yield different insights, **you will almost always benefit from using more than one of the 3S's.**

TABLE 15.2. 3Ss Summary Table

Risk assessment technique	When to use
Sensitivity analysis	• When you are focused on the behavior of individual variables in isolation • When you are searching for high impact or contentious variables
Scenario analysis	• When you want to highlight catastrophe scenarios and upside potential • When you want to explore the outcomes of changing multiple assumptions at the same time
Simulation	• When you want to calculate a risk-adjusted expected outcome • When you want to know the likelihood of a particular range of outcomes (e.g., less than zero)

Lastly, remember: **Scenarios are only meaningful if you have an accurate base case to build from.** They should not be thought of as a "free pass" for looser base-case assumptions. Whatever the scenarios, those making the forecasts are likely to be judged against the accuracy of the base case, barring extenuating circumstances such as a global recession or pandemic.

The "What You Have to Believe" Sense Check

So now you have a full-fledged revenue forecast complete with competitive adjustments and risk assessments. Are you done yet?

Almost. The last critical aspect of building a believable revenue forecast is executing a sense check. In Chapter 12, we discussed triangulation and pressure-testing in the context of adoption estimates. The same imperatives come to bear here. **Apply a "smell test" relative to any analogs or market data points that may be available.** For example, going back to our sports streaming service, showing the number of subscribers over time compared to different analogs could be insightful and could help ensure a high-confidence forecast.

As discussed previously, top-down modeling can often provide a triangulation point for your revenue forecast. Another common approach is to calculate your implied share of the market and consider whether that seems reasonable and believable. If your audience is aware of a specific data point in the market that serves as a reference, you may need to create a specific back-of-the-envelope analysis to compare your output to that data point. Ultimately, **no revenue forecast is "high confidence" unless it can be reasonably triangulated.**

The bottom line: **To satisfy your (appropriately) skeptical audiences both inside and outside your organization, you need a rock-solid revenue forecast**, complete with competitive adjustments and risk assessments. Getting there requires a lot of work, but it's work that will definitely pay off.

EXECUTIVE SUMMARY
Build a high-confidence revenue forecast.

- Identify key contentious assumptions and direct your efforts to rigorously validate them.

- Build a bottom-up model for rigor and flexibility, but triangulate with a top-down model.

- Define your adoption curve with analogs (or available technology diffusion models) and adjust for competitive impacts.

- Add confidence in your forecast through risk assessment with the 3S's.

- Sense-check your forecast with analogs, market data points, and triangulations.

SIXTEEN

Create a Bulletproof Business Case

In Parts 2 and 3, we defined the steps and the tools needed to help you reduce the risks inherent in a product launch, using careful concept development and product forecasting to increase your chances of success.

Another important requirement for a successful new product is adequate funding and resources to make everything possible. This chapter will help you assemble the ingredients needed for a persuasive business case that can help bring aboard investors, senior leaders, and other stakeholders.

As you'll recall from Chapter 9, the five key elements of a business case are:

- a clear articulation of the market need and why your product or service uniquely meets that need;

- an explanation of which groups of customers will be served, both initially and eventually;

- a projection of the size of the market opportunity and the growth you expect;

- a defendable revenue forecast that encompasses customer-adoption expectations, pricing, and competitive dynamics; and

- a clear and specific view on the resources and investments required to enable the opportunity.

But these are only the raw ingredients, right? Imagine that you're baking a cake. In addition to the ingredients, you also need a recipe—a plan for how to combine those ingredients in a way that ends up producing a great cake. It's the same with your business case. So let's review the ingredients we have introduced over the past several chapters and discuss how to combine them most effectively.

Put the Case Together with a Strong Narrative

The recipe that usually works best for a business case is **presenting a sequence of four components: (1) the problem, (2) the solution, (3) the opportunity, and (4) the ask.** We'll look briefly at all four in the following sections, paying special attention to the ask.

1. **The problem:** Certainly, your innovation must solve some problem or "do a job" that people will agree needs to be done. You should have a wealth of proof points accumulated through your early market validation (as discussed in Chapter 5), and richer customer insights from qualitative (and potentially quantitative) market research methods, as discussed in Chapter 11. You should also be well equipped to explain which customers are experiencing this problem and would be willing to adopt and pay for a solution—arguments that you can ground in your strategic segmentation and customer runway (discussed in Chapter 10).

2. **The solution:** How does your innovation *work*? How does it solve that irksome problem you've just pointed to, and how does it fit into the current (unsatisfactory) customer experience or journey? This is also where you articulate your price points (supported by customer WTP and other value bounds), pricing model, and pricing strategy (as discussed in Chapter 14). And finally, this is where you address the competitive context (as discussed in Chapter 13) and why you are positioned to win vis-à-vis these competitors (and, implicitly, *not* follow the Pebble smartwatch into the product graveyard).

3. **The opportunity:** This is where you bring together your analysis of the *market context* (discussed in Chapter 10 and comprising things like current market, SAM, TAM, and growth) with your *revenue forecast*

(Chapter 15) to demonstrate the size and nature of the opportunity represented by your innovation. Contextualizing your revenue forecast with your market sizing is critical to showing where the growth you will be generating is expected to come from (e.g., expanding current market to SAM, taking share within current market) and the potential impacts of market growth tailwinds and/or headwinds. This is where it usually makes the most sense for you to address risks, through sensitivities and scenarios (as discussed in Chapter 15).

4. **The ask:** Ultimately, your whole business case boils down to your "ask." What, exactly, are you asking of your investors, executives, partners, or other stakeholders? Yes, the answer usually involves some sort of financial investment, but it may also involve things like access to specific resources, access to a network of relationships, organizational sponsorship, or other kinds of nonfinancial support. **Every ingredient in your "cake" is important—but none is more important than the ask.**

Again: Your challenge is to create a convincing narrative that follows the logical flow outlined in steps 1 through 4 above. This usually requires thoughtful reflection on the part of you and your team members. It may also benefit from input from an external sounding board—perhaps including your formal or informal advisors and other trusted individuals who are reliably "inside the tent."

In building the case, it's also important for leaders to know themselves and their biases. Every CEO or executive leader started off somewhere—in finance, in sales, in marketing, in research, or what have you. Let's assume that you're one of them. Almost inevitably, the case you build will tend to reflect your own comfort zone. The finance person may have a brilliant model but a weaker articulation of the value proposition. The marketer may have a brilliant articulation of the customer runway and value proposition but may not be able to answer detailed questions about product materials, cost of manufacturing, and the like. The lesson? Recognize your own biases so that you can make sure you are prepared to make a well-balanced pitch. Informed investors will sense where your business case lacks depth and may not invest if you can't successfully compensate for your biases.

Even after you recognize and compensate for your own functionally de-rived biases, you still need to make sure you develop a compelling narrative. **Innovators who struggle with their narrative tend to fall into one of two traps: Either they overinvest in the narrative to compensate for insufficient rigor in their data, or they underinvest in the narrative, relying too much on what they regard as self-evident and powerful data.**

The solution may sound a bit self-evident, but it's inescapable: Invest enough in your data—in all the ways we've advocated in previous chapters—but don't assume that the narrative will write itself. After all the hard work you've done to prove out your innovation and build the case for it, it would be a shame for you to flop on delivery. To achieve your desired result, you need to **control your story and the way it's communicated to your audience.**

Define Your Ask

The key insight here is that **a good ask is a specific ask.** Rigorous research and revenue forecasting force you to build a deep understanding of what you will need to bring your product or service innovation to the market. This hard work puts you in a position to be specific in what you need—how much, when, and, most critically, *why.*

Too many start-up CEOs share pitches giving a very directional range for the dollars that they claim to need without providing much grounding in how they will use the funds, why they need the amount they need, the milestones they expect to reach, and when they will need to raise more and for what. We have seen plenty of the same among innovators in large corporate settings, who tend to focus too much on the opportunity and not enough on why what they're asking for will unlock it.

The ask must focus on the current financial needs but must also contem-plate all anticipated future financings. It does a VC no good to take 12 percent ownership in a $50 million financing if the company will need to raise $500 million in subsequent financings. Corporate investors will have similar con-cerns. You're likely to find that it's hard to get the backing of sophisticated, serious investors in either setting without *specificity* and *clarity* in your ask. Among other good things, that specificity helps give your audience confidence that you won't just burn through their cash and other resources and wind up with nothing to show for it.

For your ask to be specific, it needs to be grounded in a thorough understanding of your investment requirements, as derived from what's known as a capability assessment. The capability assessment is a fairly straightforward exercise that compares what you need to achieve your goal with what you already have. This needs to be completed with enough accuracy and specificity to be useful to those who will review your pitch. We find it most helpful to systematically compile an inventory of capabilities required by category, keeping in mind the target milestone (e.g., a development or commercial milestone). See Table 16.1.

In large organizations, innovators often have access to subject-matter experts (SMEs) who can opine on specific capability needs. In the case of startups or small organizations, innovators have to be more resourceful—for example, by asking around their networks, looking at competitors or analogs, and speaking with independent experts or consultants. **What often involves subjectivity—and therefore requires good judgment from you—is distinguishing between nice-to-have capabilities and need-to-haves.**

Once you have determined the capabilities required, you need to assess where you have gaps. This gap analysis needs to be done as honestly and

TABLE 16.1. Capabilities Framework Table

Types of capabilities	Example questions
Talent	• What expertise and skill sets will be needed? • What type(s) of resources will be needed? • How many of each type of resource will be needed (and when)?
Organization	• What organizational structure, governance, and decision rights will be required for success? • What processes will need to be developed or defined? • What reward and incentive system(s) will be required?
Technology	• What access to data, information, and analytics will be required? • What IT systems will be needed?
Infrastructure	• What physical assets will be needed (e.g., facilities)? • What intellectual property will be needed?

realistically as possible, with less of the optimism than is typically characteristic of innovators. For example, if you have part-time access to an engineer, will you really have enough of their time to get what you need done in your planned timeframe? If not, that's a gap, and a need-to-have.

Once the gaps are identified, you of course need to decide how to fill them. The options are typically (1) to build a capability yourself, or (2) to work with an external party.

Build it yourself: Can or should gaps be filled with existing resources or through hiring and training new resources? This is the less expensive way to go, and almost always the way innovators prefer to fill gaps. An important thing to watch out for: **Be honest with yourself about the caliber and fit of the talent to which you already have access.** Just because you have an engineering team creating the product or an existing sales team standing by to sell it, you don't necessarily have the right skills and expertise at hand. You may need to make some difficult judgment calls, which you'll want to make sooner rather than later. More on this when it comes to preparing your organization for launch in Chapter 20.

Work with an external party: In some cases, you may find that external organizations are the right approach for filling certain gaps. Most commonly, third parties are helpful when the capability is not critical or practical for you to own (for example, to gain access to a particular channel). There is a whole industry of outsourced service organizations providing contract manufacturing, contract development, outsourced fulfillment, contract sales organizations, and distributors that can take on many of the requirements for bringing your product concept to market. Each comes with tradeoffs, and you need to decide what is right for you, both in the near term and the long term.

The investment required flows directly from your approach to filling capability gaps. For example, hiring talent will require estimating the fully loaded costs of those new resources. It's also important to **link the timing of the investments to the revenue forecast**. This can benefit from back-of-the-envelope triangulations, such as the inside-out sense check we suggested in Chapter 15, comparing the number of sales reps you hire to the implied revenue generated per rep. **One common misstep in estimating the timing of investments results from not fully accounting for the time it takes to recruit, onboard, and yield a fully productive resource.** (A sales rep, for example, may take from six months to a year to fully ramp up.) The moral: Always build in a buffer; don't be excessively optimistic.

What else? **Don't neglect interdependencies between investments.** What are the likely synergies and possible bottlenecks created in the relative timing of building capabilities? Additionally, while your ask will need to communicate an investment timeline, in practice **you will want many investments to be triggered by** *milestones,* **not timelines**—things like "completed development of X component," "achieved X number of subscribers," and so on. To the extent that timelines are involved, try to **maximize option value.** In other words, if you don't have to make an investment yet, *don't*. Wait.

On a related note, maximizing option value isn't considered solely from the perspective of the innovator but also from that of investors. VC investors will be thinking about their exit and how value will inflect over time with milestones, so investments will need to take this into account (e.g., a VC may care less about achieving a $500 million annual run-rate in Year 8 than about achieving a $100 million run-rate in Year 4 with the option to exit at a 20 percent annual growth rate). Consequently, **investment timing and exit outcomes of comparable companies can serve as a helpful input, in addition to your revenue forecast.**

Finally, we can offer a few more tips about defining your ask. You'll find it much more difficult to raise additional funds if your progress falls behind your plan. Meanwhile, the funding environment may change unexpectedly—either on the macroeconomic level or within an organization. Based on a historical lookback of L.E.K.'s new product forecasts spanning more than one hundred products or services, we found that one of the most common reasons that products underperformed expectations was delays in coming to market. With that in mind, **best practice is to ensure you have some cushion in your ask, which you can use to mitigate hurdles and possible delays.**

For entrepreneurs, this generally translates into taking more funding when it's available, because it's more important to maximize your chances of success than to minimize dilution. For innovators in larger organizations, we advise that they "promise more but ask for more." In other words, set an exciting vision for what you can achieve—and don't hold back in asking for the resources to get you there.

Framing Your Ask for Your Audience

Once you have a specific ask grounded in a solid understanding of investment requirements, you need to frame it correctly for your audience. If you're a pitching to VCs, they tend to focus on maximizing the return on investment (ROI) they are contemplating. While your ask needs to emphasize the current financing needs, it also must contemplate all future anticipated financing needs. VCs start calculating their returns on Day 1 and will have no confidence in the current ask if you don't have an estimate of future capital needs. VCs will also have different expectations for a return than a corporate investor (and it may vary among different types of VCs). Corporate investors (i.e., senior leaders) tend to focus more on how long it takes for the new business to become profitable, the impact on overall corporate growth or their WAMGR (weighted average market growth rate), and how the proposed innovation stacks up vs. other competing funding demands. Know what metrics matter to your audience, and be prepared to frame your ask within that context.

A few additional words on funding and capital allocation in the context of large corporations. Many organizations have robust stage-gating processes for investment that involve developing discounted cash flow (DCF) models with net present value (NPV) calculations and internal rate of return (IRR) hurdles. At least in theory, there are good reasons for the company to impose this kind of standardization on new opportunities. These tools can be helpful in enforcing fiscal responsibility and can be particularly useful if a large organization is weighing capital-allocation decisions among multiple possible initiatives with different economic and risk profiles.

In practice, though, there are many drawbacks to these tools, including inaccurate assumptions and the potential for manipulations intended to derive the desired output and achieve thresholds. But the most important drawback is that NPVs are not well suited for assessing nontraditional potential investments for a business—such as novel digital products in the context of a traditional products business—because the differences in discount rate are usually poorly understood and wrongly applied. This may require innovators in these situations to work with leadership to adjust the way that their novel products or services are being assessed, rather than simply to try to play the established game.

So now you have your bulletproof business case—from compelling problem statement to well-developed ask—and hopefully you are successful in securing the funding and support required for your innovation. But a great business case, green lights, and adequate funding don't automatically translate into commercial success. For that, you also need an excellent launch. That's what we'll discuss in Part 4—and for many innovators, it's where the fun really starts!

EXECUTIVE SUMMARY

Create a bulletproof business case.

- Develop a compelling narrative encompassing the problem, the solution, the opportunity, and the ask.

- Recognize and compensate for your own biases in the business case.

- Create a specific ask based on a detailed and honest understanding of the investment requirements.

- Know your audience and make sure that your business case speaks to what they care about.

Part 3: Forecasting Revenue Checklist

Configuring for Success
- ❑ Use a systematic approach to reduce failures at every step of the innovation journey
- ❑ Manage risks by evaluating multiple indicators of success
- ❑ Avoid the seven behaviors that reduce the odds for many innovators

Developing Product and Service Concepts
- ❑ Look for what's broken, who's not being served, and how to leverage your strengths
- ❑ Take advantage of direct market feedback and rapid prototypes
- ❑ Embrace continuous upgrades and lean development for digital-led businesses
- ❑ Move up the Detect-Analyze-Act pyramid to enrich products using digital
- ❑ Use a start-up mindset for breakthrough innovation in large companies

Forecasting Revenue
- ✓ Build a business case to avoid the product graveyard
- ✓ Size the prize and identify the customers you will win
- ✓ Gather customer insights, not "voice of customer"
- ✓ Never take market research at face value
- ✓ Assume competitors are at least as smart as you
- ✓ Price to unlock the full value of your innovation
- ✓ Build a high-confidence revenue forecast
- ✓ Create a bulletproof business case

Ensuring Commercial Success
- ❑ Identify and lower the biggest barriers to adoption
- ❑ Plan enough but not too much, creating a "living" launch plan to ensure smooth execution
- ❑ Take the shortest path to value by optimizing launch scale and picking the right channels
- ❑ Prime the organization for a successful launch by tailoring capabilities and nurturing alliances

Creating Long-Term Value
- ❑ Turn a single success into an enduring franchise
- ❑ Make use of acquisitions and partnerships to accelerate innovation value
- ❑ Embrace proven pathways for long lead-time innovation
- ❑ Use incremental developments to complement breakthrough innovation
- ❑ Turn gaps into strengths for start-ups and entrepreneurs

PART IV

Ensuring Commercial Success

A deep pre-launch understanding of customer decision-making and adoption barriers is critical for the successful launch of a new product or service. Creating a flexible but sufficiently detailed launch plan that proactively aims to overcome adoption barriers is well worth the effort. This launch plan needs to incorporate decisions on the right scale of launch and the right channels to reach customers. Finally, configure the organization optimally to execute a successful launch.

SEVENTEEN

Identify and Lower the Biggest Barriers to Adoption

In Part 3 we focused on increasing your odds of success by doing your homework to develop a product or service that is compelling to customers, setting the right strategy for market success, and conveying it all effectively to investors and executives to build support. We now shift gears to talk about the process of market launch.

The launch, ironically, is a topic that gets relatively little attention. Conventional wisdom suggests that if you have the right product, it will sell itself—you just need to do well at the blocking and tackling aspects of execution, which are assumed to be more or less straightforward. But take this into consideration: **in our look-back study of product launches in the last decade, the number-one reason for underperformance when the product made it to market was poor execution of the launch**.

What should we take away from this finding? For one thing, as most leaders involved will attest, launch execution in the case of novel innovations is neither easy nor obvious. Further, launch isn't purely about execution. **Strategy needs to be continuously revisited to ensure that your plans continue to reflect market conditions**.

Throughout Part 4, we'll dig into the nuances and best practices of launch execution and planning, and we'll spotlight the missteps that innovators tend to make. And the fundamental starting point for this discussion is understanding adoption barriers you are likely to face, and how you might best overcome them. This is one of the most critical things to get right along the entire innovation journey.

Understand How Customers Buy and Which Stakeholders Will Matter

The benefit of having engaged with customers and conducted market research—and especially customer interviews—is that you understand not just what value proposition your innovation needs to deliver—and to whom—but how your customers make their buying decisions. A thorough understanding of customer-purchasing dynamics serves as the foundation for launch-related decisions such as sales and marketing investments and channels by which to reach customers; it also spotlights the barriers you will need to overcome to drive adoption of your innovation.

Exactly what do you need to understand about how customers buy? This question can be broken down into several component parts:

- **What do customers care about** when they're making a buying decision regarding your product or service? What are their **key purchasing criteria** (KPCs)?

- **Who are the stakeholders** involved in the decision? Is it just one decision-maker? Are there important influencers?

- **What is the decision-making process,** and how long does it last? What are the key steps in the process that determine the outcome?

- How, if at all, **do any of the above vary by customer segment**?

The answers to these questions should come from the customer research you conducted while building your business case. **KPCs** are typically fairly straightforward and tend to include criteria such as price, quality, service, and reputation. One caution: You need to **be sure that these KPCs are sufficiently granular to be useful to you.**

For example, drug compounding—the process by which a medication is produced in a variety of different dosages, concentrations, or formats—is

increasingly an outsourced service in U.S. hospitals due to tightening regulatory requirements and labor shortages in hospital-based pharmacies (a service
largely innovated in the early 2000s). When hospital pharmacy directors undertake to select an outsourced partner for this important role, quality is of
course extremely important—but how do they define "quality"?

A wide range of possible metrics could come into play, including, for example, the potential partner's history and status of regulatory compliance, recall
track record, quality reporting metrics, and so on. Understanding *which* definitions pertain in this particular case is critical for the supplier who wants
to win an account. Again, it's about understanding the KPCs with sufficient
granularity.

The **stakeholders** involved in the purchasing decision can be a simple
matter if the buyer and the user are the same person. But even for B2C products, this is often not the case. Take the example of flooring tiles for the home.
There are customers who buy and install tiles themselves (do-it-yourself, or
DIY), customers who hire a contractor but select and purchase the tiles themselves (buy-it-yourself, or BIY), and contractors who buy and install on behalf
of their clients (typically with their input). Further, many customers are not a
single individual but rather a cohabiting couple that is making the tile selection together. Some customers further complicate the stakeholder calculus by
involving an interior designer in the selection of their flooring tiles. In some
cases, influencers may also play a submerged but important role. In short, a
wide range of possibilities!

Purchase decision-making processes in the B2B realm can be even more
complicated. Recall the example from Chapter 5 of Edwards Lifesciences: the
innovator and leader in transcatheter aortic valve replacement (TAVR). As is
true for many B2B businesses, multiple stakeholders must be involved. In this
case, a trio of the general cardiologist, interventional cardiologist, and cardiac surgeon forms what is referred to as a "heart team" that determines what
treatment is most appropriate for each patient. Again, complex! For Edwards
Lifesciences, successfully driving adoption for a product like TAVR meant that
the company had to understand these different customer stakeholders ("call
points," from the perspective of the sales organization) and what kind of engagement and information would be needed by each to support adoption. This
meant fielding sales teams to focus on the different physicians in the heart

team and the economic decision-makers (administrators and value analysis committee members). The bottom line: **Knowing who your customers really are and the roles that different individuals play in the purchasing process is essential to your innovation's ultimate success.**

Next, you need to characterize the **purchase decision-making process** so that you can understand how the different stakeholders interact and when important decision points occur in the "customer purchase journey." This guides how and when you need to engage with your customer stakeholders. It's also important to understand how long the purchasing process takes—and, by extension, the duration of your innovation's sales cycle. Yes, sometimes this is obvious and well established, based on prior experience with more traditional product launches, but when it comes to an innovation that entails a significant need for market education, the purchasing process could take much longer than you might think.

Of course, the level of detail at which you need to understand the purchase journey will vary. A good rule of thumb, though, is that **you need enough detail to know where and when adoption barriers are likely to pop up**. Finally, it's important to **determine whether and how the KPCs, stakeholders, and purchase decision-making process vary for different customer segments** on your customer runway. How easy or difficult will it be to drive adoption within each segment? Obviously, this will have major implications for your launch and your subsequent marketing efforts. As discussed in Chapter 10, this knowledge needs to be factored into your determination of the customer runway.

Proactively Overcome Expected Adoption Barriers

Once you have a thorough handle on your customer purchasing dynamics, you need to **focus on the key initial pre-launch objective: identifying adoption barriers.**

We've referred to these in passing, but now let's discuss them in some detail. Adoption barriers are simply "reasons not to adopt." They vary by customer segment, by customer, by stakeholder, and by step along the purchasing journey. Further, you won't necessarily be able to impact all of them—but if you anticipate them, you can at least know which ones you may be able to impact.

Arguably, **the single biggest misstep taken by most innovators is insufficiently assessing and planning how they will overcome adoption barriers** *before* **launch.** All innovators learn at least *something* about their adoption barriers after launch. But the best practice is to do as much learning about barriers *before* you're in market, not after. You may or may not be able to address certain barriers once you're in market. Further, you could inadvertently poison the market for yourself (lowering long-term potential) and, especially for startups, drive dramatic unexpected delays on the road to profitability (potentially putting the enterprise at risk).

So again: Many of the barriers associated with the product or service itself ought to be identified (and hopefully addressed) as you determine product/market fit early on. Most likely, you'll discover that many such barriers have little or nothing to do with the actual innovation itself but rather with how it fits into the existing context of the customer's experience or purchase journey.

When you're identifying potential adoption barriers, you need to take a systematic approach—and a helpful approach is to use the customer purchase journey as an organizing principle. This journey can be generalized into several phases: Awareness, Consideration, and Conversion. Many other versions of the customer journey (or marketing funnel) exist, so you can tailor as needed to your specific needs.

Learning from Uber

Let's look at an example. One of the most impressive market launches in recent history is that of Uber. The ridesharing app launched its services in San Francisco in 2010. By 2022, Uber had expanded its operations to more than ten thousand cities across seventy countries, with 3.5 million drivers and nearly 120 million peak active users.[1] While not all of this growth has been pretty—a fair amount of outrage was sparked over the years by Uber's aggressive tactics as it entered different local markets—the scale and level of success is startling, especially if you consider that the odds seemed to be heavily stacked against Uber at the outset.

How so? If an outside observer had looked at the taxi industry in 2010, they wouldn't have been faulted for concluding that Uber had little chance of breaking into this mature, even stagnant, market. This was true despite the many reasons to complain about taxis—overpriced, inconsistent service with no clear visibility as to whether a cab would show up, a resistance to accepting credit cards, and limited availability at peak times and during bad weather. Yet the taxi industry's business model had stood unchallenged for more than a hundred years.

Uber represented a key business model innovation over the traditional model—taking advantage of the "gig economy" to unlock access to a massive installed base of underutilized vehicles, which allowed for disruptively low prices. From the outset, Uber's innovators understood that for its ambitious new business model to work, local network effects would be critical, and—by extension—achieving local scale mattered *immensely*. The key broad adoption barriers for Uber were (1) securing the legal right to operate locally, (2) attracting enough drivers, and (3) attracting enough customers. The company developed a systematic, thorough, and adaptive playbook to tackle each barrier as it entered each of its new markets—and also kept learning along the way.

Local regulations governing and strictly controlling taxi licenses abounded in just about every major and minor city, with taxi medallions in some places valued in the hundreds of thousands of dollars. To complicate things further, these rules and regulations were highly variable and idiosyncratic by municipality. Uber understood that it didn't have the time or the capital to navigate the local regulatory framework of each municipality in which it was seeking to operate. As CEO Travis Kalanick put it in 2012, "Every city we go to, eventually the regulators will make something up to keep us from rolling out or continuing our business."[2] Consequently, a pragmatic alternative was pursued—ignore the established regulatory framework, argue that your business shouldn't be regulated by it, and lobby extensively while buying time to establish a foothold and convert your riders into a political force. In other words, Uber took a "don't ask for permission" approach when entering markets. In numerous instances, the company continued to operate even when ordered directly by the local government to cease and desist.

Uber's approach was to systematically identify key stakeholders in local politics and to invest heavily in lobbying efforts. In some markets it hired local celebrities to drive public relations and invested in responsive marketing efforts. For example, when London's cabbies staged a protest in July 2014, Uber ran an ad campaign promoting itself as "the car service that's keeping London moving"—and apparently enjoyed an 850 percent increase in sign-ups.[3] Naturally, some of these tactics engendered significant backlash, but on the whole they also *worked*. What also helped, of course, and ultimately helped win the day, was the political support of its riders who voted with their dollars—adopting Uber in droves and providing support against the local establishment when the service was under threat of disruption. And notably, Uber didn't let its less-than-praiseworthy tactics affect customers. Some interim lessons: It certainly helps when there is significant dissatisfaction with the status quo—in this case, taxis—and the alternative is priced aggressively.[4]

The other two major barriers Uber faced were scaling drivers and riders to unlock network effects—and although one couldn't come without the other, drivers were an initial priority. To acquire drivers, Uber needed to provide enough of an economic incentive for those in the taxi industry to switch over. Consequently, it offered $1,000 sign-up incentives and referral bonuses. It also understood the opportunity to expand the eligible pool of drivers by offering a leasing program, Xchange, for those without their own car (albeit not always on attractive terms). The other key need was not just having enough drivers signed up but also having enough in the right location at the right time—the availability issue that taxis just could never get right. The solution to this was dynamic pricing, in which prices "surged," incentivizing drivers to be available at times when demand spiked (e.g., 1 a.m. on a Saturday night in downtown Chicago).

Next—and very quickly—riders had to get on board. The key insight on this side of the equation was that *safety*, real and perceived, would be a critical prerequisite to adoption by passengers. Presumably, one of the key values of taxi medallions (and their related governing authorities) was the vetting of drivers, supposedly ensuring that the drivers would (1) not harm you—after all, you're getting into the car of a complete stranger—and (2) safely get you to your destination. Uber implemented a range of features that helped give riders peace of mind, including GPS tracking for every trip, the ability to request a ride from indoors, and sharing a picture of the driver before the arrival of the car. Perhaps most important, it deployed a ratings system that captured the experiences of prior riders—roughly comparable to product reviews on Amazon. If you were paired with a driver who had earned ratings of an average of 4.8 out of 5 stars from a hundred other passengers, you could feel reasonably safe getting in the car.

Again, despite its overall success, many of the tactics that Uber employed en route to that success were not particularly praiseworthy.[5] In cataloging its approach to overcoming these barriers, we are in no way justifying them but rather attempting to highlight the lessons that can be learned from a remarkable—and reasonably recent—story of market adoption. And in that spirit, let's underscore several key lessons that are evident in the Uber experience: the power of a deep understanding of adoption barriers, even when they seem overwhelming; the value of a customer-centric approach to building rapid adoption; the value of using your customers to help overcome other barriers; and the importance of a proactive and adaptive approach to overcoming barriers once in market.

One final challenge and potential response that we should discuss—which was amply evident in the Uber example—is that **not all adoption barriers are created equal.** It turns out that in many situations, it's possible to quantitatively assess the impact of each adoption barrier, and this assessment can help you prioritize the order in which to tackle them. An effective way to do this is to conduct a **"leakage" analysis** along the customer journey—simply stated, how many customers "leak out" from the purchasing journey at each step? Understanding why such leakage occurs, where it is most significant, and what steps you as the innovator can take to minimize leakage can be very powerful.

This is in line with how e-commerce retailers think about managing their conversion funnel but taken a step further by exploring and encompassing the entirety of the customer buying journey, including how they got to the website in the first place (and if they left and came back).

To bring this to life, let's briefly go back to the world of cardiovascular medical devices. A client was developing a sophisticated, new-to-the-world cardiovascular product, and—given the complexity of the product—sought to proactively understand key barriers to adoption that the new product would face. We detailed the patient journey, quantified the flow of patients at each step, and quantified expected leakage at each step (using some of the market research techniques discussed in Chapter 11). See Table 17.1, below, for a simplified visual summary.

Once the most significant leakage steps for the appropriate patients were determined, interviews with the relevant stakeholders helped identify the key

TABLE 17.1. Leakage Analysis Example

Customer Journey		No. of patients	% of patients retained	Leakage from previous step (no. of patients)
Awareness	Eligible patients for novel treatment	20.0M	–	–
	Doctor discusses treatment with patient	4.0M	20%	(16.0M)
	Patient referred to specialist	2.0M	50%	(2.0M)
Consideration	Patient visits specialist	1.8M	80%	(0.2M)
	Recommended treatment	0.9M	50%	(0.9M)
Conversion	Patient selects treatment	0.5M	60%	(0.4M)
	Undergoes treatment	0.4M	75%	(0.1M)

barriers that they expected to drive leakage (for example, if physicians weren't convinced that their patients would benefit from the therapy). A set of options to proactively overcome these barriers were then determined—ranging from simple fixes like preparing appropriate marketing materials to complex solutions like investing in new digital tools (e.g., creating a clinical decision support tool making it easier to determine if a patient should be considered for the therapy). As you might imagine, these became valuable inputs in preparing for the launch.

There's more to say about successful launches. In the coming chapters, we will delve into launch planning and the key success factors that every innovator should think about. The goal is to ensure not only that the "simple" blocking-and-tackling execution of your launch goes well but also that all aspects of your launch are founded upon a deep understanding of customer purchasing dynamics and adoption barriers.

EXECUTIVE SUMMARY

Identify and lower the biggest barriers to adoption.

- Develop a deep understanding of your customers and their purchasing journey (including the roles of different stakeholders involved and how they make decisions).

- Systematically identify potential barriers to adoption at each step of the customer purchasing journey, from awareness to conversion.

- Identify the most impactful adoption barriers in terms of the customer "leakage" they cause along the purchasing journey and determine what steps you can take to address them.

EIGHTEEN

Plan Enough but Not Too Much

While most innovators recognize that planning for a launch is important to ensure smooth execution, too many do not invest enough of their time and energy into it. By and large, they're just too busy developing their product or service and treat launch planning as an afterthought. As a result, **many innovators pull together a launch plan that's too late, or too little, or both.**

In this chapter, we will make the case for sufficient launch planning. But first, why plan?

As you'll see in the following pages, **time invested in the launch plan can be one of the highest-ROI activities for innovators and their teams.** A great launch can increase total long-term penetration into your addressable market opportunity and also bring revenue and profit forward in time. The ROI impact in the near term and the long term can be substantial.

Look at the illustrative innovation launch curves in Figure 18.1 below. While innovators are often concerned with avoiding the "failed launch" curve, they don't often think about avoiding the "mediocre launch" curve—the realm of missed potential. **Too many innovators focus on avoiding the big launch failures—which is good—without realizing that they need to put at least as much focus on elevating their innovations to their full market potential.** The most common outcome of the less-than-successful launch isn't complete

FIGURE 18.1. Illustrative Launch Curves

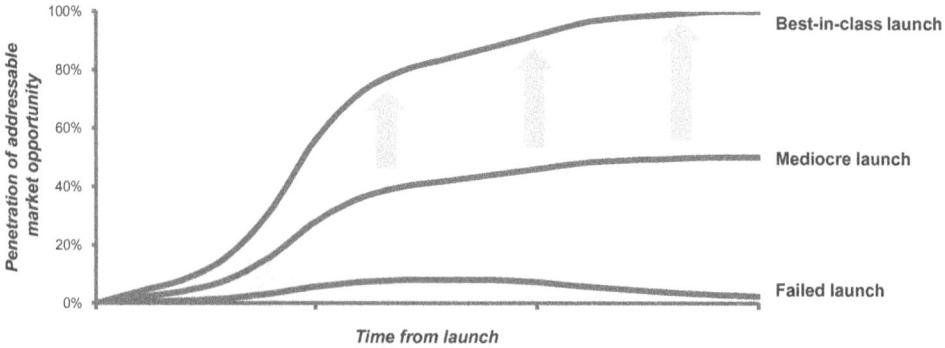

failure but mediocrity. We contend that robust, systematic launch planning will help you not only avoid a total flop but also improve your odds of achieving the full market potential of your innovation.

The Importance of a Goldilocks Launch Plan

Clearly, planning too little (and too late) is not optimal. But how much planning is appropriate? **At a high level, the more novel your innovation, the more you should invest in launch planning, mainly because you face more execution risk.** Figure 18.2 summarizes this principle.

We have labeled the quadrants in Figure 18.2 in the general order of value for launch planning. An innovation can be very new to the market, very new to your organization, or both. Breakthrough innovations are inherently new along both dimensions (quadrant 1), have the most execution risk, and therefore merit the most time and resource investment in launch planning.

As a rule of thumb, novelty to the market is a bigger driver of execution risk than organizational novelty, as it's almost always easier to mitigate internal risks. Consequently, novel products and services that are very innovative to the market but require limited new organizational capability (quadrant 2) are the next most important set of circumstances in which to invest sufficiently in launch planning.

With this construct in mind, it is easy to see why the level of launch planning is often quite minimal for an incremental innovation (quadrant 4). The launch of an incremental innovation can be a non-event if you have an existing

FIGURE 18.2. Launch Planning Requirements Framework

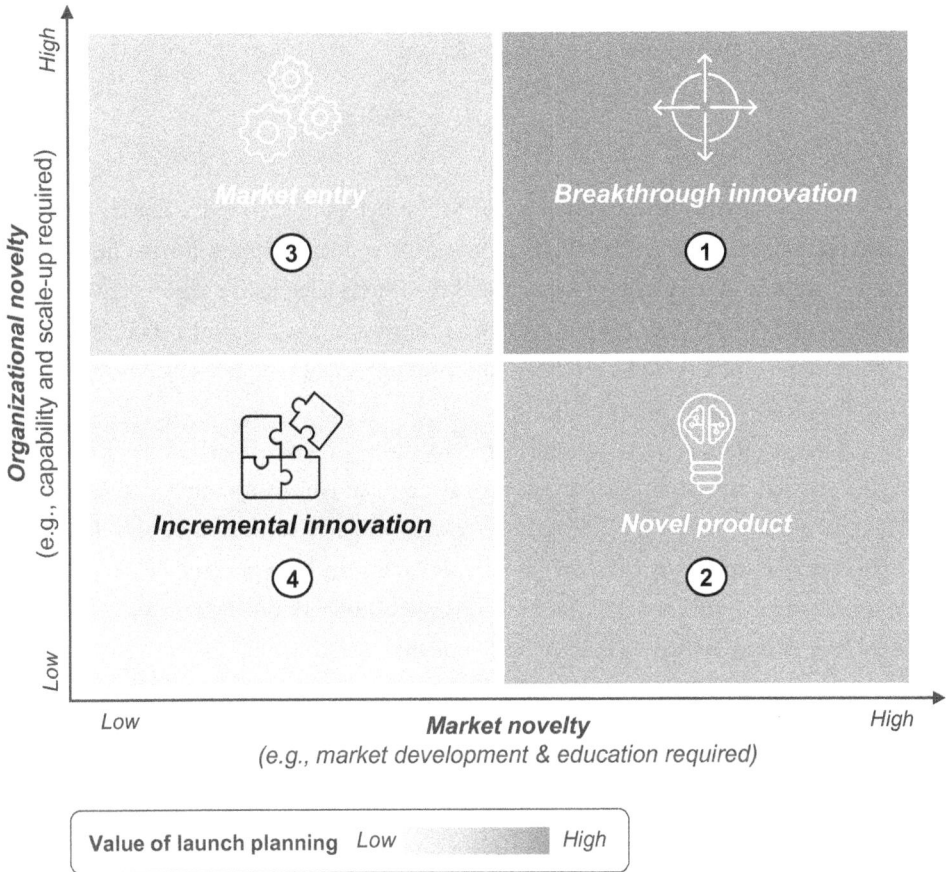

Value of launch planning Low ▓▓▓▓ High

channel and an existing customer base, making it easy to add the new product into the "bag" of the sales team. By contrast, for a start-up organization or a company entering a market with which it has limited or no experience (quadrant 3), there may be a need to build substantial internal capabilities or scale up the organization entirely from scratch.

Our focus in this book is primarily on the launch of innovations that fall into quadrants 1 and 2 of this framework, which is where we'll focus this launch-planning discussion.

So far, we have focused on the risks of planning too little. This is by far the more common issue for innovators, but *too much* planning can also occasionally be a problem. In the relatively rare situation when an organization plans too much, it risks insufficient flexibility for executives to make decisions based on the evolution of the market situation. So **your goal should be to plan enough, but not too much**—a Goldilocks launch plan, if you will.

Creating a "Living" Launch Plan

What exactly constitutes a launch plan? A launch plan is simply a document (although not a simple one!) that lays out what needs to happen at what juncture and who is responsible for making those things happen. It's a project plan, focused specifically on the launch of an innovation. The plan often takes the form of an Excel spreadsheet or a project management template (e.g., using a web-based tool like Smartsheet).

Launch plans tend to be structured in three phases: pre-launch, launch, and post-launch. Done well, they serve as an invaluable communication tool for all of those involved in the launch. **A well-prepared launch plan becomes the indispensable "true north" that drives each launch team member's daily, weekly, and monthly priorities and activities.** Furthermore, it is meant to be a living document that is continuously updated as the launch progresses. This is why it is such a helpful tool for driving organizational focus and alignment.

A good launch plan needs to be comprehensive. If a launch plan is incomplete, you can't trust it, and therefore its usefulness as a planning and communication tool is substantially undermined. To make the plan comprehensive, a systematic, structured approach to creating it is required. There are several steps that we have found consistently helpful for innovators:

- Designate your **launch team.**
- Define the **key success factors (KSFs)** for your launch.
- Identify the **deliverables that each function needs to contribute** to achieve the key success factors.
- **Assess the readiness of each deliverable** to determine the remaining activities needed.
- Lay out the **detailed plan to complete each deliverable.**

Let's start with the launch team. First, there's a distinction between the team that runs the launch and the team that participates in putting together

the launch plan (granted, in a start-up environment there may be no difference). For the launch plan to be right and for it to serve as an effective communication tool, it needs to be created cross-functionally, with a range of
stakeholders providing input—R&D/product development, sales, marketing,
manufacturing, finance, HR, legal, etc. The constellation of stakeholders will
depend on your industry and your scale. **Best practice is to err on being more
inclusive in creating the launch plan,** while at the same time **limiting the
team responsible for the launch to only the essential members across key
functions.** This approach gathers the knowledge needed to get the plan right
(and to build consensus among relevant stakeholders) while ensuring that the
actual launch team remains nimble.

Key success factors (KSFs) are usually obvious fundamentals without
which the launch will either not take place (e.g., gating factors like a regulatory
approval, key product functionality) or success will be compromised (e.g., un-
addressed barriers to adoption). The intent of the KSFs is to focus the team on
tackling these priorities. For example, for Uber's launch, discussed in Chapter
17, rapidly recruiting sufficient drivers and building rider trust in Uber's safety
were KSFs.

One approach that can be useful for identifying KSFs is to think about
what is required of different functions (e.g., commercial, R&D/product development) across three areas of the launch plan: preparing the product (or
service), preparing the market, and preparing the organization. With respect
to the product/service, what needs to be in place to successfully launch and
succeed post-launch? What needs to be understood about or communicated to
the market (especially if market development is an important part of the innovation challenge)? What organizational preparations are critical (as identified
through the capability gaps analysis in Chapter 16, for example)? Notably, it's
at this stage that you really make good use of the in-depth understanding you
developed regarding adoption barriers, as discussed in Chapter 17. **The launch
plan should clearly define the steps to be taken to address each key adoption
barrier.**

Using this same approach, you can create a systematic list of **deliverables**
needed to ensure that each KSF is achieved. Deliverables are specific items that
need to be completed (e.g., Uber developing a driver rating feature to support
its safety KSF). Practically, it's helpful to lay out the deliverables by function so

TABLE 18.1. Launch Plan Sample Output

	KSF: Build rider trust	Owner
Prepare the Market	**Deliverable 1.1**: Create driver rating feature	Product Development
	Deliverable 1.2: Capture driver picture during sign-up process	HR
	Deliverable 1.3: Create background check process for new drivers	Operations
	Deliverable 1.4: Create a marketing campaign to spread awareness of safety features/procedures for consumers	Marketing
	...	

that you understand what each team needs to contribute to achieve each KSF. In Table 18.1, we've provided an illustrative example, once again focused on Uber.

Once we have our deliverables, we know what needs to be achieved. The next step is assessing how far along we are with each deliverable. This is the **launch readiness** assessment. For example, if the pricing strategy still needs to be determined, that may be a deliverable that is partially complete—perhaps you already have your WTP data and a potential price range but still need to decide whether or how you will segment pricing and the ultimate price point at launch. Some deliverables may not yet be initiated, while others may be complete. It is helpful to complete this step so that you know how far from "launch ready" you are and have a good sense of the key deliverables along the critical path, based on importance and progress.

Finally, it's time to create the **detailed plan** itself. For each deliverable, you need a comprehensive list of activities and for each of these activities, you need to know:

- Timing (when to start) and duration (how long it will take)
- Any interdependencies (prerequisite activities, co-dependent activities, downstream dependent activities)
- Sequencing based on timing relative to other activities

- How many and what resources will be required
- Who is accountable and who needs to be involved (a responsibility matrix like a RACI can help)
- Any key milestones other than deliverable completion
- Any metrics you may need to track

You can see why it is easiest to put all this into Excel or, better yet, a dedicated project management tool. This part certainly isn't rocket science, but thoroughness pays off, and ensuring that you have the right folks making the plan is critical (hence the prior point on inclusiveness). One watch-out: **Avoid insufficiently precise descriptions of activities.** If you don't actually know what you would do to undertake the activity, then either it shouldn't be there, or it needs to be expressed differently. A launch plan can easily become a source of frustration if activity descriptions are too high-level, or if they lend themselves to varying interpretations.

All in all, as you can see, plan development can be an involved process. Depending on the complexity of the innovation and situation, the time and effort involved in creating a launch plan will vary. **Typically, you should budget four to eight weeks to develop a reasonably robust launch plan.**

How long before launch should you develop a plan? Well, that depends. Launch planning approaches vary across industries. It has become a near-science in the world of biopharma, where every day a drug is on market is worth incredible value, and the opportunity cost of not having done sufficient planning is extraordinarily high. In the pharma world, therefore, launch planning often begins up to *three years* prior to expected commercial launch of a drug.

This is one extreme, of course. The other extreme is planning a launch merely a few weeks ahead of time, which is what happens with some B2C digital products. For most innovations in less regulated and less complex markets, planning can start three to six months prior to launch. For more complex markets or innovations, six to twelve months may be more appropriate. The key determinant of how much time you need is the level of market development and priming required.

The more work required to ready your market, the farther out from launch you should start planning. "Planning to plan" can be well worth the investment!

EXECUTIVE SUMMARY

Plan enough but not too much, creating a "living" launch plan to ensure smooth execution.

- Focus on maximizing market potential from your launch—avoiding not just failure but also mediocrity.

- Invest in launch planning commensurate to the novelty of your innovation (the more novel the innovation, the more value there is in planning).

- Err on being more inclusive of organizational stakeholders when creating the launch plan, but limit the team responsible for the launch to essential members only.

- Create a comprehensive launch plan with enough detail that it can be relied upon as an indispensable "true north" for driving launch priorities and activities but not so much detail that it is inflexible in the face of changing market realities.

- Ensure that the launch plan clearly defines the approach to address each key adoption barrier identified.

- Treat your launch plan as a "living" document that is updated continuously as the launch unfolds.

NINETEEN

Take the Shortest Path to Value, Not to Market

As you craft your launch plan, you'll need to make a few critical decisions about how you'll get your innovation in the hands of customers. These include how rapidly and broadly you'll launch as well as what channels you'll use to reach your customers. **Innovators tend to rush—pursuing the fastest path to get products or services in front of customers—but this can come at the cost of long-term revenue potential and/or profitability.**

In this chapter, we help you think through what your options are and how to weigh them appropriately.

"Go Big or Go Home" Launches

Not all launches are the same. Broadly speaking, you have two options: a **full-scale launch or a limited launch**. The main difference is how expansively and rapidly you enter the market. But first, let's clarify some terms. The "soft" launch, often used with new digital products, is a tool deployed in the product development process to gather market feedback and refine an innovation, as discussed in Part 2. A limited launch, by contrast, is a more focused, measured entry into the market. For example, you might limit the customer segments that you pursue or the geographies you enter. Obviously, a full launch is at the opposite end of the launch spectrum—you pull out the stops and go after your market as quickly as you can.

Typically, companies pursue a full launch when they want to bring forward their opportunity. **In situations where barriers to entry are low and/or generating network effects is critical, a rapid, full-scale launch is imperative.** This is particularly true for digital products and digitally enabled services. Sometimes a full launch is necessary because there is a market land grab occurring, as in the cases of Uber and Groupon (an online marketplace for "group" deals). Remember our Uber example: Within ten years of launch, the company was operating in seventy countries and more than 10,500 cities worldwide.

In general, **if you've done your homework and planned well, you should try to launch as rapidly and broadly as possible.** But be aware that if you *didn't* do your homework or plan well, a full-scale launch is very likely to reveal problems—and *fast*. For example, when Samsung rushed its Galaxy Note 7 smartphone to beat the iPhone 7 to market, it didn't do enough testing on the product, which resulted in a massive recall and reputational hit when it became clear that the device's batteries were at risk of overheating and catching on fire (which inevitably generated embarrassing headlines). Similarly, when Atari, the leading video game company in the early 1980s, rushed development of an *E.T.* video game (based on Steven Spielberg's blockbuster movie), it created a product that was incredibly difficult to play and frustrating to gamers. Millions of unsold copies of the game ended up in a landfill in New Mexico.

How do you de-risk a full-scale launch? The answer lies in part in preparing the market (see the related discussion of launch plans in Chapter 18). For many markets, it is critical to win over not only early adopters—to build market traction and word of mouth—but also the *right* early adopters. **Purposeful, intentional relationship-building with influential or key opinion-leading customers, who can later serve as references, can be extraordinarily powerful.** Many fashion and athletic brands do this with celebrity endorsements, for example. In healthcare, targeting leading academic institutions is likewise a common strategy.

Early wins can also have important internal organizational benefits, such as building confidence and refining your sales team's capabilities (more on this in Chapter 20). In businesses where network effects can play an important role in enhancing the value of the product or service, as well as in driving rapid adoption, exercising care in finding the "nodes" in the network with the most potential to drive viral spread of your innovation can be extremely valuable. This is one reason why successful YouTube and TikTok influencers have been able to make a surprisingly good living over the last decade.

Limited Launches and the Art of the Lean Launch

If you've spent all of the time and money needed to develop and refine your fantastic innovation, why on earth would you execute a limited launch? Why would you not try to maximize the value of your innovation immediately?

Most often, the answer is that you don't have the resources for a full launch. Cash-strapped start-ups often pursue a limited launch and use the anticipated initial market traction to raise more capital or fund further growth. This can be a mistake. To put it bluntly, it's a failure in funding (whether your own or market-driven) if a full launch is merited and you can only afford a limited launch.

That said, there are certainly special situations in which a limited launch is exactly the right approach. For example, **a limited launch can be attractive if your innovation requires substantial market development, and if by launching too rapidly, you risk jeopardizing the innovation's long-term potential value.**

While you should learn as much as possible in advance of the launch, it is worth recalling a topic discussed in Chapter 17: that there is always more learning that takes place when you launch. In a particularly complex launch situation, you may need to buy yourself some more time for that learning. In the world of medical devices, for example, many start-ups with innovative new products opt for limited launches because (1) it can take time to change the way physicians practice medicine, and (2) it can be very complicated and time-consuming to navigate B2B purchasing processes at hospitals.

For example, Intersect ENT—an innovator of implants used in sinus procedures—pursued a strategy of launching in sequential metro areas to build local scale and gain market traction. This served Intersect ENT exceptionally well and helped earn the company a billion-dollar-plus payout when it was acquired by medtech behemoth Medtronic. But many examples pointing in the opposite direction are also evident in the same industry. Some challengers to Intuitive

Surgical—a leader in robotic surgery discussed in Chapter 10—have tried to move quickly to place robots at accounts but then struggled to drive any meaningful utilization by customers, which completely derailed their razor/razor blade monetization model.

While a full launch may be advisable most of the time, you shouldn't execute a full launch when a limited one is more appropriate—that is, if your innovation requires significant market education, exhibits a long sales cycle, or targets a narrow set of large B2B customers. This mistake is most common in large organizations that have significant scale and place strong incentives on executives to deliver value sooner—sometimes to the detriment of long-term value creation. Start-ups are certainly much less likely to fall prey to the lure of a full launch when they really should start with a limited launch, especially given capital constraints. **In this context, a limited launch can be viewed not as an obstacle for hamstrung start-ups but as a lean-launch approach to maximizing capital efficiency and long-term value creation.**

Tradeoffs of Direct vs. Distributor Channels

Now let's move from launch to channel. Beyond the rate and scale of your launch, you also need to decide how best to reach customers—in other words, which channels to use. When we say "channels," we mean whether you plan to sell directly to customers or through other intermediaries—for example, a consumer products company will likely sell direct to consumers, through brick-and-mortar retailers or online marketplaces like Amazon, or a combination.

For many other products and services, distributors and wholesalers exist that can offer efficient routes to market. This may be related to different market segments (for example, you can buy a tennis racquet at a sporting goods store, at a tennis club's pro shop, on Amazon, or through an online tennis retailer), or it may be related to geography (e.g., direct sales channels in large or established markets like the United States or Western Europe as opposed to distributors in developing countries). Most companies end up using multiple channels, which means they have to consider possible channel conflicts: Does one channel undermine another? Ultimately, you need to weigh the pros and cons of different channels to figure out the right mix for you—both at launch and over time. We'll discuss the pros and cons of direct and distributor channels below, but

FIGURE 19.1. Sales Channel Framework

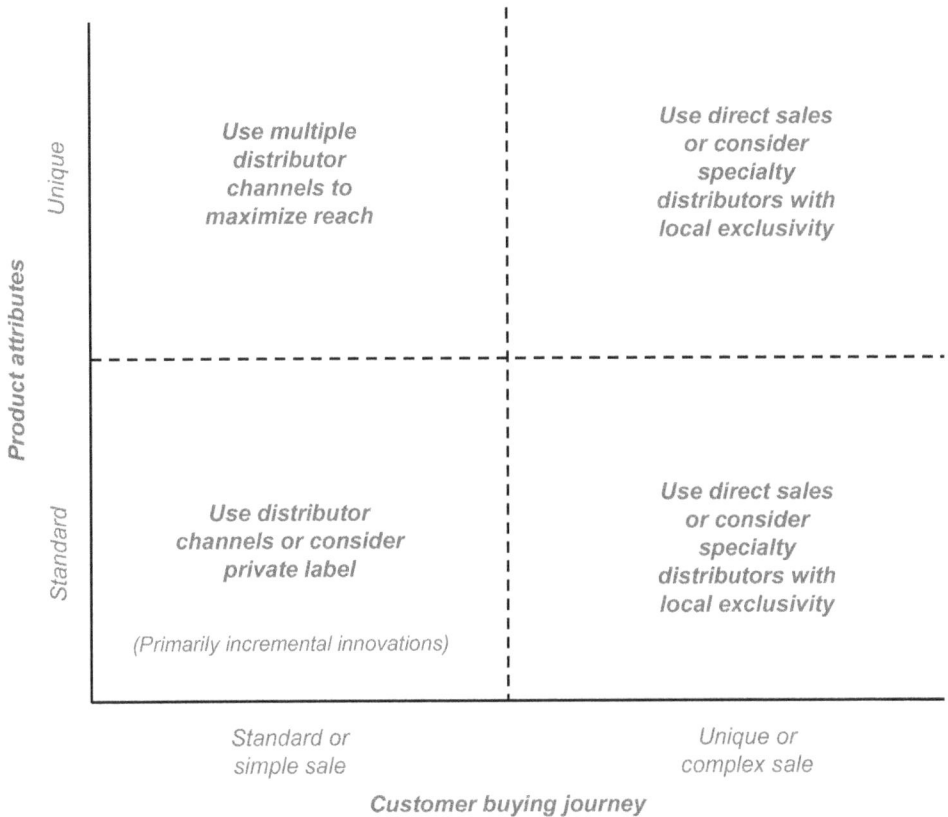

Figure 19.1 provides some direction depending on how unique your product and its customer buying journey is. **In general, the more unique the customer buying journey and the more unique or difficult to sell your product, the more value there may be in emphasizing direct channels or a limited number of specialty dealers.**

Why go direct? To some extent, the answer is obvious: You retain control of the customer and keep all the economics you generate. **A direct channel establishes a relationship between you and your customers—you control the customer journey, the full experience around your product or service, and create an engine for generating ongoing customer insights as well as feedback loops to product development.** This is very helpful for creating an enduring franchise rather than a one-hit wonder (a subject to which we return in

Chapter 21). You also do not need to give up economics to a third party, which can range from just a few percentage points in highly efficient markets to 20 to 40 percent in other markets. On average, for example, companies pay around 15 percent of their selling price in fees to Amazon.

The negatives of going direct are largely around expense: It can be costly—sometimes *extremely* costly—to create a direct sales channel. It can also be a time-consuming and ultimately inefficient way to access customers. For example, the creator of a new single-use product for restaurants is likely to be better off going through a food service distributor like Sysco and thereby reach thousands of customers immediately and not have to worry about logistics. But the creator of a new type of high-speed oven may require a direct sales force to educate restaurants about the benefits of the new technology.

Sometimes, though, even in cases where efficient channels already exist, it can be worthwhile to go direct. Apple, Nespresso, lululemon, and Tesla all built their own brick-and-mortar retail presences to control the customer journey, which is an important aspect of their aspirational and higher-end brands. This can also help prevent disintermediation, whereby distributors can leverage their relationships with customers (and their resulting insights into demand) to try to swap in their own private-label products (e.g., Amazon Basics).

And while we're on the subject, let's take a brief detour into the strange and unique channel that is Amazon. At the risk of stating the obvious, Amazon represents a special conundrum for many B2C (and increasingly, B2B) brands.

The scale and reach of the Amazon marketplace are unlike any other, and they have given the platform incredible value. How do you ignore the dominant online retailer in twenty-eight countries, with 200 million global Prime members and a commanding position in the United States?[1] Not easy! For many products, Amazon is perceived as an absolutely vital channel. At the same time, it introduces significant challenges. Competition is fierce—not only from your competitors but also, in many categories, from resellers and Amazon private label. Margins are significantly impacted by Amazon's fees and the increasing need to spend on search positioning and advertising. Data-sharing on customers is limited, preventing many brands from forming meaningful relationships or gathering insights from their customers. For those products that are subject to counterfeiting, this is particularly problematic. And for other kinds of products—including those that are logistically complex, expensive to ship (e.g., large/bulky, fragile, refrigerated), require customization, or are regulated (e.g., tobacco)—Amazon is not a preferred or even a viable channel.

For many products, though, it *is* possible to sell through Amazon, so the choice comes down to a consideration of the costs and benefits. For a small innovator, reaching a large number of customers early can be worth the lower margin you capture, but this also depends on your channel alternatives. Are there other established channels, and do you have access to them? Will being on Amazon cause channel conflict with others, such as big box retailers? The answer to this may also change over time: As you build your brand and market awareness, you may be able to open new channels and rely less on Amazon.

The level of competition and commoditization in your category should also drive your decision. The more competition you face, the harder it will be for you to capture customer mindshare and the more difficult it will be to maintain pricing discipline.

It's also important to decide how important managing the customer experience and capturing insights on customers is to you. Most high-end brands avoid Amazon not just because of concerns over counterfeiting but also because they want to preserve margins and loyalty at high-end retail partners as well as deliver on a brand promise of a higher-touch, higher service-level experience than is achievable through Amazon. If this powerful channel is off-brand for you, you may want to stay away from it.

Take Bombas, for example, an innovator in socks and other comfort apparel with a unique social mission addressing homelessness: For every item of clothing that is purchased from Bombas, another is donated to a homeless shelter, totaling something like 100 million donated items to date.[2] Given the nature of its products, the company could logically be on Amazon—but it has steered away from such a channel relationship to ensure that it controls its message and brand positioning, which Bombas sees as critical to its differentiation versus the myriad of other brands in its space.[3] Notably, as of this writing, Amazon does have a handful of resellers of Bombas products, which further points to the challenge of managing this channel.[4] If Amazon is an option for your innovation, you need to consider both the financial and strategic benefits and the costs of taking advantage of the channel. **In general, if you are worried about controlling the customer experience and building your brand, Amazon may not be the best channel for you.**

But to return from our detour through the world of Amazon: **Distributors and third-party partners can be, and usually *should* be, a part of a company's go-to-market strategy.** In some markets, there's just no choice—if you want to sell products into many markets in Latin America or China, for example, you have to use local distributors who essentially serve as gatekeepers to customers. And this can be a good thing: In fragmented markets, distributors can add tremendous value by bringing efficiency to both suppliers and customers, including providing sales support and handling many tedious back-end processes like billing, fulfillment, and cash collection. And as you may recall from our discussion of pricing in Chapter 14, channels can also be an effective way for you to vary pricing to capture different willingness to pay across customer segments who access your product or service differently.

The experience of United States Gypsum (USG), a Fortune 500 company and the leading manufacturer of wallboard in North America, provides insights into weighing channel tradeoffs for a novel innovation. Wallboard—the stuff most modern walls and ceilings are made out of—is used extensively in both residential and commercial construction. By most reckonings, this isn't a category known for its innovation. And yet in early 2010—a very difficult time for the construction industry, which was emerging from the Great Recession–related housing crisis—USG was sitting on a new product that seemed positioned to disrupt the market. USG's Innovation Center had created a new kind of wallboard that was 30 percent lighter and 20 percent stronger than the conventional product used in home construction.

The calculus regarding the market appeal of Sheetrock UltraLight Panels (as the product came to be branded) was complex. For obvious reasons, the product appealed strongly to the laborers who were responsible for hanging wallboard. Homeowners, by contrast, didn't care one way or the other unless they were do-it-yourself-ers (DIYs). The value to builders and contractors was moderate (e.g., lower freight costs, higher productivity of laborers), and it varied for different channels that sell wallboard (e.g., retailers like the Home Depot, professional broadline dealers, and gypsum specialty dealers).

USG also faced the complicating factor of launching a novel premium product into a market with prices depressed by a glut in supply of wallboard, thanks to the housing crisis. Furthermore, it's worth noting that USG was the only wallboard manufacturer vertically integrated with its own distribution channel, which coexisted with other channels. The challenge for USG lay in navigating the different customer segments with varying willingness to pay (WTP) and determining the right channel(s) by which to go to market, given the financial and strategic considerations—for example, the possible cannibalization of existing products with a leading market position and the emergence of channel conflicts, including its own.

USG determined that residential renovation was the use case with the highest WTP, because (1) remodelers were less price-sensitive (as they could pass costs on to homeowners) and valued the ability for one laborer to carry the wallboard around the job site, and (2) DIYs similarly appreciated the lightweight benefits. Wallboard subcontractors also valued the product benefits but had a slightly lower WTP. Notably, remodelers and DIYs tended to shop at big box retailers like The Home Depot and Lowe's, while wallboard subcontractors shopped primarily at specialty stores. These subcontractors were distinct from builders and general contractors, who valued the product less and who purchased more commonly through channels like professional broadline dealers.

This sophisticated level of understanding enabled USG to create a segmented strategy for targeting different customer segments through these channels at slightly different price points, reflecting their respective WTP. And while this strategy created a relatively elegant segmentation hedge for USG's pricing strategy, it also required the company to manage some complexities. Large retailers like The Home Depot needed to be convinced that the benefits of carrying the new product would overcome the potential cannibalization risk of a proven, lower-carrying-cost product. Further, at launch, USG had to hold off on distributing Sheetrock UltraLight Panels through its own vertically integrated channel to minimize market confusion, given that the product wouldn't be made available to lower-WTP channels.

Who would have guessed that innovating in the realm of wallboard could be this complicated? But the story presents a compelling example of the complicated tradeoffs that can at times accompany a channel decision. To recap: USG needed to consider the different profit potential of each channel based on mix of customers being served, the size of the customer segment, their WTP, and the potential cannibalization of existing products. Furthermore, different channels competed with each other to some extent, such that managing these conflicts and appropriately sequencing channels post-launch was important for preserving relationships while maximizing profit potential—that is, after establishing a high market price point.

Was it worth all this upfront investment of time, energy, and money? Absolutely! For USG, the results were nothing short of stupendous. The product won innovation accolades and awards in the industry and was a significant financial success that helped the company take meaningful share in a more or less commoditized market, which it was able to retain even after competitors introduced their own lightweight wallboard options. In short, effective channel management was an important enabler of this success story.

Casper Mattress provides a direct vs. distributor channel story that points in a somewhat different direction. Casper's innovation was creating a direct-to-consumer channel for mattresses—made possible by new technologies for fabricating, compressing, and shipping.[5] It's not an overstatement to say that Casper's disruptive approach to the mattress industry revolutionized how people shop for and buy mattresses. Unlike the traditional mattress shopping experience—which requires visiting showrooms to try products and interacting with commissioned salespeople—Casper introduced a simplified and convenient model that resonated with modern consumers. First, it established a user-friendly e-commerce platform through which customers could browse, select, and purchase mattresses online from the comfort of their homes, thus eliminating the need for physical store visits. Second, instead of overwhelming consumers with numerous mattress options, Casper offered a relatively pared-down selection of mattresses that were designed to appeal to different styles of sleepers and make the decision-making process more straightforward.

Casper's most distinctive feature was its delivery method. The company compressed its high-quality mattresses into compact boxes, making them easy to ship directly to customers' doorsteps. The approach not only reduced shipping costs but also allowed for a hassle-free unboxing experience. This innovative DTC channel strategy resonated with consumers looking for convenience, transparency, and affordability—and, not surprisingly, soon prompted other mattress companies to follow suit. Casper has struggled in recent years for a variety of reasons,[6] but the company's broader lesson—of the potential value of creating and leveraging DTC channels—is evident in many markets, and that approach is becoming a more viable option for a growing number of innovators, as consumers become savvier and the internet makes it easier than ever to reach them at a relatively low cost.

Manage Channels, Don't Let Them Manage You

To wrap up, as you consider the right mix of channels for your innovation, you should:

1. identify your different channel options across customer segments and geographies;

2. evaluate the financial and strategic tradeoffs;

3. determine your priority channels and any conflicts that need to be managed (making use of the framework in Figure 19.1); and

4. revisit your decisions over time as your launch unfolds, your market position changes, and you glean more insight into the effectiveness of the different channels you are using.

It's worth noting that this process may look quite different in a large organization vs. a start-up. In a large organization, you usually have established channels in the form of existing sales teams or distribution partnerships. As a result, there is likely an existing approach to bringing product to market and the decision may already be made for you. In this situation, you just need to make sure that the channels are right for your innovation (i.e., you're not just using what's available even if it is not well suited for your product). For a start-up (or a new business within a larger organization), you're likely starting with a blank sheet of paper and have more need to go through this full decision-making process.

Whether you're at a large organization or a start-up, if you've concluded that it makes sense to leverage third-party channel partners, it's important to understand the differences in their capability, reach, and motivation. Some have a greater focus on private label and can be expected to behave more as a "frenemy" than a partner. Some have much more customer reach and selling capability, which likely translates to a stronger negotiating position and higher cost for you (e.g., Amazon). **Understanding the reputations of potential partners by gathering market intel from others who have worked with them can be of great value, especially if the channel will be critical to your launch expectations and difficult to change.**

If you have specialist or exclusive distribution partners, you will likely benefit from **creating a channel partner management plan.** In managing channel partners, you need to onboard them appropriately in order to ensure that they understand the value proposition, target customers, and other nuances of your innovation; to define financial and nonfinancial metrics (e.g., service levels) for performance; and to ensure that incentives are correctly aligned (and sufficiently strong) and that communication expectations are set. You need to establish, *upfront*, proactive rules of engagement for managing potential conflicts (e.g., territories/fences vs. other partners or direct channels, pricing expectations). Failing to invest adequately in this kind of rule-making can lead to a host of problems like "gray market" dynamics (e.g., when your distributor sells products from one market segment or geography to a different one than intended in order to take advantage of differences in pricing).

Ultimately, though, what's most important is to **ensure that you are proactively and purposefully managing your channel partners with frequent evaluations of their performance.** Keep the horse in front of the cart. You don't want to end up altering your strategy to meet the needs of your channel partners; rather, you want to adjust your channels to fit your strategy.

EXECUTIVE SUMMARY

Take the shortest path to value by optimizing launch scale and picking the right channels.

- Decide on the best way to get your innovation in the hands of customers based on maximizing long-term opportunity potential, not just speed to market.

- Launch at scale and rapidly if you've prepared adequately, and especially if barriers to entry are low and/or network effects are important.

- Consider a limited launch when your innovation requires significant market education, exhibits a long sales cycle, or targets a narrow set of large customers.

- Determine the right mix of direct vs. distributor channels based on the uniqueness of your product and the buying journey.

- Develop a plan to proactively manage your channel partners, including frequent evaluations of their performance.

TWENTY

Prime the Organization for
a Successful Launch

Suppose you've built the *fastest aircraft ever*. Great! Unfortunately, if you don't have the pilots and the crew needed to get it up in the air and fly it, you're going to go nowhere very fast. Whether it's an aircraft or a new business, the people at the controls—and behind the scenes!—are a critical part of getting where you want to go.

Your success from here on out depends largely on having the right organization to execute the launch. Without that in place, you're likely to find yourself in a plane without a flight crew. The "right organization" means the right team, structure, incentives, and processes.

Of course, your specific organizational needs (and challenges) grow directly out of your context. Are you a start-up? A business unit within a larger organization? A brand team operating in a larger organization? These are all different—but they also present some commonalities. We've collected some observations and organizational best practices that can be applied in each of these situations.

Organizational Priorities for Start-Ups

In some ways, the start-up has it best. You (usually) have the flexibility to create a customized organization for your launch from scratch. Looking at your launch plan and adoption barriers, you know what types of resources and configuration make the most sense, and you (most likely) have the decision-making authority to make it happen.

This is all to the good, because flexibility is usually essential to the launch of a novel innovation. Your requirements for success may look nothing like those of other products and services on the market; if so, you don't want to have to adapt an organization that was designed for something different to this new purpose. In addition to flexibility in resources and structure, you also (most likely) have some flexibility in designing incentives to drive alignment with outcomes, often including equity.

Unsurprisingly, however, the key organizational challenge for start-ups tends to be limited resources. The opportunity cost of every investment is significant, given this resource scarcity. Consequently, **it's critical to prioritize organizational investments in sales, customer service, and quality control.** A good bottom line: If you can generate sales and happy customers, you will create opportunities to add resources in other parts of the organization.

Organizational Priorities for Established Companies

If you're an innovator within a larger organization, you probably have different constraints and different problems than you'd encounter in a start-up. As a business unit within a larger company, you likely have a reasonable degree of flexibility to structure your team and focus your organizational investments (especially if you are running a separate P&L), but all of this will have to be done within corporate guidelines (e.g., HR, compliance). While you may have your own sales, marketing, and product development resources, you are likely to depend on corporate shared services in many other areas, including legal, HR, purchasing, manufacturing/operations, and so on.

The most common challenge here is maximizing your leverage of shared corporate functions—in other words, getting support that is tailored to your needs, and enough of it. This means building meaningful relationships and ensuring that these functional partners understand (1) what your launch priorities are, (2) how they contribute to them, and (3) what you expect of them.

This is a juncture for reflection. If you can't get enough out of these functional partners despite your best efforts, and if those deficits threaten to hurt your launch performance, you will need to find ways to get dedicated resources.

If you're operating **a brand team within a larger organization**, you're on the opposite end of the organizational spectrum from the start-up: You have very limited flexibility but (we hope!) access to lots of resources. The product team typically manages product development and marketing strategy but relies on shared services for all the key functions, including sales, marketing, HR, manufacturing/operations, and so on. In this context, it is critical to build alliances both within the various functions and with other product and service teams, as there will surely be areas in which priorities overlap and it will be important for you to collaborate effectively.

In many cases, the biggest challenge is getting the appropriate attention from the sales organization, especially if your innovation is just one of multiple priorities. **You absolutely need to understand the sales team's incentives and whether those provided to support your innovation are compelling.** You need to know this upfront, before launch, when a change is most feasible and most impactful (incentive changes on the fly are notoriously difficult).

Finally, it's important for you to understand whether the sales team has the skill set and capabilities required to successfully sell your product or service (more on this shortly). If the answer is "no," you may need to look for support from senior management to get the right (and likely separate) sales resources in place. If it is not possible to build a separate sales force, it's often beneficial to add a separate team of product specialists to communicate the value proposition of the innovation to customers, as you leverage existing sales resources in ways they can add most value (e.g., broader contracting, potential bundling opportunities with existing products).

Importance of Building Internal Alliances

Regardless of the specific context, **when you're working as an innovator within a larger organization, the importance of building alignment and investing in allies can't be overstated.** We've seen all too many situations in which the success of a team was undermined by other stakeholders in the organization, who for one reason or another weren't willing to provide the support needed. Those reasons differ from organization to organization, but most commonly they result in reluctance, denial, or just a lack of prioritizing the help needed (e.g., lead generation/sharing from a parallel sales team, responsiveness of shared services).

The National Football League in the United States provides a helpful example of successfully managing these dynamics. The NFL, the top league for professional American football teams, manages the distribution of all the games played throughout the season. Starting in 2018, the NFL began planning for a complete revamp of its direct-to-consumer (DTC) streaming service called NFL+. This was a big deal. Why? Because most of the NFL's revenue streams were derived from content licensing—as opposed to operating its own content platform—which made streaming services a sensitive addition to the league's traditional business model. Furthermore, a streaming service needed to navigate complexities related to issues such as content rights (e.g., in and out of market) and pricing (e.g., wide ranges in existing market pricing for content consumption, ranging from free to monthly subscriptions that were themselves complicated by season length and so on).

So aligning an organization like the NFL behind this new and very different opportunity proved a significant lift. The team—led by Gil Moran, Head of Direct-to-Consumer and Media Strategy for the NFL—had one big advantage, which was that they had undertaken extensive research using extended diary studies for football fans. This showed that despite the wide availability of NFL football on network TV, there were still situations in which consumers were missing out on content. For example, they were willing to pay for broader access if they could watch games of interest while on the go and away from home.

Moran and his team engaged with a wide range of stakeholders across the organization to build alignment and ensure that they had the support needed for launch. In some cases, they learned that they needed to bring on board some functions they had not initially realized would be critical for their success (e.g., sponsorship), which is exactly what they did. By the time the team launched NFL+, the organization was well aligned to support the launch. Ultimately, the effort paid off. The streaming service was highly successful and—despite high targets—surpassed its Year 1 budget.

In retrospect, the lessons are clear: **You need to invest in learning about the businesses that sit next to you—what they want and how they will perceive your efforts—and in building good working relationships.** In general, as discussed in Chapter 18 in the context of launch plan development, it's better to err on the side of being more inclusive and engaging a broader set of stakeholders. Remember: No one ever gets offended by being included. With that maxim in mind, try to eliminate potentially detrimental organizational blind spots proactively.

Organizational Best Practices for Launch

As suggested above, we can also point to a handful of common organizational themes for launch success, regardless of whether you're in a start-up or a larger organization. Below are several of the more important of these lessons:

- **Use metrics that drive performance.** Of course, sales are a key metric, probably at the top of the list, but it's also valuable to identify a handful of key performance indicators (KPIs)—usually fewer than five—on which you and your commercial team can focus. For example, looking back to Intuitive Surgical in Chapter 10, *placing* a new surgical robot is an important metric for success—but so is the *level of utilization* (i.e., the number of procedures performed per month using the robot, at the account, and by an individual surgeon), which has significant implications for long-term account productivity.

- **Align incentives.** We've already discussed incentives, to some extent, but we can't overemphasize the old adage that "if you pay for A, don't expect B." You need your customer-facing teams to have incentives aligned with your goals. That goal may solely be converting new customers, but it may also include driving sustained usage, facilitating referrals, or delivering a certain level of customer satisfaction. Incentives should tie to your KPIs, not just to sales. Additionally, incentives need to reflect the level of effort required. For example, converting a new customer is usually much more difficult than generating a repeat sale, so incentives should be higher for new customer conversions. Finally, it's worth noting that incentives need to be directed with clearly communicated goals and reinforced with reviews for performance accountability.

- **Focus.** As we pointed out in Chapter 8, It's always better to have one person spending 100 percent of his or her time on something than to have ten people spending 10 percent of their time on it. Where you can dedicate resources to a specific job to support your launch, you should do so. In fact, focus is a broader theme that should carry forward from your launch plan—a relentless focus on your stated goals and KPIs, as well as ensuring that leadership stays focused on launch success and isn't siphoned off in service to other pressing needs.

- **Build the right sales team.** There's more to getting the right sales team than meets the eye. We spoke about this briefly in the context of making sure an existing sales team has the right capabilities. But ask yourself *what a successful rep really needs to be able to do* and what background will therefore be valuable. Is your innovation one that requires solution selling? Is it a complicated enterprise sale? Does it require a certain level of specific expertise or jargon fluency? Is it a market-development or market-share play? Will customers only respond to a salesperson with a specific type of background or profile? Sometimes it's obvious that a certain background, certification, or experience is critical. Often, the specifics of a prior experience or existing customer relationships matter little. What you *really* need to make sure of is that a salesperson has the skill set required to engage with your target call points and to sell your story. Have they sold comparable products and services before? Don't fall into the trap of hiring (and sometimes overpaying) for the wrong type of rep. For example, we've seen companies struggle to commercialize a product because they have a bunch of "farmers" (i.e., reps focused on account maintenance/continuity) trying to do the work that "hunters" ought to be doing.

- **Invest in commercial tools.** The effectiveness of salespeople can be dramatically enhanced if they are armed with the right tools. This can speed up training, shorten ramp time, and deliver higher productivity. Tools can include data for prioritizing customers (e.g., which customers in which order and estimated opportunity by customer—both particularly valuable in

B2B contexts), insights into customer decision-making dynamics (e.g., decision-makers, influencers, processes), and marketing collateral tailored to overcome specific adoption barriers (e.g., ROI calculators, white papers, reference customers). For example, pharma companies—famous for their selling organizations—are known to purchase data such as prescribing volumes and physician referrals for their reps to leverage. Often these tools entail making investments in enabling functions like sales operations, which are critical for maintaining and analyzing data and customer relationship management (CRM) systems. Many organizations make the mistake of overinvesting in sales reps and underinvesting in commercial tools—even though the latter may yield much higher ROI by meaningfully enhancing the productivity of *all* reps.

- **Maintain commercial discipline.** It can be tempting to stray from your launch plan and try to sell to anyone who shows interest in your product or service. Often, early on in your customer runway, you're focusing on specific customer targets, and it can require real discipline on your part to prevent opportunism from driving commercial activities. As unnatural as it may seem, sometimes the right answer is to turn away lower-priority customers—even ones who seek you out!—to avoid getting distracted from your objectives.

- **Inspire with aspirational goals.** Translating a revenue forecast into monthly and quarterly goals for launch can be tricky. You need to manage the expectations of your stakeholders—including investors and senior executives, in the case of a larger company—but you also need to drive and inspire your team. It is best to define an aspirational goal that can inspire but also has a clear, articulable path to being achieved. Once a revenue forecast is developed, it shouldn't be that difficult to determine sales goals—but it can certainly be a delicate matter to settle on goals that are aspirational enough to inspire the troops but not so ambitious as to demoralize them when they prove difficult to attain.

- **Adjust priorities dynamically.** Remember that your launch plan should be a living document that evolves with the launch. While maintaining focus is important, it is equally critical to reevaluate your plan and to ensure that your launch priorities and the assumptions underpinning your launch goals remain sound. Market traction, competitive responses, internal organizational dynamics—all of these can contribute to needing to course-correct your plan. Stay focused, but adaptable.

An inspirational example can help bring these lessons to life. It concerns an innovative healthcare start-up, which we'll call "BestHealth." BestHealth, which enjoyed a successful half-billion-dollar exit a few years back, exemplified many of the best practices outlined above in the launch of its flagship product targeted at electrophysiologists (physicians who treat issues with the heart's electrical system). Interestingly, the company had started with a modestly successful product for the broader cardiovascular space but then recognized that if they modified it for a different use case for an adjacent customer target (electrophysiologists), they could address a much more acute unmet need (reducing a patient's hospital stay from overnight to same day) and carve out a more differentiated market position.

This investment in customer research paid off. The new product took off and quickly became the dominant part of the business. But what was notable was BestHealth's approach to its launch. The company invested heavily in commercial tools, including a detailed prioritization of customers, which determined that their top three hundred prospective customers represented something like two-thirds of the market opportunity, based on the scale of these physician practices. They hired skilled sales reps—with relevant "hunting" experience—and armed each of them with a list of electrophysiologists prioritized by estimated opportunity potential.

BestHealth also realized through its pre-launch research that prospective customers with a specific set of workflows (e.g., post-treatment protocols) were more likely to see immediate value in the product. With this in mind, the company developed an app that reps could use in their customer interactions to understand whether the workflows fit the profile of an early adopter, allowing for both swift triage and focus during the early stages of launch.

Sales leadership also focused the team on two KPIs: (1) the number of new customers per quarter and (2) the level of penetration of existing customers. Because the sales team was equipped with opportunity size by customer, they could easily see their level of sales penetration into any given customer. This metric was helpful in ensuring that customers stuck with the product and that share grew over time at an account. The sales team couldn't just open an account and move on; sustained success was heavily incentivized. Furthermore, the organization looked at new accounts in cohorts and monitored their maturity of product usage relative to their cohort on a quarter-by-quarter basis.

All in all, the commercial discipline of the launch was impressive. For example, reps weren't allowed to go after customers who were not on their specific list. The sales leadership hosted a weekly "war room," during which each frontline sales manager was expected to update peers and sales leaders on progress against the two KPIs listed above and also to share any learnings. This kept the group focused on what mattered, drove a culture of accountability (while injecting some healthy competition) and enabled accelerated sharing and adoption of best practices. The result was a best-in-class launch in the industry.

As we stated at the outset of this chapter, just as an aircraft needs the right pilot and crew, you need to get your organization right to maximize the success of your launch. Don't underestimate the people aspects of commercial success. Every launch is different, which requires that you architect the organization for the specific situation, but some best practices have proven to be effective across a wide range of innovation contexts.

EXECUTIVE SUMMARY

Prime the organization for a successful launch by tailoring capabilities and nurturing alliances.

- Build a strong organization to execute on your launch including the right team, structure, incentives, and processes.

- If operating in a start-up context, prioritize investments in sales, customer service, and quality control.

- If operating in a larger company, focus on maximizing leverage of shared corporate functions, ensuring that sales team incentives are effective, and investing in internal allies.

- Follow the most critical launch best practices: relentless commercial focus, clear metrics aligned with sales incentives, and investment in commercial enablers.

Part 4: Ensuring Commercial Success Checklist

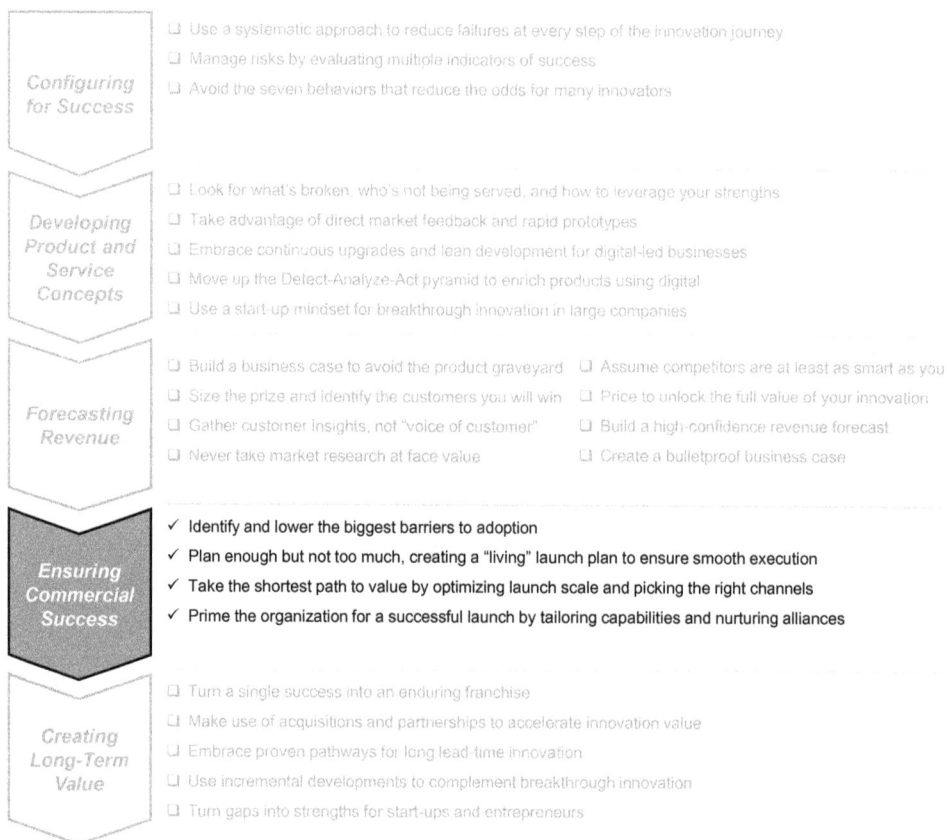

Configuring for Success

- ❏ Use a systematic approach to reduce failures at every step of the innovation journey
- ❏ Manage risks by evaluating multiple indicators of success
- ❏ Avoid the seven behaviors that reduce the odds for many innovators

Developing Product and Service Concepts

- ❏ Look for what's broken, who's not being served, and how to leverage your strengths
- ❏ Take advantage of direct market feedback and rapid prototypes
- ❏ Embrace continuous upgrades and lean development for digital-led businesses
- ❏ Move up the Detect-Analyze-Act pyramid to enrich products using digital
- ❏ Use a start-up mindset for breakthrough innovation in large companies

Forecasting Revenue

- ❏ Build a business case to avoid the product graveyard
- ❏ Size the prize and identify the customers you will win
- ❏ Gather customer insights, not "voice of customer"
- ❏ Never take market research at face value
- ❏ Assume competitors are at least as smart as you
- ❏ Price to unlock the full value of your innovation
- ❏ Build a high-confidence revenue forecast
- ❏ Create a bulletproof business case

Ensuring Commercial Success

- ✓ Identify and lower the biggest barriers to adoption
- ✓ Plan enough but not too much, creating a "living" launch plan to ensure smooth execution
- ✓ Take the shortest path to value by optimizing launch scale and picking the right channels
- ✓ Prime the organization for a successful launch by tailoring capabilities and nurturing alliances

Creating Long-Term Value

- ❏ Turn a single success into an enduring franchise
- ❏ Make use of acquisitions and partnerships to accelerate innovation value
- ❏ Embrace proven pathways for long lead-time innovation
- ❏ Use incremental developments to complement breakthrough innovation
- ❏ Turn gaps into strengths for start-ups and entrepreneurs

PART V

Creating Long-Term Value

Traps that cause many organizations to destroy value after the first launch can be avoided, while incremental innovation can be used to build on the success of a breakthrough in the long term. The requirements for driving sustainable success from innovation vary for different types and scale of businesses.

TWENTY-ONE

Turn a Single Success into an Enduring Franchise

Let's imagine that a company has pulled it all off. It has succeeded in bringing to market its first product, and that product is clicking with a well-defined base of customers. Milestones are being met; hurdles leapt; money and plaudits are pouring in. At this point, the management of our imaginary company might be forgiven for expecting a shift in its cadence—say, from that long uphill slog they've just lived through to a relaxed jog, somewhere along a sunlit upland.

Sounds great! But for most companies, even for those that hit the jackpot on their first time out, this is *not* the best plan.

In fact, it's exactly at this point that many companies come up short. According to a recent study of first-time product launches in the life sciences sector, only 27 percent of companies showed increased shareholder value twelve and twenty-four months after their first product, while more than 50 percent of companies destroyed value over both time intervals.[1]

Why? The central dilemma for most innovating companies is that once their product comes to market, there are new challenges to overcome, including scaling a commercial organization and managing investor expectations. Much of what needs to be done to address these challenges is covered in earlier chapters of this book. In this chapter, though, we focus on issues that are particularly important for new companies launching their first commercial product.

Five Areas Where Many Companies Fall Short

Since 2015, there has been significant growth in the number of first-product companies deciding to stay independent, rather than partnering or merging with larger organizations. This can be an attractive pathway if you're able to manage the transition from a development company to a scaled commercial business. But experience shows that **many enterprises pay insufficient attention in five key areas: operations, competition, international expansion, resourcing, and investor management**. Let's look at these in turn.

Scaling up commercial operations. For a successful launch, the company needs to build up its commercial team, which means both identifying (and possibly recruiting) a strong leader and building all the related customer-facing infrastructure that he or she needs to succeed. For an established company, these elements are usually already in place, but for many first-time launchers, the pieces all need to be assembled. As these commercial and supply-chain organizations get built up, there needs to be a corresponding expansion in the related staff ranks—which in turn is likely to create the need for more formalized HR management, enhanced communications, and so on. Eventually, the company's physical infrastructure probably will need upgrading as well.

Dealing with competitors. New companies are often shocked at how fast competitors come to market, creating new demands on the commercial organization to stand out from the crowd. As we explained in Chapter 13, companies that have a strong market idea need to anticipate strong and rapidly emerging competitive threats and have a plan in place for dealing with them.

Going (or not going) international. An added complication for many new companies today is the need for a rapid transition to international markets. What if a new business enjoys good success in its home market but then sees imitators quickly popping up internationally? That company then faces the choice of (1) accelerating its own international rollout, (2) ceding international markets to competitors, or (3) pursuing an international partnering strategy. This choice must be made *quickly*. Hertz had the luxury of waiting twenty years before making its first international expansion (to Canada). Uber, by contrast, expanded to forty international locations in its first three years.

Meeting your growing resource and capital requirements. The combined effects of the rapid build-up of commercial operations and the need to stay

ahead of competitors means higher cash demands, often sooner than originally anticipated. Accelerating international rollout means that multiple build-
outs need to happen at once, rather than engaging in the kind of self-funding
sequence in which each maturing market helps fund the next market entry.

Managing investor expectations. Whether your company continues to be
privately backed or has transitioned to a public listing, your investors need to
be carefully managed. The combination of factors described above means that
capital demands may be greater and may arrive sooner than originally anticipated. If expansion to new markets is accelerated, then the time to achieve
profitability may become extended. The desire to please investors—to accentu-
ate the positive—can easily lead to unrealistic expectations. The safer path is
to be realistic, which means asking for more and promising more in return but
further into the future.

The Challenge of Going Beyond the First Product

Even if you do everything right to achieve a successful product launch and international rollout, the job is not complete unless you are able to develop a self-sus-
taining pipeline of successful new product additions and extensions. To illustrate
this challenge, we will consider two first-product companies: GoPro and Garmin.

Founder Nicholas Woodman, a surfer from California, began selling GoPro
cameras—wide-angle action video camcorders—through the QVC shopping
channel in 2004.[2] The launch was a huge success, and it was soon followed by
a series of upgrades. The cameras quickly developed a loyal following. By 2012,
GoPro was responsible for over 21 percent of digital camcorders in the United
States and was hailed as one of America's fastest-growing companies. The company went public in 2014 with a valuation of more than $5 billion.

Fast-forward to late 2023: The company was still reporting around $1 billion
a year in sales, but profits were uneven, growth was going backwards, and more
than 90 percent of the IPO valuation had vanished. What went wrong? Put
simply, GoPro failed to broaden its reach and appeal beyond its initial product
concept. The company made a big push into drone cameras in 2016—a device
called the "Karma"—but that device turned out to be a complete flop, with all
2,500 units eventually being recalled. Partly due to powerful competition from
the very successful Chinese company DJI, GoPro withdrew permanently from

the drone market. Backed by several state-owned entities, DJI's sales are now estimated to be around four times those of GoPro.

GoPro is a cautionary tale of how hard it can be for a first-product company to build an enduring franchise with a sustained growth outlook and that delivers an attractive return to investors. The company did everything right with its first launch—but it wasn't enough. Here's the main point of the GoPro story and of this chapter: **Established companies tend to have much of the infrastructure and talent needed to turn a first breakthrough success into a series of incremental new product platforms and extensions, but new first-product companies have to build all of that on the fly.**

The Value of a Multi-Platform Product Plan

Garmin was one of the first companies to see the potential of GPS navigation. It was founded in 1989 by Gary Burrell and Min Kao, in Lenexa, Kansas. By 2007 Garmin had achieved more than $3 billion in annual sales of products that used moving-map displays and turn-by-turn directions for cars, boats, and aircraft, with automotive being by far the largest segment. But the company was about to face a series of challenges that could easily have destroyed the business. First, in 2007, Apple released the iPhone, which put powerful new GPS capabilities in the pocket of every user. Then, in 2009, Google launched the Google Maps app for *free*. Said one analyst: "I don't see much positive growth for . . . Garmin. . . . Why would you pay for something you can get for free?"[3]

Garmin responded by adjusting its existing businesses and placing bets on two major new growth platforms. In its existing automotive businesses, Garmin transitioned to becoming an OEM supplier for automotive navigation systems that are part of the manufacturer's dashboard displays. Yes, this new direction lacked the margin potential of the direct-to-consumer model, but it was still a large and growing business. Meanwhile, the company did not stand still in its other established businesses. In its marine and aircraft segments, the company launched a series of refinements and new capabilities, including autopilots and integrated instrument systems (and thereby following in the path laid out by Collins Aerospace, described in Chapter 5). The company's integrated aircraft cockpit systems have become the standard for personal aircraft and small business jets.

One of the two new platform bets was Nüvifone, which essentially took on Apple with a GPS navigator that also had a built-in mobile phone. Perhaps not surprisingly, going up against mighty Apple in its wheelhouse, the Garmin product was a complete flop. Garmin's other new platform bet was in wearable devices. The company had entered the fitness space in 2006 with the acquisition of Dynastream Innovations, a specialist in fitness tracking devices. Garmin built on this platform to create a whole range of wearable fitness tracking devices. Competition in the fitness and outdoor segment was fierce, but Garmin's human-centric designs had broad appeal. By 2015, outdoor and fitness had overtaken automotive to be the largest segment for the company, with over $1 billion in sales. Analysis of uploads from marathon runners in major events such as New York, Boston, and Chicago showed that more than 70 percent of the tracking watches were from Garmin.[4] By the end of 2023, Garmin's market capitalization exceeded $20 billion, with the negative reverberations of the 2007–2009 iPhone disruption far behind in the rearview mirror.

Garmin succeeded by having a multi-platform product plan *before* adversity hit. Of course, there's no guaranteed path to a second or third success. One of Garmin's major initiatives—the Nüvifone—was a complete dud. As we've stressed in previous chapters, *innovation is risky*. And this is exactly why your emerging company, as it looks down the road, needs a plan that encompasses multiple bets. Garmin succeeded by **maturing from an emerging company embracing a breakthrough innovation to an established company with a mix of breakthrough and incremental innovation**, with constant upgrades and expansions that have made it a respected leader in navigation and tracking across all four of its key platforms: outdoor/fitness, automotive, marine, and aircraft.

After an initial product success, companies have to face the broader question of what business they're in over the long term. Often the answer is not a straight line but a series of successive generations and adaptations. Having multiple platforms tailored to different market segments can give your company the resilience it needs to withstand a massive disruption in your largest market and positions you to make the transition from a first-product phenomenon to an enduring innovator.

EXECUTIVE SUMMARY

Turn a single success into an enduring franchise.

- Be aware of the challenges in transitioning from a development company to a scaled commercial business, particularly in the areas of operations, competition, international expansion, resourcing, and investor management.

- Understand how hard it is to maintain success and growth beyond the first product, and be prepared to invest accordingly.

- Recognize the value of a multi-generational product plan as part of the transition from a product breakthrough mindset to a mix of breakthrough and incremental innovation.

TWENTY-TWO

Make Use of Acquisitions and Partnerships to Accelerate Innovation Value

Ask anyone in the developed world who the world's most innovative companies are, and you'll probably get an answer that includes some combination of Apple, Amazon, Facebook (now Meta), Microsoft, and Google (now Alphabet). But what most people *don't* know is just how much of what made those companies what they are today came from technology they brought in through acquisitions.[1]

Let's look at some concrete examples. Apple's iTunes was built on the SoundJam MP music service it acquired in 2000. Siri was acquired in 2010; it was originally a U.S. Defense Department program. Apple Music was based on the acquisition of Beats Electronics in 2014. Amazon's cloud computing business (which accounts for the majority of its operating income) grew out of thirteen acquisitions made between 2012 and 2020. Facebook acquired Instagram in 2012 and WhatsApp in 2014. Facebook's revenues from digital advertising (a market in which Google and Facebook have more revenue than all other companies combined) was bolstered by the acquisitions of advertising technology companies Atlas in 2013 and LiveRail in 2014. Microsoft PowerPoint was based on the acquisition of Forethought way back in 1987. Microsoft Teams was based on technology from the acquisitions of Parlano around 2007 and Skype in 2011. Google's Android is built on technology from an acquisition in 2005. After their acquisitions, Writerly became Google Docs, and Tonic Systems became Google Slides. Google acquired YouTube in 2006 for $1.6 billion; by 2023, the acquisition price was equivalent to *three weeks* of YouTube advertising revenue.

Of course, it's certainly true enough that Apple, Amazon, Meta, Microsoft, and Alphabet are fantastically innovative companies. But going back to the point we made in Chapter 1, they have gained that identity in part because **they start with an agnostic approach regarding internal or external innovation. They focus on *finding the best ideas*—wherever those ideas come from—and making sure that internal teams can build on the latest developments in those realms.**

What's an illuminating contrast? Consider the example of Intel, by many measures, a brilliant and highly successful technology company. Over the last twenty-two years, though, its share performance has disappointed, with a lower market capitalization in 2023 than it had in 2001. Arguably, Intel's subpar value creation in this period can be blamed largely on its lack of a successful acquisition strategy. As described in Chapter 7, the company has a proud history of pursuing breakthrough innovation through internal development. Yes, acquisitions have been undertaken, but on a more limited scale and without the transformative impacts we saw in the case of Apple, Amazon, Facebook, Microsoft, and Google. Intel's biggest move was the 2017 acquisition of autonomous driving technology developer Mobileye for $15 billion—but Mobileye persisted in burning cash, and in 2023 it was spun out in an IPO. The lesson here is that **large companies that struggle to access external innovation will find it hard to match the growth of those able to bring in new capabilities from the outside through targeted acquisitions.**

The Five-Point Framework

To be successful in this game, companies wishing to include acquisitions as part of their innovation and development efforts need to apply the same systematic rigor as we advocate for internal innovation. Toward that end, we advise companies to use a five-point framework for finding, evaluating, and completing successful acquisitions, as summarized in Figure 22.1.

The approach starts by having a **clear strategy for how the acquisition can supplement the company's organic development**. For example, this could be

FIGURE 22.1. Five-Point Acquisitions Framework

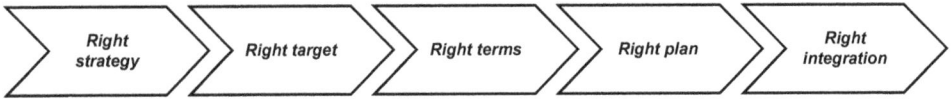

| Right strategy | Right target | Right terms | Right plan | Right integration |

by providing a foothold in a high-growth new area, as we saw with Google's acquisition of YouTube, or it could be by accessing a critical new technology, as in the case of Apple and Siri. Note that "starting with the strategy" does *not* mean the strategy has to originate in-house. We are strong advocates of constant vigilance of developments in and around a company's competitive space. Sometimes that kind of vigilance uncovers ideas for a new growth vector—but ultimately, it should also lead to a clear strategy for how this new departure can create value within the company's portfolio of offerings.

In addition to helping spot new growth opportunities, **constant vigilance should help inform companies about which are the ideal acquisition targets to access the required capabilities.** When Facebook acquired WhatsApp in 2014 for more than $16 billion, many observers were shocked by the price. After all, the company had revenues of only $16 million and losses of more than $230 million. On the other hand—as Facebook had figured out—WhatsApp had a unique proposition, offering messaging services to users without using wireless networks or sustaining data fees, which gave it strong consumer appeal, especially in developing markets. Since then, the platform has grown to over *two billion* subscribers. The lesson for acquirers? **It pays to find the right target— one that delivers unique and potentially transformational capabilities.**

This brings us to the "terms" block in Figure 22.1. Price is a big piece of this, but only one piece. Acquiring a company to help fulfill a company's strategy for innovation and growth is not like trading shares on the stock market. We are big believers in finding the right strategy and the ideal target first and worrying about price second. Why? Well, even if you overpay for a good company, if it is part of a well-defined strategy, it should still pay off, even if that's a lower overall return than anticipated. But most situations are not like WhatsApp, in that there is usually more than one potential target in sight. When that's the case, **successful acquirers have both a target price and a walk-away price**, with the goal of getting as close to the former if possible. The walk-away price should be based on the same disciplined approach to revenue forecasting described for new products in Chapter 15. In an acquisition where the goal is access to new capabilities, you also need to pay close attention to terms beyond price, such as the retention of key talent.

For acquisitions that are part of an innovation strategy rather than just acquiring mature businesses, **the plan for integration and development is just as important as it is for a breakthrough new product developed in-house**. The plan needs to touch on all the elements of this book's Part Four, including identifying and mitigating barriers to broader adoption, having a clear post-acquisition plan covering the first one hundred days, assembling and fielding the right team to implement the plan, and sharpening up the strategy for how the acquisition can unlock further growth by accelerating organic new product development.

Finally, **the acquiring company needs to do what's required to make the acquisition a success**. Disney Animation is the heart of one of the world's most creative and successful companies, with an unmatched history of creating many of animation's most iconic and best-loved characters. But in 2005, Disney Animation was struggling in the wake of a series of box office disappointments—at the same time that the upstart Pixar was soaring, with fresh ideas and a huge lead in computer-generated animation.[2] Disney CEO Bob Iger was convinced that the best path forward was not only to acquire Pixar but to put Disney Animation under the direction of Pixar visionaries John Lasseter and Ed Catmull. It was a tough pill for the traditionalists at Disney to swallow—and Iger faced serious pushback from the Disney board—but it turned out to be absolutely the right thing to do. Disney paid $7.4 billion for Pixar in 2006, which in the ensuing fifteen years turned in $11.5 billion in ticket sales alone.[3]

The Power of Partnerships

Let's imagine a parallel situation: What if your organization discovers a potentially life-changing innovation but lacks the capability to bring it to market? This was exactly the situation facing the University of Pennsylvania (UPenn) in 2010. Researchers led by immunologist Carl June had been experimenting with a new type of therapy for patients with advanced chronic lymphocytic leukemia (CLL) who had exhausted all other treatment options. The treatment involved modifying a patient's immune T cells to program them to multiply and attack cancer cells, and it proved extraordinarily effective for most patients who participated in early trials.

It soon became obvious that UPenn would need a partner—both to maximize the number of patients (mostly children) who could be helped with the therapy, and to ensure that UPenn had the resources to continue with its groundbreaking research. How to find such a partner? The answer is outlined in Part 3 of this book. **Only by understanding the market potential, the barriers to adoption, and the requirements for success can you assess potential partners and negotiate favorable terms.**

And that's exactly what UPenn did, resulting in a global licensing agreement with Novartis in 2012. By 2022, the treatment now known as Kymriah had improved the lives of nearly seven thousand children and young adults and enabled UPenn to create a brand-new Center for Advanced Cellular Therapies.

Breaking New Ground: A Nonprofit
Enterprise Bets on a New Subsidiary

In 2013, Children's Hospital of Philadelphia (CHOP) embarked on an alternative approach to monetizing innovation: starting a new company. Entrepreneur Jeff Marrazzo had approached Steve Altschuler, CEO of CHOP, in 2010. Marrazzo knew Dr. Altschuler from having served as an observer on CHOP's board as part of his UPenn business school studies. Did Altschuler know of any potential new venture opportunities? In fact he did: He was convinced that CHOP could be doing a better job of commercializing innovation, and he also knew that it was important for CHOP to develop new sources of funding for its research. Altschuler agreed to have Marrazzo talk to researchers across CHOP. Marrazzo spent three months doing just that, and one of his last interviews, with Dr. Kathy High, was the one that intrigued him. As Marrazzo recalls, "I was scheduled to talk to Kathy for one hour. Our meeting lasted seven hours, and I missed four trains back to New York City."[4]

High was experimenting with adeno-associated viral (AAV) vectors to create gene therapies that addressed certain rare inherited disorders affecting children. At the time, gene therapies had a poor reputation, resulting in part from some conspicuous failures, but after meeting with High, Marrazzo was convinced of the opportunity and the need for a new company to help it reach its potential and benefit patients. For example, one promising therapy was a treatment for pediatric blindness related to retinal dystrophy—a wrenching disease for children and their parents.

Marrazzo persuaded CHOP this was something worth putting more effort into. The group hired consultants to conduct a detailed assessment of the revenue potential and ultimate value that the program could generate.[5]

Armed with that assessment, Marrazzo—along with Drs. Altschuler and High—spent the next two years developing the detailed plan to create a new subsidiary using AAV technology. They explored licensing and different funding options, but none were compelling compared to the value potential from internal development. In 2013, CHOP made the decision to launch a new company—Spark Therapeutics—with Marrazzo as CEO.[6] The twofold goal: to keep together a successful academic team with a unique pipeline of promising research and to bring breakthrough new therapies to market. CHOP initially committed $10 million of funding to the venture, with a promise of more to come.

Although the team was tasked with developing new commercial therapies, they were not starting from scratch, having already developed preliminary capabilities in AAV gene therapy manufacturing and regulatory pathways that were ahead of most pharma companies. Over the next two years, the clinical development advanced successfully. In a pivotal Phase 3 trial, the drug for retinal neuropathy—now called Luxturna—showed 93 percent of children who were functionally blind at the start of the study gaining functional vision. In 2015, the company raised $161 million in an IPO. Two years later, Luxturna was launched. The price was high, but the company introduced a novel pricing plan that provided a refund if the drug was not successful for the patient. In 2019, Spark was acquired by Roche for $4.8 billion: a total payout to CHOP of more than $750 million, creating what was effectively an endowment to fund continuing research at CHOP.

While in retrospect this transition might sound straightforward, for the academic team at CHOP the prospect of being part of a new company—and carrying their clinical research through to commercialization—was a daunting one. At the start, the established venture capital firms were reluctant to invest in unproven technology, an unproven backer in CHOP, and an atypical founding team of entrepreneur Marrazzo and researcher High. Asked how he balances the belief in the product against being realistic about the challenges, Marrazzo's advice for his fellow entrepreneurs is, "Keep your eyes on the stars but your feet on the ground. It is good to have a bold vision, but you need concrete, step-by-step plans for how you are going to make it happen."

Figure 22.2 illustrates a high-level framework for using acquisitions or partnerships to accelerate innovation strategies:

The greater a company's commercialization resources and capabilities, the more sense it makes to in-license or acquire emerging technologies that fit with the company's product extension and go-to-market capabilities. Conversely, the less robust a company's resources and capabilities for bringing a new technology to market, the more sense it makes to out-license or partner. For AAV gene therapies in 2013, potential pharma partners had no greater development capabilities than CHOP, and the funding demands were not overwhelming given the small number of patients and required trial sizes. For CHOP, developing Spark themselves—at least until the first product came to market—created far more value than any other option.

FIGURE 22.2. M&A and Partnership Innovation Acceleration Framework

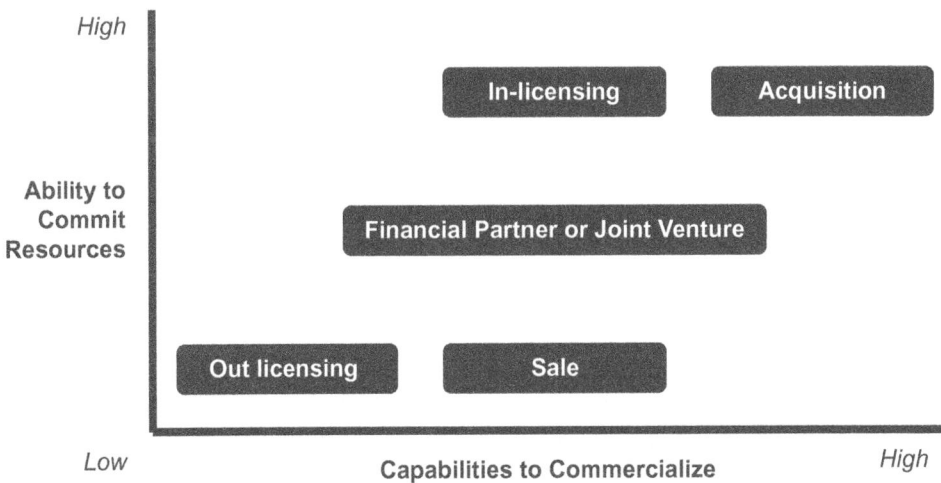

The first takeaway from the brief case studies in this chapter is that **innovation strategies and ideas aren't worth much if they can't be successfully brought to fruition—and sometimes that requires tapping expertise and capabilities from outside your organization**. This can happen in a variety of ways: through acquisition, a licensing deal, or new management with a financial partner.

The second is that whatever route your company chooses to pursue, **the key to maximizing value is to undertake the same detailed assessment and forecasting that you would perform if you were planning to launch the technology entirely in-house—but under alternative scenarios associated with the different external options**. Only then can your organization fully understand the value of your options as well as the options facing potential partners.

And finally, a partnership or sale will be the last step for many innovators and entrepreneurs. This often makes the most sense when a company has already made considerable progress in bringing a new product or service to market—but it's clear, nevertheless, that a new owner could do even more. Stated differently, if *untapped potential* is still there, and *other organizations have critical capabilities that the company lacks*, then that company may be better off out-licensing with a royalty stream or even going for that outright sale, using a detailed assessment and forecast to assess the value of the alternatives.

EXECUTIVE SUMMARY

Make use of acquisitions and partnerships to accelerate innovation value.

- Maintain an agnostic approach regarding internal or external innovation. Focus on *finding the best ideas*—whether those ideas come from internal teams or potential acquisition targets.

- Use a systematic framework to find, assess, and execute successful acquisitions that can complement internal development programs.

- Be aware of the opportunities and tradeoffs for both established and emerging companies in assessing when it creates most value to buy, sell, or partner an innovative new product.

TWENTY-THREE

Embrace Proven Pathways for Long Lead-Time Innovation

Back in Chapter 3, we stressed the importance of *thinking both short-term and long-term concurrently*. This is particularly important for industries such as the life sciences, aerospace, and energy, in which innovations can take years or even decades to come to market. But how do you maintain a sense of short-term urgency for a launch that may be a decade away?

The answer—which we explore in this chapter—is to **break down your development process into a series of distinct milestones that (1) set interim deadlines, (2) serve as indicators of success, and therefore (3) correspond to increases in valuation.**

Managing Your Business as a Series of Inflection Points

Let's start by considering the typical development cycle for a new drug.[1] Although the following sequence tracks the governmentally supervised process for drug development in the United States, European and other agencies follow similar approaches:

1. **Lead identification.** This involves research to identify target molecules within the body that impact disease progression and potential "leads"— that is, chemical or biologic matter that appears to regulate the drug

targets up or down. Leads may come from the screening of existing libraries of molecules or the synthesis of new compounds designed to react with the target.

2. **Lead optimization.** Typically, multiple leads are tested and refined to resolve potential issues around toxicity, how the drug is absorbed in the body, and how it impacts the target. Not all programs result in a promising lead.

3. **Preclinical development.** If a promising lead is found, it may advance to the next stage of testing to make sure it is ready for human studies. This involves animal testing and pharmacokinetics (how the drug interacts with the body). Tests must meet FDA criteria prior to any such human studies.

4. **Phase 1.** The first human studies are conducted, generally with healthy people, to assess safety and select appropriate dosing.

5. **Phase 2.** If the drug is shown to be safe, it then moves onto preliminary testing of the drug's effectiveness in patients who have the disease. If successful, Phase 2 informs the requirements for the Phase 3 study.

6. **Phase 3.** This is the pivotal study to determine the drug's effectiveness. The number of patients involved is informed by factors that include the expected effectiveness of the drug; if the drug is expected to help only a fraction of involved patients (as we recently saw with trials of Alzheimer's-related drugs), then correspondingly more patients will be required to warrant statistical confidence in the benefit.

7. **FDA submission.** Assuming that the outcome of Phase 3 is mostly positive, the company submits all of the relevant data and evidence to the FDA for approval.

8. **Commercialization.** If the drug is approved by the FDA, then the company is free to begin marketing the drug, although the FDA still has the option of mandating special handling or warnings.

Figure 23.1 shows how the cumulative probability of reaching different stages generally diminishes as we look further ahead in the development process.

FIGURE 23.1 Drug Probability Of Success Chart

Valuation at beginning of development stage

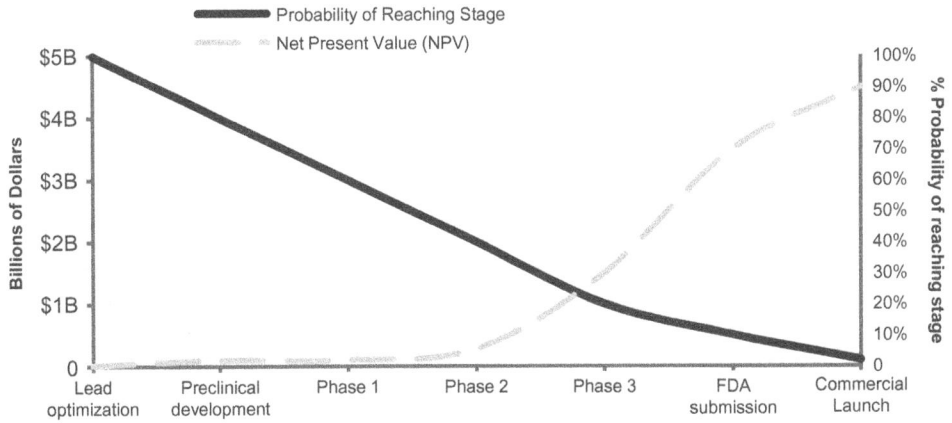

Of course, this is just an illustrative chart; the probabilities of success vary significantly for different disease states and therapeutic approaches, and the program values in the chart are averages, which vary enormously from drug to drug. But the *overall direction will be similar across drugs*, with values steadily increasing from almost zero at the early stages to the potential for billions of dollars in Phase 3 and beyond.

Not surprisingly, then, innovators in the pharmaceutical field manage their businesses around a series of inflection points. If you can complete all the requirements to get to the next stage, then value will increase, and you will have lots of options for new funding and resources. Conversely, if the program fails, the value goes to zero and you are back at the starting line.

A Different Pathway: Aviation

In the case of a new drug, the inflection points are well defined because they are controlled by independent regulators. Other long lead-time innovations have their own distinct pathways. By all accounts, it's not easy for a new entrant to carve out a space in the highly concentrated commercial aircraft market—but Brazil-based Embraer found a way and has pursued that path successfully for more than half a century. Let's look at that example to illustrate this very different approach to long lead-time innovation.

The story begins back in 1941, when the Brazilian government created a Ministry of Aeronautics to advance its ambitions in the field and—a decade later—established a technical institute of aeronautics. In 1965, the government commissioned the R&D needed to build a Brazilian prototype aircraft, which in 1968 made its first successful test runs.

It was a graduate of the government-sponsored school, Ozires Silva, who in 1969 founded Empresa Brasileira de Aeronautica—Embraer, for short—in which the Brazilian government held a 51 percent stake.[2] Embraer took over the government's prototype project, which meant first designing planes that could serve military purposes. It signed its first contract with the government with a target of eighty turboprop planes—the so-called Bandeirante, also known as the EMB-110—for use by the Brazilian Air Force. In 1975, the first plane emerging from this effort was delivered to the air force. In that same year, Embraer exported its first aircraft, to Uruguay, and in 1977 successfully sold small numbers of planes in France and the United States.[3]

But Embraer also had in mind a longer-term and larger-scale commercialization strategy. The company had identified a market niche: smaller turboprop planes for relatively short regional flights, which the larger airplane manufacturers weren't particularly interested in, in part because regional airports tended to have short runways and other technical limitations. The Brazilian government encouraged Embraer's emerging commercial aspirations, because it wanted to foster the kind of short-hop air travel that could help that relatively large country "feel small."

The company soon developed a fifteen-seat commercial version of the EMB-110. Like its military predecessor, it was a small turboprop plane—designed to carry between fifteen and twenty passengers—and it was produced as inexpensively as possible, which meant, among other things, importing parts as necessary. Embraer eventually sold around 500 EMB-110s. Its successor, the EMB-120—the Brazilia—became the most widely used regional aircraft in the world, operated by twenty-six airlines in fourteen countries.[4] Next came the EMB-220, which was faster, accommodated up to thirty passengers, and boasted a pressurized cabin.

Despite the traditional reluctance of Brazilian companies to go the multinational route, Embraer soon acted on its international ambitions, targeting both the United States and European Union.[5] An early success came in the form of a partnership with the low-cost carrier Ryanair, which begin operations in 1985 flying the fifteen-seat Bandeirante. Ryanair flew the EMB-110 until 1989 and continues to fly Embraer aircraft to this day.

Along the way, there certainly were major bumps in the road. In the early 1990s, for example, Embraer partnered with Argentina-based FAMA to design and build a high-speed turboprop. The project ran over budget, and the resulting plane badly underperformed in the market, plunging Embraer into deep financial straits.

Despite these corporate disruptions—which included privatization in 1994 and a WTO ruling protesting the Brazilian government's continuing involvement in the company—the company in 1996 introduced the ERJ-145: a twin-engine, narrow-body jet that accommodated between thirty-seven and fifty passengers, which within four years held a 29 percent share of the world market for regional jets.[6] The ERJ (Embraer Regional Jet) family, which originally had four models, soon proved a success. This led to a successful diversification into both larger commercial jets (70 to 130 passengers) and executive jets. One of those products—the Phenom 300—became the best-selling executive jet in the world. By the beginning of 2000, Embraer was the fourth-largest manufacturer of commercial aircraft—and also the most profitable.[7]

The company kept tabs on its direct competition—most notably the much larger Bombardier, which was the other market leader in short-hop regional jets.[8] Fortunately for the Brazilian firm, that Canadian-based manufacturer decided to place a large bet on competing in the large-jet arena, marketing its CSeries jet to compete directly with the Boeing 737 and the Airbus 320, two of the best-selling jets in the history of aviation. Bombardier had been tempted by the higher profit margins on larger-capacity planes, and in fact produced a more fuel-efficient jet than those manufactured by its giant competitors. But Boeing and Airbus simply cut their prices while they improved their products' fuel efficiency, thereby beating back the Bombardier challenge.

Again, Embraer took note, deciding that it would forgo the most lucrative part of the industry in favor of competing in its own niche. It launched its E-Jet family in 1999 and the E-Jet E2 in 2018. Notably, the E2 was built on an investment budget of $1.7 billion, whereas Bombardier's equivalent plane cost $4.4 billion to develop. The E2 was launched on time—showing up unexpectedly at the European Airshow in 2016 and landing 215 orders—whereas the Bombardier model launched two years later than expected.[9]

The company has focused on three product lines that, while closely related, are nonetheless distinctive: commercial, executive, and military. It has centralized its R&D and product development in its Brazilian headquarters, which helps it move quickly—developing products in average of five years, as opposed to the industry average of seven years.[10]

Embraer is now the third-largest manufacturer of commercial aircraft in the world, with facilities in the Americas, Africa, Asia, and Europe.[11] By 2021 it had become the world's segment leader for aircraft of up to 150 seats.[12]

What innovation lessons should we take away from this story? Well, certainly enjoying some degree of government protection for your first several decades doesn't hurt. But even under that welcome shelter, Embraer did a lot of things right on its own. It defined and stuck to its original two market niches (military and commercial) but added a third (executive) when a new market emerged. Even in truly dark days, it innovated constantly, at a centralized location—which helped it stay relatively nimble. It set delivery targets that many in the industry thought outlandishly optimistic, and then delivered on those targets. It understood who its real competitors weren't (Boeing and Airbus) and were (Bombardier) and focused on beating out that real competitor.

Balancing High-Risk, Long-Term Innovation with Near-Term Wins

Embraer also illustrates a more subtle, but equally important, lesson: Once a business becomes established with long lead-time innovation, business gets easier. **Barriers to entry are high, and established companies can often find lower-risk growth opportunities that build on their innovation platform**. For Embraer, this was executive jets. In the case of a pharmaceutical company, opportunities might include expansion into new indications or new, more convenient drug formulations.

For the life sciences, data on drug launches shows how established pharmaceutical companies are putting more of their efforts into incremental innovation rather than breakthrough new platforms. A study by *Science* magazine showed that pharmaceutical companies originated 58 percent of the 252 new drugs launched over an eight-year period (with the remainder being universities and biotechs), but only 44 percent of the 118 drugs were deemed to have scientific novelty.[13] Put another way, 65 percent of the drugs developed by pharmaceutical companies were classed as "non-innovative."

Innovative organizations that lack established products can sometimes offset high-risk, long-term programs with near-term wins. For example, licensing deals or other service revenues can provide short-term cash flow.

Public-sector research and contracting are other important pathways for long-term innovation. For example, academic research often provides the basis for early-stage life science innovation. Government contracts play a key role in aerospace and defense industries. Finding ways to take advantage of these is a critical success factor in these industries. As Embraer certainly illustrates, major aerospace and defense companies have been able to use long-term contracts to smooth out much of the volatility that they've learned to expect, given the nature of their businesses.

Long lead-time innovation is hard, but the rewards can be correspondingly higher. Organizations need to be creative in finding ways to manage through technological uncertainty, external disruptions, and funding challenges, **managing toward the next value inflection points and using cash flows from established products and line extensions to fund new breakthrough innovations.**

EXECUTIVE SUMMARY

Embrace proven pathways for long lead-time innovation.

- Recognize that long lead-time industries bring challenges in funding requirements and time to market but also benefits in terms of barriers to entry and long life cycles for successful innovations.

- Maintain accountability and a sense of urgency by managing the business as a series of value inflection points that are consistent with the established milestones that are relevant for the industry where you compete.

- Nurture support from government and the broader community that recognizes the outsized role that long lead-time businesses often play in supporting both community priorities and regional economic development.

TWENTY-FOUR

Use Incremental Developments to Complement Breakthrough Innovation

All innovations can be located along a spectrum, ranging from incremental to breakthrough changes. At the more adventurous end of that scale, we have breakthrough innovation, which involves creating new markets and tapping previously unmet needs. In this book, we have spent more time on these kinds of breakthroughs—not because they are more important but because breakthrough innovation has more unknowns, making it more difficult to successfully develop, forecast, and launch new-to-the-world products and services.

In this chapter, though, we focus on the other end of the spectrum: incremental innovation. We also look at the question of why incremental and breakthrough innovation sometimes coexist uncomfortably.

Why discuss incremental innovation? Because most new products or services are not radical departures. Instead, they are updates to existing offerings that provide some new features or increased performance. In these cases, the market size, customer segments, sales channels, and competition are all very familiar, since they are the same as, or similar to, the prior version.

Incremental innovation is important, because it helps businesses realize the full potential of their existing service lines, including any past breakthrough innovations. Incremental innovation plays a range of roles: adding new features to match or stay ahead of competitors, refreshing the product or service's appeal to keep up with evolving consumer tastes, maintaining support from channel partners, and many more. And yes, sometimes an incremental innovation can have an outsized impact on a product if it proves a major hit with consumers.

One example of this is Kellogg's Special K Red Berries, launched first in Europe and then quickly introduced in the United States in 2001.[1] Prior to the Red Berries introduction, Special K was a rather sleepy niche cereal. Its sugar- and fat-free, 110-calories-per-serving pitch was targeted at people who were managing their weight and were willing to put up with the bland taste. Freeze-dried fruits had been floated in the marketplace way back in the 1960s—when consumers were eager to sample food technologies associated with the Apollo space program—but that early version of the experiment did not last.

The new effort we're looking at here began in 1999 in France and the U.K., where French focus groups indicated that consumers craved fruit on their cereal. The company engaged a Polish fruit supplier, built the fruit into the product, and then shrank the size of the box while keeping the price the same—thereby recouping the extra cost of the fruit. According to Jeff Montie, Kellogg's vice president of innovation in Europe at the time, the product "took off like a rocket." Other cereal brands were quick to emulate that success, and soon the dried-fruit cereal category was exceeding several hundred million dollars in annual sales.

So a relatively modest innovation had a big impact on the cereal category, and helped Kellogg's leapfrog ahead of rival General Mills, at least for a while. But it is worth noting that the leading competitors, product economics, and sales channels remained unchanged.

The speed with which dried fruit cereal was adopted at Kellogg's and General Mills illustrates how incremental innovation can happen quickly, even within the kinds of large organizations that might seem ill equipped to speed up their own evolution. But again: incremental innovations don't present the kinds of challenges that we see in breakthrough products. Nobody's organization needs to be blown up and replaced; the same factories, marketing teams and salespeople can be kept in place; and the existing channel customers stay happy or perhaps get even happier. Most organizations have established metrics that proposed product variations are held up to, such as threshold performance levels from taste panels or test markets. If the new concept meets the criteria—as dried fruit cereals clearly did—then the whole organization can quickly get behind the innovation.

Incremental Innovation: What's Required?

First things first: **Developing new concepts for incremental innovation does not require inspiration. The more important attribute is extreme vigilance.**

This comprises the monitoring of evolving consumer tastes, learning about competitive developments in product features or new production capabilities, listening to distributors and sales teams, and looking for ideas in other countries or even back in history. The fruit-cereal idea illustrates several of these: After listening to consumers, Kellogg's revived a freeze-dried fruit technology from forty years earlier, then brought the idea over from Europe to the United States. For General Mills, it was a case of monitoring the competition and then rapidly introducing its own market entry with the "Berry Burst" version of Cheerios.

In technology industries, vigilance can take the form of monitoring competitive developments in processing speed or battery life and then figuring out how those rivals are accomplishing that particular feat. The airline industry is a notably vigilant context. As major airlines realized that their low-priced competitors were attracting customers with no-frills offerings for lower fares, they began to respond. These airlines therefore began shifting their revenue streams to focus on add-on fees vs. the initial ticket price, initially through the checked-bag fee (usually after the first checked bag). Research by one of the early implementers of this strategy revealed that the incremental revenue the company would generate from new fees was *four times* greater than the walk-away revenue loss from customers who were dissatisfied with the new, more restrictive ticket terms. They also investigated the likelihood of other airlines following suit and ultimately concluded, based on their models, that shifting to add-on fees represented greater upside, *regardless of competitor responses.*

In fact, others in the industry quickly followed suit on baggage fees, and more, leading to an industry in which add-on fees—checked baggage, on-board snacks, priority boarding, extra legroom, and so on—emerged collectively as a significant revenue generator. The result has been twofold: billions in extra revenue for the industry from add-on fees and more competitive pricing for base fares.

In many examples of incremental innovation, **it is good to be first, but it's usually not crucial**. It's unrealistic to think that your company can always be first—but if you're nimble enough, most of your competitors' moves probably can be matched. And this may well create a virtuous circle: in industries with the benefit of a group of well-run competitors, incremental developments on the part of one player often end up benefiting the whole industry and its customers.

Incremental and Breakthrough: Conflicting Imperatives?

Arguably, the agility of the major cereal players in adapting their products to consumer tastes with small but impactful innovations is one reason why the same leading players have remained in control of the business for many decades. But as with many successful businesses, that same success makes it hard for them to embrace breakthrough innovation. As the CFO of one such company remarked to us: "We like products where the ingredients cost less than the packaging." If that's truly your target, then *any* breakthrough innovation is going to struggle to get support. Ironically, though, as the cereal makers' category has faced an extended slow decline over the past quarter century, they have increasingly faced the need for breakthrough innovation.

These challenges to the breakfast cereal category have not come from a lack of real or potential features in the cereal products themselves. Instead, it has come from gradual changes in consumer tastes and consumption patterns—specifically, more emphasis on food on the go (as opposed to sitting down to eat a bowl of cereal) and trends toward coffee and hot breakfast offerings provided by the likes of McDonald's and Starbucks. Aware of these trends, Kellogg's has emphasized growth in its frozen-breakfast line, spearheaded by Eggo frozen waffles. General Mills has not made a similar push, perhaps because it was insulated by the strong growth in its Yoplait division prior to the introduction of Greek yogurt. Notably, however, both missed the rapid development of the frozen egg and meat sandwiches, which Jimmy Dean, a division of Tyson

Foods, helped launch and which has since evolved into a major new category. In 2023, for example, an estimated 91 million Americans consumed frozen breakfast entrees or sandwiches.[2]

This evolving breakfast story illustrates the point that **focusing on product features is fine for incremental innovation, but breakthrough innovation requires solving for the customer experience and unmet needs**. This, in turn, requires the more customer-centric approach described in Chapter 4: What is broken or missing from the customer experience? Are there potential customers that are not being served today? How can we use our company's capabilities to help address these needs?

Answering these questions requires you to have a good understanding of the contrasting characteristics of incremental vs. breakthrough innovation, as summarized in Table 24.1.

TABLE 24.1. Breakthrough vs. Incremental Innovation Summary

Components	Breakthrough	Incremental
Customer segments	• Both styles of innovation are targeted to address the same customers' evolving needs	
Competitors	• Opportunities for new challengers • Innovations are more difficult to replicate (often conflicts with existing business models) • Winners and losers are likely to emerge based on adoption of "the new"	• Incumbent competitors • Innovations likely to be quickly replicated by competitors • Opportunities for all competitors to grow and capture more value
Channels	• Potentially new channels, including both new to the business as well as first in class (e.g., Metaverse, App store)	• Existing channels or potential adoption of new channels from other industries
Technology	• Embraces new organizational capabilities	• Leverages existing capabilities
Risk	• Higher risk, uncertain returns • Longer-term payback • Creates new options for future growth	• Low risk, moderate return • Short-term payback

The Role of Execution in Determining Whether a Product Becomes a Breakthrough

As noted at the outset of this chapter, incremental vs. breakthrough innovation can be located on a spectrum—and where you land on that spectrum often depends on your execution and the reactiveness of competitors. This is well illustrated by the response of a leading spring mattress manufacturer—let's call the company "Sweet Dreams." In the premium market, traditional spring mattress companies had been losing share to disruptive leaders: Tempur-Pedic, with its premium foam mattress, and Select Comfort, with its adjustable pneumatic system and direct-to-consumer (DTC) sales model. Tempur-Pedic and Select Comfort had been gaining market share, driven by mattress performance and DTC advertising. Given the brand awareness Tempur-Pedic and Select Comfort had achieved, Sweet Dreams knew they needed to do something beyond their established line of traditional spring mattresses.

Their original plan was to jump into the market with a competitive foam mattress. But they wanted to be *sure* about what to do. Through consumer testing (specifically, conjoint analysis across a 2,000-plus consumer survey), the company tested a range of options, including foam mattresses, spring mattresses, and various other options—notably including a new hybrid that combined elements of both spring and foam. Consumers were enthusiastic about the new hybrid spring-foam concept, which combined the softness and support of foam but mitigated the heat retention that some consumers complained about.

Of course, the "hybrid mattress" is now a defining term for the product class, but at the time, it was a first-in-class product. The new product profile yielded a 25 percent preference share of the total premium market vs. existing Tempur-Pedic foam products and other premium spring products. In other words, Sweet Dreams was onto something special.

Assuming proper execution, this now represented the opportunity for true breakthrough innovation: the opportunity to define a new market. Today the hybrid mattress accounts for roughly one-third of all mattresses sold. Unfortunately for Sweet Dreams, however, the company failed to claim the lion's share of this new market. They underinvested in DTC advertising, perhaps reflecting the fact that there was pressure from the established spring-mattress part of the company not to change the sales model. They failed to register the "hybrid mattress" name, thereby allowing competitors to quickly come in and claim a majority of the new hybrid market. The upshot? The opportunity for breakthrough innovation with new technology had become more like an incremental innovation.

Incentives in Large Organizations

One reason why large and successful organizations find it hard to embrace breakthrough innovation is that they tend to create a culture of risk avoidance. Career advancement generally goes to those who are considered a "safe pair of hands" with a track record of keeping business on track and avoiding negative outcomes. This creates an asymmetry of rewards for risk. A new product feature may have limited upside but almost no downside risk. On the other hand, a breakthrough innovation may have much more upside but a greater risk of failure. It is also likely to require much more effort and commitment from those involved, making them more tied to its eventual success or failure.

Returning to our cereal example after the launch of Special K Red Berries, it would have been easy to find a product manager at General Mills ready to lead the launch of Cheerios' Berry Burst. The concept had already been proven by Kellogg's. Who wouldn't want to be associated with an almost certain winner? Far safer for someone at General Mills to champion that product than to try to meet the needs of consumers for hot, on-the-go breakfast foods, perhaps by experimenting with some kind of microwavable breakfast burrito concept.

Safer but arguably short-sighted: Hot Pockets microwave sandwich wraps were launched by Chef America Inc., originally targeted at restaurants, and were later acquired by Nestlé, with the category eventually reaching $2 billion in sales.

Perhaps most important, someone pushing for breakthrough innovation will find fewer supporters and more people likely to resist developments that upset the status quo. Much has been written in the last twenty years about the organizational barriers to breakthrough, or disruptive, innovation, but our favorite commentary comes from many centuries ago. In *The Prince,* Niccolò Machiavelli—although writing about government—provided sound advice about breakthrough changes:

> It must be considered that there is nothing more difficult to carry out, nor more doubtful of success, nor more dangerous to handle, than to initiate a new order of things. For the reformer has enemies in all those who profit by the old order, and only lukewarm defenders in all those who would profit by the new order, this lukewarmness arising partly from fear of their adversaries, who have the laws in their favor; and partly from the incredulity of mankind, who do not truly believe in anything new until they have had the actual experience of it.[3]

That wisdom from long ago, aimed at the political realm, is surprisingly pertinent for many business organizations today.

Innovation Challenges for Large Organizations

For these organizational reasons, the larger and more successful a corporation becomes, the more likely that breakthrough innovation requires a separate structure to be able to thrive and experiment. On the other hand, smaller businesses have less to lose, and can attract people who are motivated by the prospect of challenging the established organizations.

The challenge for large corporations is to **find ways to develop both incremental innovation and breakthrough innovation**. Incremental innovation is needed to meet near-term changes in customer tastes and competitive challenges and realize the full potential from existing businesses. Breakthrough innovation is needed to address fundamental gaps in customer needs and long-term threats to existing businesses. In Chapter 8, we discussed ways to address the structural challenges described above. But as we noted in Chapter 23, some large organizations will still find it more effective to "outsource" breakthrough innovation, pursuing promising opportunities through acquisition rather than internal development.

And there's no harm in that. By and large, the truly great companies are agnostic about where they find their great ideas.

EXECUTIVE SUMMARY

Use incremental developments to complement breakthrough innovation.

- Incremental innovation involves lower risk than breakthrough innovation and plays a critical role in realizing the full potential of mature product lines and any breakthrough product launches.

- Incremental and breakthrough innovations have very different characteristics across customers, competitors, channels, and risk. This makes it a challenge for the same organization to pursue both at the same time.

- Using the approaches described in earlier chapters, organizations must configure themselves to deliver both incremental *and* breakthrough innovation if they are to maximize long-term success and value to shareholders.

TWENTY-FIVE

Turn Gaps into Strengths for Start-Ups and Entrepreneurs

Much of this book is targeted at unlocking breakthrough innovation in both large and small organizations, sometimes by learning from the start-up world. But what if you *are* one of those start-ups?

It may seem difficult for you to embrace and apply some of the advice in this book. You don't have specialists in your organization you can turn to for help with manufacturing, design, competitive intelligence, marketing, or customer research. You don't have an established customer base or brand that you can build from. You almost certainly don't have a corporate mentor looking out for you. How can you make sure you are using whatever strategies are available to improve your odds of success against organizations with far greater resources and capabilities?

In this final chapter, we call out the unique circumstances for entrepreneurs and emerging companies and discuss how they can apply the lessons of this book to their own advantage.

How Entrepreneurs Can Turn Weaknesses into Strengths

First, a few statements about the *context* for success: Chapter 8 detailed some of the challenges faced by in-house start-ups as compared to more agile, independent emerging companies. If you are an entrepreneur at one of those start-ups, then ideally, you've made it a point to choose industries or sectors where start-up advantages count most.

For example? **People-critical industries with low barriers to entry play to start-ups' ability to attract top talent**, both through equity incentives and through the appeal of being part of a close-knit team. As recent history amply illustrates, software and digital businesses are prime examples. Others include early-stage life sciences development and all kinds of "virtual" organizations in which capital-intensive activities such as manufacturing are outsourced to more flexible contract organizations. For the years 2018–2021, digital businesses accounted for 59 percent of the fastest-growing start-ups between $20 million and $100 million in revenue.[1]

Having worked with both multinationals and tiny start-ups over the years, we are often impressed at how well the leadership team for a quality $2 million start-up stacks up against equivalent teams for organizations five hundred times their size. To some extent, of course, this is a competitive necessity: The low barriers to entry in the start-up realm mean that there often end up being far more competitors than many entrants initially expect. This puts a premium on the requirement for companies to have unique capabilities—including great leaders—if they are to rise above the crowd of competitors.

Industries with unclear liabilities or regulatory boundaries give advantages to firms willing to move fast, even if it involves some regulatory or liability risks. As described in Chapter 18, Uber was able to move quickly by being willing to bet on demand by customers overwhelming objections from incumbents. Imagine how the general counsel of Marriott would have reacted if someone at the company had proposed starting a new division for people to rent out rooms in their own homes. With no training for hosts, no safety standards for the homes, and no discernable quality control, such a notion would go against everything that an established company like Marriott stands for.

Which is exactly why there was a gap in the market for Airbnb to fill.

Conflicts with incumbent business models can be another high-potential opportunity for new entrants. As described in Chapter 5, Netflix was effectively given a free pass against home entertainment giants such as Disney, WarnerMedia, and Comcast because the streaming model conflicted with their highly profitable bundled cable offerings. Whenever you read about an incumbent company's infrastructure advantages—and it's surprising how often you see stories like this, once you start looking for them—it's worth questioning whether they're really advantages or liabilities. Before the advent of electric vehicles, for example, almost no one would have given a California start-up any chance of succeeding against the largest automakers in the world, with their high-volume automated factories, thousands of dealers, and century of history.

But when you consider closely the case of Tesla—and increasingly, other entrants—those existing factories, powerful union workforces, and expensive dealer networks start to look more like liabilities.

Small, underserved markets create opportunities for new entrants. Honda started life by producing motorized bicycles—an unglamorous but highly functional niche in which no one else wanted to specialize. Retail giant Walmart got its start by serving rural towns that were being neglected by other discount retailers such as Kmart.[2] Tesla started with a niche market open-top electric sportscar. In each case, starting with smaller, underserved markets provided the opportunity to hone the company's skills and increase its capabilities before taking on (and succeeding against) larger mainstream competitors. The climb up the ladder often begins with the unglamorous bottom rung.

Configure to Maximize Advantages

Beyond choosing the right market segments, emerging companies need to **configure to maximize their advantages**. Successful emerging companies develop informal networks (1) to recruit top talent and (2) to keep them on board with equity incentives that only pay out if the company succeeds. Arguably, **the number-one requirement of an aspiring start-up CEO is the ability to recruit the best people he or she knows and trusts from prior relationships.** Emerging companies can use all the tools described in Chapter 7 to go to market with low-cost prototyping and testing. They can take a nuanced approach to risk: being willing to tolerate uncertainty around how regulatory, market, and competitive developments will unfold, in part because they're willing to "overinvest" in satisfied customers to ensure repeat business and free (word of mouth) marketing. Social media becomes ever more important here. Who are the influencers, and what are they saying about you?

In Parts 3 and 4 of this book, we went into detail on how to build a robust revenue forecast and business plan. This road map applies to start-ups as well as to large organizations. Put simply, we advise entrepreneurs to **be a garage start-up with a Fortune 500 business plan**. The value is not just in the final product (although that will certainly help your fundraising, discussed below); the *process* of developing a robust forecast and business plan forces you to conduct the necessary information-gathering and thereby elicit the kinds of focused market feedback that may well improve your odds of success.

Now let's turn to what for many start-up entrepreneurs is the elephant in the room: funding. Over the twenty-five year period that ended in 2022, there was a rapid expansion in venture capital investing—driven by the success of a number of high-profile start-ups—with funding averaging more than *$400 billion per year* in the final two years of that quarter century.[3]

This flood tide of venture funding has changed the dynamics for many emerging companies—but maybe not as much as you might expect. First, as described in Chapter 1, yes, there are millions of ideas for new products and services each year—but for every entrepreneur with a new idea, the chances are pretty good that there are several others working on something intended to meet the same need or solve the same problem. What happens in that case? If one start-up based on that good idea raises $2 million from friends and angel investors while another raises $30 million from larger funds—a discrepancy that gives that second company a huge advantage when it comes to developing and launching the product—what's likely to happen? We don't need to spell it out.

Of course, big venture capital funding does not *guarantee* success. There are exceptional situations, such as the founders of Wayfair, who achieved substantial scale before tapping outside capital. But in many arenas, probably even most arenas, **the race to conceive and shape a great new idea is burdened— even overshadowed—by an arms race for funding**. We don't mean to sound like Eeyores here—but once again, this is one more compelling reason for emerging companies to do the homework outlined in Parts 3 and 4.

So let's say you've found an attractive market, recruited a strong team, secured the necessary funding, and successfully brought your first product to market. Now what? Do you keep growing and building, or do you look for a suitable exit partner and declare victory? If you have majority external investors, of course, this may not be your decision to make. Even if that's *not* the case, sooner or later you need to acknowledge the different kinds of skills that are likely to be required for your company's continued development and growth. New challenges may well require tools that aren't in your toolkit.

Knowing When to Exit or Find a Partner

As described in Chapter 21, many growth companies underperform expectations after their first successful product launch. For this reason, and others, you need to **maintain an understanding of your company's value to others**. If you can find an investment bank willing to invest in a long-term relationship, they can be helpful in this process. Maybe your business could be a potent platform for growth within a larger organization. (If you haven't tried that idea on for size, try it now.) What big company *really needs* to learn what you already know? In the Spark example described in Chapter 23, the premium paid by Roche was 122 percent over the previous trading value for the company's shares. Working independently, it could easily take five or ten years to unlock the same value. If you wind up going this route, you won't be alone. Over the five years ending 2022, *more than 80 percent of venture capital-backed exits* went to strategic buyers.[4]

Meanwhile, what happens to *you*? Successful **entrepreneurs need to assess whether they can create more value by staying with a now-established business or by starting over with a new opportunity**. Staying with the established enterprise may have lower business risk, but again, it will require different skills compared to a typical start-up context (as described in Chapter 8). Are you well positioned to step out and then step forward? Probably. Studies show that successful entrepreneurs attract two to four times more funding than novices.[5] They tend to put that money to good use, with success rates for their next venture that are 50 percent higher than average (which is likely also due to better access to funding).[6]

All of this is food for thought—and your circumstances are nothing if not unique. But most likely, you are a distinctive blend of capabilities and experience. Given the right market opportunity, you are a strong candidate to create yet another new product or service that gains traction in the market.

Your past success is likely to be a powerful option-generator. Regardless of the direction you go, we hope that this book helps you achieve the kind of success that opens up those options—and that you find a rewarding way to exploit them!

EXECUTIVE SUMMARY

Turn gaps into strengths for start-ups and entrepreneurs.

- Choose industries or sectors in which entrepreneurial advantages count most—people-critical businesses, low barriers to entry, unclear regulation, conflicts with established business models, and underserved markets, among others.

- Configure to maximize advantages. Use personal networks and powerful incentives to recruit an exceptional team.

- Be a garage start-up with a Fortune 500 business plan.

Part 5: Creating Long-Term Value Checklist

Configuring for Success

❑ Use a systematic approach to reduce failures at every step of the innovation journey
❑ Manage risks by evaluating multiple indicators of success
❑ Avoid the seven behaviors that reduce the odds for many innovators

Developing Product and Service Concepts

❑ Look for what's broken, who's not being served, and how to leverage your strengths
❑ Take advantage of direct market feedback and rapid prototypes
❑ Embrace continuous upgrades and lean development for digital-led businesses
❑ Move up the Detect-Analyze-Act pyramid to enrich products using digital
❑ Use a start-up mindset for breakthrough innovation in large companies

Forecasting Revenue

❑ Build a business case to avoid the product graveyard
❑ Size the prize and identify the customers you will win
❑ Gather customer insights, not "voice of customer"
❑ Never take market research at face value
❑ Assume competitors are at least as smart as you
❑ Price to unlock the full value of your innovation
❑ Build a high-confidence revenue forecast
❑ Create a bulletproof business case

Ensuring Commercial Success

❑ Identify and lower the biggest barriers to adoption
❑ Plan enough but not too much, creating a "living" launch plan to ensure smooth execution
❑ Take the shortest path to value by optimizing launch scale and picking the right channels
❑ Prime the organization for a successful launch by tailoring capabilities and nurturing alliances

Creating Long-Term Value

✓ Turn a single success into an enduring franchise
✓ Make use of acquisitions and partnerships to accelerate innovation value
✓ Embrace proven pathways for long lead-time innovation
✓ Use incremental developments to complement breakthrough innovation
✓ Turn gaps into strengths for start-ups and entrepreneurs

Appendices

In this final section of *Predictable Winners*, we present four appendices that dig deeper into several topics introduced in Part 3 of the book, which focused on forecasting revenue. They are:

- Appendix 1: Tools for Market Research
- Appendix 2: Real-World Data Resources to Complement Market Research
- Appendix 3: Estimating Purchase Intent
- Appendix 4: Revenue Modeling Best Practices

To win support from investors and other stakeholders, your revenue forecasts need to be both rigorous and compelling. This means figuring out where you can win, testing your value proposition, gathering customer insights, and assessing the quality of your market feedback—all processes that require depth and detail. These appendices give you the granularity needed to achieve that.

APPENDIX 1

Tools for Market Research

In Chapter 11 we delved in depth into two of the most used forms of market research: qualitative interviews and quantitative surveys. In this appendix we provide additional detail on the best practices for executing this research. We should stress up front that the tactical relevance of the following best practices will vary depending on whether you're planning to conduct the research yourself or outsource it to a third party. If you're doing it yourself, this section should help accelerate your efforts or refine your already established approaches. If you are outsourcing, this section should help you know what "good" looks like and act as a discerning purchaser of market research services.

Best Practices for Interviews

In Chapter 11 we introduced the considerations for determining who you should plan to interview and where you might find those interviewees. After you've settled upon your likely source(s) of interviewees, you will have more clarity on how long it will take to conduct the research as well as the cost. Most interviewees will expect to be paid an honorarium for their time, especially in regions with well-established market research infrastructure like North America and Western Europe and in industries like healthcare, in which such research is very common. Keep in mind that interviews can also be leads for early adopters, so you want interactions to be positive and valuable for them as well.

One other consideration on this topic: there may be situations in which you don't want to or legally can't interview someone. You may not want to interview someone, for example, who might be close to a competitor and inadvertently guess what you're working on. From a legal perspective, privacy laws in certain geographies—for example, Canada and many European countries—can pose some challenges to your research, as can your obligation to appropriately manage compliance when you're speaking with certain types of stakeholders. These can include, for example, foreign government officials (possibly governed by the U.S. Foreign Corrupt Practices Act, or FCPA) and medical practitioners in the United States (whose participation may be regulated by the U.S. Physician Payments Sunshine Act, or PPSA). It's worth keeping these kinds of nuances in mind—and checking with legal counsel, if needed—as you plan your interview campaign.

Before moving on to develop your interview guide, it is important to think through the format and structure of your interviews. The interview format typically flows from the interviewees you plan to target and what you plan to ask them. Most of the time, interviews lasting 45–60 minutes work best. That said, in-depth discussions dissecting a customer journey or soliciting feedback on a product concept with a prompt or demo can make the interview longer (e.g., up to two hours), whereas discussions focused on validating specific hypotheses can be as short as 15–20 minutes. Part of your challenge here is balancing the depth of the interview with your interviewee's time commitments and, eventually, mental fatigue. Interviews can be conducted over the phone, in person, or virtually via tools like Zoom or Teams, with the "appropriate" format often being driven by practicality or necessity. For example, in Japan, in-person interviews have often been part of the cultural status quo, while in the United States, phone calls are the accepted norm. Video calls have become more common and can be particularly helpful if you're sharing a demo or more immersive product prompt, because video helps you read body language and facial reactions.

As a reminder, the interview guide should follow the structure as shown in Table A2.1.

TABLE A1.1. Interview Guide Structure

Interview guide sections	Key components	Percent of interview time
Introduction	• Welcoming background statement (who you are, goals of call) • Estimate of interview length (time) • Assurance of confidentiality and anonymity (if required) • Thank you for participation	5%
Qualifying/ warm-up	• Critical questions used to qualify for participation (screener) • Only questions essential for eligibility • Avoid asking sensitive questions if possible	10%
Main guide	• Follows the interview guide blueprint • Starts with easy, less threatening questions and builds to more challenging and sensitive questions • "Nice-to-have"/secondary questions at the end	80%
Closing	• Reinforcement of value of participation/thank you • Permission to follow-up (if wanted) • Referrals (if wanted/needed) • Honorarium (if needed)	5%

Obviously, you should plan on opening with a polite and accurate self-introduction and confirm the qualifications of the interviewee. The warm-up should also help you gain a sufficient understanding of the person's experiences, role, and organization (if relevant) to contextualize their answers. (This may be quite helpful later if you need to understand why answers have varied across interviewees.) In addition, the warm-up gets the flow of the conversation going and builds trust with the two participants in the conversation. Interviewees share more when they are comfortable, so the initial goal of the interview should be to put the interviewee at ease. For this reason, it's important not to pose sensitive questions too early in the conversation.

Once you're finished thinking through the warm-up, it's time to write the main guide. With the blueprint in hand, you are well positioned to break your questions up into logical sections (e.g., unmet needs and pain points, current solutions and perceptions of competitors, decision-making processes and key purchase criteria, reactions to product concept). **Identify the "must-have" vs. the "nice-to-have" answers to ensure that your questions are appropriately prioritized.** There are some basic best practices in formulating your questions to ensure they are clearly and consistently interpreted and elicit useful and specific responses. See Table A2.2 for common best practices we find helpful in question writing. A final thought on the question-writing process: Be wary of introducing biases that can influence the validity of your research. For example, instrumentation bias—that is, question-wording or sequencing that can negatively impact the validity of responses—can be avoided by keeping in mind some of the best practices presented in Table A2.2.

Back to the components of the interview guide: Your closing section can be quick and simple, but you should remember that it's an important opportunity to leave the door open for future conversations and ask for referrals, if needed.

Best Practices for Surveys

In Chapter 11 we introduced the need to determine the sample size and quotas for your survey. If you've had the pleasure (or misfortune!) of studying statistics, you might recognize that the right way to determine the sample size is to estimate the total population, determine an acceptable margin of error (e.g., ±5 percent) and desired confidence level (e.g., 90 percent confidence that the answer is within the margin of error), estimate the level of variation (i.e., expected standard deviation from average among responses), and plug all of this into one of several available formulas (instructions for manual calculation as well as many easy-to-use calculators and pre-calculated tables are available online).

That said, real life dictates a more pragmatic approach. A statistical formula can help anchor you on a preferred sample size, but in practical terms, cost, respondent accessibility, and required timeline usually play a bigger role in determining the ultimate sample size collected. Fortunately, these constraints can often be reasonably balanced to collect useful results with confidence in

TABLE A1.2. Interview Question Best Practices

Key question writing best practices	Don't do this:	Do this:
Avoid leading questions	"What do you dislike about the payroll system?"	"What, if anything, do you dislike about the current payroll system?"
Separate double-barrelled questions	"How satisfied are you with the clarity and frequency of the email updates you receive?"	"How satisfied are you with the clarity of the email updates you receive?" "How satisfied are you with the frequency of the email updates you receive?"
Be as specific as possible	"How likely would you be to purchase the following office product?"	"How likely would you be to purchase the following office product for use at your place of business in the next 12 months?"
Use basic and familiar language	"Please elucidate upon the aspects of your professional skill set that are relevant to this profession."	"Please provide a brief background on your professional experience and how it fits with this job."
Make it easy for the interviewee to answer your question	"How is the industry split? How has this trended over time, and will the trend continue?"	"How is the market currently split among these segments (for example, out of 100%, what percent would you attribute to each segment?)" "What was the split three years ago and what do you think it will be three years from now?"
Allow respondents the choice not to answer unless necessary	"Can you share what you perceive as Company A's strengths?"	"If you're familiar, please share what you perceive as the strengths of Company A."

a timely and cost-effective manner. The magic of statistics is that **there are diminishing returns with larger and larger samples**. Stated positively, **you can get a long way toward your goal even with a relatively small sample**. For example, in a population of 10 million, you can achieve a 90 percent confidence level with a 5 percent margin of error with approximately 275 respondents. In our experience, **most consumer surveys are effective with sample sizes in the hundreds and low thousands, while most B2B surveys are effective in the 100–200-respondent range.**

Once you set your target sample size, you need to set your quotas for different groups within that sample. You can think of your quotas as smaller sample sizes within the total and run similar calculations to those discussed above. Keep in mind though that your quotas will limit how granular your analysis of the data can be with any confidence. For example, we've found that thirty respondents is a reasonable minimum rule of thumb in B2B surveys. To ensure that you successfully gather enough responses from potentially different quota groups, you can set rules so that the survey automatically rejects any more respondents from that group. Alternatively, you can monitor completion as the survey is fielded and then adjust as needed. **Usually, it is simplest to set quotas as a specific number, but sometimes a minimum or a maximum is more appropriate**, especially if you are trying to collect responses from multiple groups with different levels of priority and different likelihoods to fill out the survey.

For example, in a survey for a finance app designed for high school students, you might set a minimum and a maximum for parents (buyers) and students (users), depending on who is more likely to respond. You will also need to keep in mind if one respondent can fill multiple quotas and count as a "two-fer" in your quota rules.

One last note on quotas: you may need to be flexible in how you define qualifying criteria for a group. If you set rules too strictly, you can risk eliminating many otherwise qualified respondents, which can increase the fielding time and cost of your survey unnecessarily.

Having defined your audience, sample size, and quotas, you also need to figure out where to find respondents to take your survey. You can use customer databases if relevant and accessible; in addition, third-party panels or individually purchased respondent lists may be useful. Third-party survey panels are relatively expensive, but they tend to be of much higher quality (i.e., fewer irrelevant or miscategorized respondents) and yield their results faster (i.e., fielding time typically shorter). Buying lists of contacts can be helpful and is usually less expensive upfront, but this approach is typically best thought of as a supplement to a third-party panel, especially if you're struggling to find specific types of respondents. The fact is, these lists are often of poor quality—resulting in low hit rates—and usually do not end up being less expensive on a per-completed response basis.

Here' s a list of tips that should meaningfully improve the quality, flow, and respondent experience of any survey:

- Invest up front in organization and navigation.

- Group questions covering similar issues into specific subsections (e.g., product usage, concept evaluation, etc.).

- Include section/subsection headings to make it easier for the respondent to follow.

- Use transition statements so the respondent knows what's coming next (e.g., "In this next section, you will be asked to evaluate two new product concepts").

- Use programming logic so that the respondent only has to deal with relevant questions (i.e., avoid branching structures like, "If you answered yes to the previous question, then"; instead, make it automated).

- Invest in the quality of your questions and your layout.

- If asking questions about multiple product categories, ask all questions about one category at the same time, rather than asking each question across categories.

- Separate complex response grids into smaller "chunks," to make them less daunting and easier to complete on a smartphone.

- Avoid using drop-down boxes (they tend to be time-consuming and frustrating).

- Minimize the amount of scrolling that is required by keeping your questions brief so that they will fit on one smartphone screen.

- Avoid layouts that make the screen appear "dense" (especially for complex response grids with multiple data-entry columns).

There are also a variety of best practices when it comes to survey question-writing. Respondents are notoriously bad at answering certain types of questions, including:

- spending and purchasing behaviors more than a year in the future;
- adoption intent for new products and services (we will come back to this); and
- admitting to socially undesirable or illegal activities.

Your survey needs to anticipate these limitations, especially if the answers to one or more of the questions are important to you. Very specific wording and question format selection can help. Adjustments for overstatement biases—as mentioned in Chapter 12—will also come in handy.

One of the most common challenges encountered in survey writing is deciding on the mechanics of *how* to ask a question. Which question type, selection options, and quantitative scales should they use? **The key to deciding on the right question type and answer options is to envision the end goal.** What output will you need to generate, and how will you want to present it to stakeholders? With those anticipated outcomes in mind, how would you want to cut the data? How might you want to group responses, based on your hypotheses?

In Table A1.3, we have summarized the most common question types, when it's appropriate to use them, and several other key considerations regarding their use. In the end, most surveys use a mix of these question types. While there is a veritable treasure trove of academic literature on research methods and surveys, Table A1.3 provides a practical working introduction to the most useful tools in the survey toolkit.

At this stage, we should discuss another versatile and useful tool that can be incorporated into a survey—the conjoint analysis (which was briefly introduced in Chapter 14 in the context of pricing). This is a heavily analytical technique in which respondents are shown several product or service concept profiles with different attribute combinations—such as price, features, or brand—and asked to select which option they prefer. These "buying simulations" are repeated multiple times to discern how much participants care about any unique attribute. The data is then analyzed using a mathematical model to determine the relative importance of each attribute and to estimate the total value of each

TABLE A1.3A. Survey Question Types And Uses – Part 1

Common question types	When to use	Example(s)	Key considerations
Basic: e.g., dichotomous and multiple choice	Use when response options are known and manageable	Dichotomous: "Have you purchased casual footwear within the past 12 months?" (a) Yes (b) No Multiple Choice: "Which of the following best describes how often you shop for 'casual footwear'?" (c) Once a week (d) Once a month (e) 2–3 times per month	• Response options must be mutually exclusive and exhaustive • Numeric answer ranges should not overlap • Include "Other/Specify" as an option. • Consider "Don't know" or "Prefer not to answer" for some questions
Forced choice: e.g., paired comparison and rank order	Use to determine order of preference or importance between multiple items	Paired Comparison: "If you had to choose between shopping for casual footwear at the new Brand X retail store versus a competitor's retail store that offered similar products, which one would you prefer?" (a) New Brand X retail store (b) Competitor's retail store Rank Order: Rank your preferred methods for purchasing casual footwear from 1 (most preferred) to 3 (least preferred). Use each number only once. (a) Online using a computer or laptop (b) Online using a smartphone or tablet (c) Going to the actual retail store	• Does not capture the degree or magnitude of differences between items • Must be limited to 5–8 items due to "cognitive complexity"

TABLE A1.3B. Survey Question Types and Uses – Part 2

Common question types	When to use	Example(s)	Key considerations

Rating scale e.g., Non-Numeric, Numeric Partially Anchored	Use to measure the intensity and direction of attitudes toward specific items	Non-Numeric (e.g., Standard Purchase Intent Scale): "Based on the description, how interested would you be in shopping for casual footwear, clothing or accessories at this new Brand X retail store?"
		
		 a) Will not shop
		 b) Unlikely to shop
		 c) Undecided about shopping
		 d) Likely to shop
		 e) Will shop
		
		 Numeric—Partially Anchored: Rate your agreement on a scale of 1 to 7 for the following statements
		
		 Strongly Disagree 1 2 3 Neither Agree or Disagree 4 5 6 Strongly Agree 7
		
		 Constant Sum: Allocate 100 points across these criteria based on their importance in your decision to purchase our brand of casual footwear.
		
		 a) Comfort: ___
		 b) Quality: ___
		 c) Price: ___
		 d) Reputation: ___
		 Total Must Add to 100
			• Primary type for key survey questions
			 • Facilitate calculating averages to test for differences
			 • Some scales are pre-defined (e.g., Net Promoter Score)
			 • Best practice for scales:
			  – Non-Numeric: 4 or 5 categories (unidirectional or bipolar)
			  – Numeric: 7-point Likert scale with anchors
			  – Use a balanced scale (i.e., as negative as it is positive)

attribute to customers. This is a very effective approach for arriving at the right configuration of product features, bundles, and potential price points.

In addition to having the right question formats, wording, and selections, your questionnaire also needs to follow the right programming logic. This is one of the key differences between a short, do-it-yourself survey and an in-depth survey. There are three commonly used types of logic in a survey.

The first and simplest is **skip logic**. This is usually straightforward: You want respondents to skip questions that are irrelevant to them (e.g., product non-users may skip questions for users).

A second common and simple type of logic is **randomization** or **rotation**. Always showing the answer options in the same sequence introduces the possibility of order bias. Showing options in a random order minimizes this.

The third common and more complicated type of logic is **piping**, in which responses from one question get "piped" into the question wording or response options of a later question. This is particularly useful if you want the respondent to reference or anchor on something they previously stated (e.g., "You made X percent of your shoe purchases online last year. What percent of your shoe purchases do you expect will be online next year?"). Piping logic can at times become very complicated if multiple criteria or responses from multiple questions are used together. It can also take the form of inclusion or exclusion of question text or response options, based on a prior response. For example, if a respondent is being asked to rate satisfaction with all suppliers they have used in the last year, those that were *not* used may need to be excluded. All these types of logic typically require clear communication and notes in the questionnaire for the programmer (whether done internally or with a third party).

One last consideration for ensuring you have a well-written survey is any needed **adaptations for differing geographies**. Obviously, conducting primary research (interviews as well as surveys) across different countries can create complexities. One essential starting point is to ensure that your questionnaire is translated well. Respondents need to see a native-tongue translation that can even account for differences in the same language across regions—like, for example, British vs. American English. You may also need to account for sampling limitations, cultural sensitivities, and structural market differences (e.g., different buying channels, competitors, regulations, purchasing norms). In some countries, it may not be practical to run a survey online, which can require phone surveys (akin to a hybrid between an interview and online survey), or your ability to reach the preferred sample size may be quite limited.

A more complicated challenge—and one that is often missed—is being able to **compare survey data across regions**. The topic of response-style variances from country to country has been studied extensively; responses are known to differ depending on question format type and the "personality" of a society. Dutch social psychologist Geert Hofstede's "Cultural Dimensions Theory" characterizes cultures on several dimensions that are useful for understanding response variability: individualism vs. collectivism, uncertainty avoidance, long-term vs. short-term orientation, among others. Respondents in Latin American countries, for example, tend to "tilt" toward the more positive end of the rating scale, while those in Asian countries tend to use mid-points of the scale and therefore typically award lower ratings than their Latin American counterparts. These differences sometimes make it difficult to determine meaningful distinctions across countries in survey results, and should be accounted for.

Real-World Data Resources to Complement Market Research

In Chapter 11 we introduced the value of identifying and potentially using different sources of real-world data to complement, direct, and validate market research. Below we share some specific suggested resources that a practitioner may find useful.

Real-World Data Resources

There is a wide variety of available datasets that can be used for customer behavior analytics, including segmentation. This is most evident with retail point-of-sale data for CPG products (e.g., via vendors like NielsenIQ, IRI, and SPINS) but can also be found in other industries like healthcare (e.g., claims data, prescribing data, referral data). Unfortunately, these datasets can be prohibitively expensive, especially for innovators whose pockets aren't yet very deep.

But in many situations, you can create your own aggregated customer datasets, often in very cost-effective ways. For example, in the online world, there is a broad selection of tools used for capturing insights such as web-scraping (i.e., systematically extracting data from websites using vendors like Stackline and JungleScout), customer review aggregation (which can be combined with text mining), and social media sentiment analysis (e.g., using vendors like Brandwatch). Additionally, if you are fortunate enough to be working for an organization with substantial amounts of existing customer data, this can be an extremely valuable source of behavioral insight (e.g., sales data for analyzing purchasing behaviors, customer relationship management, or CRM, data to link to sales). Although the usefulness of this data is likely to vary for new products vs. existing ones, it should usually be explored.

In addition to these real-world data sources, keep in mind the value of customer feedback from live testing of products—especially digital ones—in the development phase (e.g., beta testing), as discussed in Part 2. In later phases, this remains a potent source of insight into customers and how they segment.

Finally, you can consider incorporating or starting with a preexisting segmentation to build upon. For example, L.E.K. offers a segmentation of U.S. hospitals (Provider Pulse), and Experian offers a segmentation of U.S. households (Mosaic®). Another approach is to try mining a primary research vendor's panel. Dynata, for one, allows you to search its respondents to identify common characteristics among certain types of target individuals. These models may serve as a useful foundation for modification or at the very least as a conceptual template.

APPENDIX 3

Estimating Purchase Intent

In Chapter 12 we discussed the role of asking prospective customers about purchase intent of an innovation. There are a variety of techniques used for purchase intent. The most commonly used approach is stated purchase intent: "How likely would you be to purchase Product X?" You can ask this without a price point at all, but at a minimum, it's better to ask purchase intent assuming what they would consider a reasonable price point (you can derive what customers think "reasonable" means later). If you are planning to test price sensitivity, you will test at a range of specific price points. You can also ask this question with a timeframe (e.g., "In the next 12 months . . ."), which can aid with accuracy, as customers have been shown to more accurately predict purchases for shorter time horizons.

Purchase intent is most often solicited using a five-point Likert scale (named after psychologist Rensis Likert): 5: Definitely would, 4: Probably would, 3: Might or might not, 2: Probably would not, and 1: Definitely would not. A seven-point Likert scale can also be used, but the five-point approach is usually easier for customers to understand, and substantial research exists to help you interpret results based on the five-point scale.

Arguably, stated purchase intent is *not* an ideal predictor of actual purchasing behavior. This is particularly evident when you consider that in many product categories and situations, a customer does not plan to make a purchase but ultimately does. The research suggests that stated purchase *probability* is at times a more accurate predictor of actual purchasing behavior than *intent*. In this situation, instead of asking purchase intent, you ask about the likelihood or chances of making the purchase and provide an associated probability. The best-known and validated purchase probability scale is the eleven-point Juster scale: 10: Certain, practically certain (99 in 100), 9: Almost sure (9 in 10), 8: Very probably (8 in 10) . . . 1: Very slight possibility (1 in 10), 0: No chance, almost no chance (1 in 100).

In reality, both approaches have merit, but again, most market research professionals prefer the simplicity of five-point Likert scale purchase intent. Why? It's easier for respondents to understand, simpler for you to analyze, and—given its extensive use to date—gives you the benefit of many potential data points with which you can compare your results (for example, comparing results across different innovations evaluated). We also see that in some cases, the results on an eleven-point scale tend to "clump," so that respondents are in effect not using several of the scale options, which in practical terms results in a five- or seven-point scale anyway.

Adjust for Overstatement Bias

Unfortunately, even if we ask the right people, use the right prompt, and ask in the right way, we still may end up with adoption estimates that are inaccurate. The bad news, as stated earlier, is that customers tend to be quite bad at predicting future behaviors like purchasing. In fact, **most respondents tend to overestimate their likelihood to purchase or adopt a new product or service.** This level of overstatement varies based on characteristics of the product or service and of the respondent group. For example, purchase intent accuracy (as a predictor of purchasing behavior) is worse for novel products vs. existing or replacement products (unsurprisingly), and worse for nondurable vs. durable products. It also varies across consumers, business professionals, and healthcare providers as well as across countries.

The good news is that prior studies provide us with some tools for making overstatement adjustments. **To adjust for overstatement, it is best practice to assign a probability weighting on each of the scores 1 to 5 (for a five-point Likert scale).** Some market researchers use simple rules like the "top 2 box" approach: 75 percent for "5," 25 percent for "4," and 0 percent for all other scores;

TABLE A3.1. Adoption Adjustment Calculation Example

5 Point Rating Scale	Example		Consumer Products; Tech/ Services (Durable)	Consumer Products; Goods/Retail (Nondurable)	Example Calculations	
	# of Responses	Percent	Weight Set 1	Weight Set 2	Set 1	Set 2
Definitely Would: 5	50	20%	0.70	0.90	14%	18%
Probably Would: 4	75	30%	0.30	0.40	9%	12%
Might or Might Not: 3	75	30%	0.10	0.10	3%	3%
Probably Would Not: 2	38	15%	0.00	0.00	0%	0%
Definitely Would Not: 1	12	5%	0.00	0.00	0%	0%
				Adjusted adoption		
					26%	**33%**

however, there is a developed body of literature with different adjustment factors that can be used for different situations. **Use the adjustment scale that best fits your innovation, based on product or service type and audience.** Table A3.1 provides an example for consumer products.

To ascertain the level of bias, you may want to create a control group (like those used by researchers in medical studies). In the high-speed rail example cited in Chapter 12, we asked survey respondents about current use of different modes of transport and were able to compare to actual data. This helped ensure that we used the correct overstatement adjustment.

One last note on adjusting for biases: while we most commonly face the challenge of overstatement, respondents occasionally will underestimate adoption. This usually occurs when they are presented with a truly novel concept that they struggle to fully appreciate or for which they have no good frame of reference. In such situations, you'll need to be creative to figure out why the adoption numbers are as low as they are and use analogs or triangulations to sense-check.

APPENDIX 4

Revenue Modeling Best Practices

In Chapter 15 we discussed at some length the topic of building a revenue model. In this appendix we provide some additional tactical best practices to help ensure that your model is as accurate and error-free as possible.

Once you have developed a revenue model methodology, you can start thinking about actually building the model. At first, you start with just the skeleton (typically in Excel), where you replicate the logic and mathematical relationships between each of your inputs and outputs in accordance with your methodology. From there you move on to populating the model with your collected data and adding further functionality—for example, building a control panel to enable you to change inputs and run scenarios.

As you build your model, you'll probably encounter the ever-present tension between simplicity and flexibility. Remember: **The more flexibility you try to build in the model, the more complexity you introduce.** "Flexibility" usually translates into adding functionality, such as the ability to tweak more assumptions, split the market into more segments, and summarize outputs in more ways. And while more flexibility can be valuable and tempting, complexity is not. Complexity dramatically increases your odds of making errors, the difficulty of spotting errors, the time it takes to build and update the model, and the difficulty of explaining (and teaching someone else to use) the model. As a rule, therefore, **your model should be as simple as possible and only as flexible as your specific context requires.**

In our experience, there are a number of helpful best practices for modeling:

- Logic and format

    - Logic should flow to the right (i.e., moving forward in time) and down (i.e., never feeding (linking) information from below).

    - The model should follow a clear hierarchy with colored sections, indentation, and limited use of text formatting.

    - Every section should be labeled so that the purpose is clear.

    - Each input should appear only once and should be highlighted (e.g., boxed), and subsequent references should all feed from this one cell.

    - You should group inputs in your model so that it is clear where they can be found.

    - Inputs should be documented with explicit sources (or labeled "dummy").

    - Numbers should be color-coded by type so it is easy to identify their derivation (e.g., input, feed, calculation, and so on).

- Mechanics

    - Use as few assumptions as possible (to minimize compounding of errors).

    - Break calculations down into component parts.

    - Keep formulas as simple as possible (e.g., split complex formulas into multiple steps).

    - Do not hardwire numbers (i.e., only inputs should be hard pasted, and only once).

    - Distant lines of data being referred to should be fed/linked nearby for clarity.

As you build your model, you need to *consistently invest time in quality control (QC)*. Your revenue forecast is only as good as your QC. If you have a "bust" in the model, it can output completely wrong results. If you aren't diligent and do not do a proper sense check, you may not catch your error. Fortunately, there are many ways to minimize the risk of errors in your model. Some of the modeling best practices cited above are specifically intended to reduce the room for error or make it easier to spot errors (e.g., changes in the model will not flow through because your "hardwiring" of data has introduced errors). We have also observed and developed several modeling QC best practices:

- If you can reach the same result through two or more different calculations—and you usually can—include a "check line" that compares them.

- Any complex functions or extensive segmentation should be followed by check lines (e.g., anything that should add to 100 percent should be confirmed).

- Wherever possible, calculate ratios and growth rates (e.g., compounded annual growth rates, or CAGR), because this helps you see the big picture and sense-check outputs.

- Add simple graphs of key items and display them side by side for easy comparison.

- Test your calculations by inputting extreme values (very large, small, zero)—e.g., if price goes to zero, so should the revenue.

- Use triangulations to sense-check both intermediate and final outputs (e.g., via market or competitor data points).

Notes

Chapter 1

1. See, for example, Innosight's Corporate Longevity Forecasts, Huron, www.innosight.com/insight/creative-destruction.

2. We will define *innovation* as a method that visualizes transformative future success and works backwards to define requirements to achieve it.

3. Going forward, we'll simply use the word *product* as an umbrella term for both products and services.

4. Hendrik Bessembinder, "Wealth Creation in the U.S. Public Stock Markets 1926 to 2019," *Journal of Investing*, 2021, 47–61.

5. Stuart E. Jackson, *Where Value Hides*, 2007.

6. In this example, the proportion of spending on "winners" = (60%*3 + 40%*0)/(60%*3 + 40%*1) = 81.8%.

7. Sydney Finkelstein and Shade H. Sanford, "Learning from Corporate Mistakes: The Rise and Fall of Iridium," *Organizational Dynamics*, 2000, 138–48.

8. And going forward, "we" in this manuscript will generally refer to your two authors.

Chapter 2

1. Manny Picciola and Stuart Jackson, "Why the Greek Yogurt Craze Should be a Wake-Up Call to Big Food," *Harvard Business Review*, 2014.

2. Growth statistic from Wikipedia, https://en.wikipedia.org/wiki/Chobani.

3. The single best account of the 737 MAX saga is Peter Robison's *Flying Blind: The 737 MAX Tragedy and the Fall of Boeing*, Doubleday, 2021. Also illuminating is the "Summary of the FAA's Review of the Boeing 737 MAX" online at https://www.faa.gov/foia/electronic_reading_room/boeing_reading_room/media/737_RTS_Summary.pdf.

4. Jeffrey Cruikshank, *The Apple Way*, 2006.

5. Our source for "best-selling" is Wikipedia, https://en.wikipedia.org/wiki/Tesla_Model_3.

Chapter 3

1. This version also comes from Wikipedia. Walter Isaacson's biography of Steve Jobs (Simon & Schuster, 2011) gives more detail, including how Jobs leaned on Corning Glass to manufacture what Corning referred to as "gorilla glass"—a material developed decades earlier that had never found a market.

2. See "The Rise and Fall (and Rise Again?) of BlackBerry," February 1, 2018, in the HBS Digital Initiative, online at https://d3.harvard.edu/platform-digit/submission/the -rise-and-fall-and-rise-again-of-blackberry/.

3. See "BlackBerry's Quest: Fend Off the iPhone," April 27, 2008, in CNET, online at https://www.cnet.com/tech/tech-industry/blackberrys-quest-fend-off-the-iphone/.

4. This story is told in Chaim Gartenberg, "The BlackBerry Storm Showed Why You Should Never Turn a Touchscreen into a Button," *The Verge*, March 31, 2022, online at https://www.theverge.com/23002238/blackberry-storm-surepress-screen-button-touchscreen -technology.

5. Elon Musk's approach to innovation across several industries in summarized in Andy Wu and Goran Calic, "Does Elon Musk Have a Strategy?" *Harvard Business Review,* July 15, 2022, online at https://hbr.org/2022/07/does-elon-musk-have-a-strategy.

6. Vipin Kumar, "Corporate Failure of Kirch Media, Vivendi and Parmalot," *Reviews of Literature*, 2014, https://oldrol.lbp.world/UploadArticle/138.pdf.

Chapter 4

1. Although it's not really an innovation story—at least as we're using the term in this book—we shouldn't fail to mention the roller-coaster ride that Hertz went through in the early 2020s. The global COVID pandemic caused business and pleasure travel to plummet, and car rentals crashed accordingly. Hertz, struggling as a result, filed for Chapter 11 bankruptcy in May 2020 and eventually got delisted by the NYSE. But during the second half of that year, the company sold off a third of its rental fleet into a scorching-hot used-car market, which brought in welcome cash and drove up rental prices on the remaining vehicles. Hertz was refinanced in 2021 and announced plans to add 100,000 Teslas to its fleet. See Kevin Dowd, "How Hertz Went From Bankrupt to Buying 100,000 Teslas," *Forbes*, November 7, 2021, online at https://www.forbes.com/sites/kevindowd/2021/11/ 07/how-hertz-went-from-bankrupt-to-buying-100000-teslas/?sh=54cc6e2fd8bb. More recently, it appears that Hertz has turned over some fifty thousand of its Teslas to Uber drivers for use as long-term rentals. See Fred Lambert, "Hertz Took Delivery of Half Its Massive Tesla Order of 100,000 Electric Cars," *electrek*, February 8, 2023, online at https:// electrek.co/2023/02/08/hertz-half-massive-tesla-order-100000-electric-cars/.

2. For details, see Square's website at https://squareup.com/us/en/payments/payment -platform.

3. Sarah Nassauer, "How Dollar General Became Rural America's Store of Choice, *Wall Street Journal*, 2017.

4. We will talk more about growth tailwinds in Chapter 10.

5. Alan Lewis and Dan McKone, *Edge Strategy*, 2016.

Chapter 5

1. From the Whisker website at www.litter-robot.com/about-us.html.

2. Authors' interview with Katherine Dudley, September 19, 2023.

Chapter 6

1. Statistics from "Statista," https://www.statista.com/statistics/267209/global-app-economy/.

2. See Mansoor Iqbal, "App Download Data (2024)," Business of Apps, online at https://www.businessofapps.com/data/app-statistics/.

3. From John Wu and Robert D. Atkinson, "How Technology-Based Start-Ups Support U.S. Economic Growth," Information Technology and Innovation Foundation, November 28, 2017, online at https://itif.org/publications/2017/11/28/how-technology-based-start-ups-support-us-economic-growth/.

4. Authors' interview with Craig Wills, September 28, 2023.

5. Authors' interview with Halem Sellami, September 27, 2023.

6. See, for example, *HBR's 10 Must Reads on Leading Digital Transformation*, 2021, and *The Digital Transformation Playbook*, Columbia Business School Publishing, 2016.

Chapter 7

1. Raytheon Technologies recently renamed itself RTX Corporation.

2. Authors' interview with Erin McCleave, October 9, 2023.

3. From the Saga website at https://www.saga.co.uk/careers/purpose-values-strategy.

4. "Business Model," Saga, online at https://corporate.saga.co.uk/about-us/business-model/.

Chapter 8

1. Lydia Ramsey, "Take a Look Inside Walmart's Newest Health Clinic That's Just the Start of its Push into Healthcare," *Business Insider*, September 15, 2019, https://www.businessinsider.in/take-a-look-inside-walmarts-newest-health-clinic-thats-just-the-start-of-its-push-into-healthcare/articleshow/71142150.cms. Our account was based largely on web pages and press releases, many of which are no longer available.

2. Sharon Terlep, "Amazon Buys Online Pharmacy PillPack for $1 Billion," *The Wall Street Journal*, June 28, 2018, https://www.wsj.com/articles/amazon-to-buy-online-pharmacy-pillpack-1530191443.

3. Ramsey, "Take a Look Inside Walmart's Newest Health Clinic." See also Lori Flees, "One Year in, Walmart Health is Delivering Affordable Health Care—and Expanding," Walmart, September 17, 2020, online at https://corporate.walmart.com/newsroom/2020/09/17/one-year-in-walmart-health-is-delivering-affordable-healthcare-and-expanding.

4. Walmart press release, April 5, 2022, online at https://corporate.walmart.com/news/2022/04/05/walmart-health-expands-to-florida-with-five-new-health-centers.

5. David Carmouche, "Walmart Health Nearly Doubles in Size with Launch Into Two New States in 2024," Walmart press release, March 02, 2023, online at https://corporate.walmart.com/news/2023/03/02/walmart-health-nearly-doubles-in-size-with-launch-into-two-new-states-in-2024.

6. From "Walmart Health is Closing," Walmart press release, April 30, 2024, online at https://corporate.walmart.com/news/2024/04/30/walmart-health-is-closing.

7. See the Google Ventures website writeup at https://www.gv.com/about. "We focus all our energy," says Google, "on meeting and supporting founders at the earliest stages of company-building."

8. Mikey Campbell, "Intel to Shutter New Devices Group, Disband Team Behind AR Smart Glasses," *AppleInsider*, April 19, 2018, online at https://appleinsider.com/articles/18/04/19/intel-to-shutter-new-devices-group-disband-team-behind-ar-smart-glasses.

9. Alex Sherman, "Hulu Is Facing an Existential Crisis as Disney Approaches a 2024 Deadline to Buy Comcast's 33% Stake," *CNBC*, July 6, 2022, https://www.cnbc.com/2022/07/06/hulu-faces-existential-crisis-as-disney-decides-how-to-move-forward.html.

Chapter 9

1. Geoffrey A. Moore, *Crossing the Chasm*, 2014.

2. Eric Migicovsky, "Success and Failure at Pebble," *Medium*, April 11, 2022, https://medium.com/@ericmigi/why-pebble-failed-d7be937c6232#. See also the engaging YouTube account at https://www.youtube.com/watch?v=SRdMQwQT47k, which includes a description of Pebbles's second triumphant Kickstarter campaign: $20.4 million from 78,471 backers.

3. This was based on a Slidebean web page that has since been taken down, formerly at https://slidebean.com/story/what-happened-to-pebble-smartwatch.

Chapter 10

1. This assessment is based on Scrapehero.com locations for Whole Foods and Winn-Dixie.

2. This assessment is based on Statistica, via the National Automobile Dealership Association.

3. Note that the higher the growth rates, the less accurate this is.

4. Stuart E. Jackson, *Where Value Hides*, 2007.

5. From the lululemon Form 10-k, March 17, 2011, https://www.sec.gov/Archives/edgar/data/1397187/000139718716000089/lulu-20160131x10k.htm.

Chapter 12

1. See, for example, "Apple iPhone Overtakes BlackBerry Sales," *The Economic Times*, November 8, 2008, online at https://economictimes.indiatimes.com/industry/telecom/apple-iphone-overtakes-blackberry-sales/articleshow/3689193.cms. Apple was still slightly behind Nokia in sales at that point.

Chapter 13

1. This story is well told in Ed Cumming, "How Nespresso's Coffee Revolution Got Ground Down," *The Guardian*, July 14, 2020, online at https://www.theguardian.com/food/2020/jul/14/nespresso-coffee-capsule-pods-branding-clooney-nestle-recycling-environment.

2. Statistics from "Nestlé Reports Full-Year Results for 2022," Nespresso pressrelease, February 16, 2023, online at https://www.nestle.com/media/pressreleases/allpressreleases/full-year-results-2022.

3. Nespresso was late getting into the U.S. market, and its technology originally produced only small, espresso-sized servings—in other words, not to the American taste. As a result, "in the U.S., Nespresso exists in the long, dark shadow of the K-Cup." Cumming, "How Nespresso's Coffee Revolution."

4. Some literature—like Tim Calkins's *Defending Your Brand: How Smart Companies use Defensive Strategy to Deal with Competitive Attacks*—exists on this topic.

Chapter 14

1. In 1997, the company was something like ninety days away from bankruptcy. See, for example, "How Apple Almost Went Bankrupt In the Mid-90s," the interesting You-Tube video on the topic, https://www.youtube.com/watch?v=312gQ8ugzPE.

2. See, for example, "Disney+ Hikes Prices as Sales Sink Across the Company," CNN Business, August 9, 2023, online at https://www.cnn.com/2023/08/09/business/Disney-reports-quarterly-earnings/index.html.

3. In specialists' circles, this is referred to as the van Westendorp approach.

4. Again, for the specialists among us, this method is known as Gabor Granger.

5. Additional detail on conjoint analysis can be found in the appendix.

6. A measure of their ubiquity: We now live in what some refer to as the "subscription economy."

7. See, for example, Josh Howarth, "80+ SaaS Statistics and Trends," *Exploding Trends,* February 12, 2024, online at https://explodingtopics.com/blog/saas-statistics.

8. Sara E. Needleman and Angus Loten, "When Freemium Fails," *The Wall Street Journal,* August 22, 2012, online at https://www.wsj.com/articles/SB10000872396390443713704577603782317318996.

Chapter 15

1. Christian Bauckhage and Kristian Kersting, "Strong Regularities in Growth and Decline of Popularity of Social Media Services," arXiv:1406.6529 [math-ph], June 25, 2014. See an online précis at https://www.researchgate.net/publication/263424759_Strong_Regularities_in_Growth_and_Decline_of_Popularity_of_Social_Media_Services.

Chapter 17

1. Pamela Duncan, "The Worldwide Scale of the Uber Files—in Numbers," *The Guardian,* July 15, 2022, online at https://www.theguardian.com/news/2022/jul/15/the-worldwide-scale-of-the-uber-files-in-numbers.

2. See Ingrid Lundgren, "Uber's Travis Kalanick on Regulators," *TechCrunch,* September 12, 2012, online at https://techcrunch.com/2012/09/12/ubers-travis-kalanick-on-regulators-you-have-to-grit-your-teeth-to-be-a-warrior-or-do-something-less-disruptive/.

3. Olivia Solon, "How Uber Conquers a City in Seven Steps," *The Guardian,* April 12, 2017, online at https://www.theguardian.com/technology/2017/apr/12/why-everyone-hates-uber-seven-step-playbook.

4. Uber pursued a penetration-pricing strategy, offering lower-cost rides to passengers and subsidizing economics for drivers.

5. It's worth noting that Uber did not turn a profit as a public company until 2023.

Chapter 19

1. Ayelet Israeli, Leonard A. Schlesinger, Matt Higgins, and Sabir Semerkant, "Should Your Company Sell on Amazon?," *Harvard Business Review,* September-October 2022, online at https://hbr.org/2022/09/should-your-company-sell-on-amazon.

2. Through its network of 3,500 "giving partners," Bombas donates the #1, #2, and #3 most-requested items in homeless shelters. See their website at https://shop.bombas.com/.

3. In the eyes of the company, this was especially true early on. See Krystal Hu, "Why Brands like Bombas and Warby Parker Don't Sell on Amazon," *Yahoo!Finance,* May 1,

2019, online at https://www.yahoo.com/video/why-dtc-brands-like-bombas-dont-sell-on
-amazon-115401931.html.

4. We note, too, that Amazon calls out products that are "more sustainable" and that are "climate-pledge friendly" but doesn't choose to similarly identify companies that (for example) support people who are homeless.

5. We shouldn't minimize the company's design innovations. On its website, Casper emphasizes the R&D that's conducted by the forty-five researchers, scientists, and engineers who work in the Casper Labs. See https://casper.com/casper-labs.html.

6. See, for example, Stephen Moore, "Casper Disrupted the Sleep Economy; Then the Covers Came Off," *Marker,* November 18, 2021, online at https://marker.medium.com/casper-disrupted-the-sleep-economy-then-the-covers-came-off-5307b71fc190.

Chapter 21

1. This was an internal L.E.K. study, summarized at https://www.lek.com/insights/hea/us/ei/shareholder-value-creation-first-time-launchers-two-decades-learnings.

2. Julian Mitchell, "The Rise, Fall, and Rise Again of the Illustrious GoPro," *PremiumBeat,* September 22, 2021, online at https://www.premiumbeat.com/blog/rise-fall-of-the-gopro/.

3. Jordan, "You'll be Lost Without it: The Rise, Fall and Rise of Garmin," *Harvard Digital Initiative,* November 17, 2016, online at https://d3.harvard.edu/platform-rctom/submission/youll-be-lost-without-it-the-rise-fall-and-rise-of-garmin/.

4. Robert Ferris, "How Garmin Survived the iPhone and Started Growing Again," *CNBC,* October 6, 2020, online at https://www.cnbc.com/2020/10/06/how-garmin-survived-the-iphone-and-started-growing-again.html.

Chapter 22

1. Chris Alcantara, Kevin Schaul, Gerrit De Vynck, and Reed Albergotti, "How Big Tech Got So Big: Hundreds of Acquisitions," *Washington Post,* September 26, 2023, online at https://www.washingtonpost.com/technology/interactive/2021/amazon-apple-facebook-google-acquisitions/.

2. This story is well told in Chapter 9 of Bob Iger's 2019 book, *The Ride of a Lifetime: Lessons Learned from 15 Years as the CEO of the Walt Disney Company.*

3. Iger called it his "proudest decision." See Sarah Whitten, "Bob Iger Says Pixar Was 'Probably the Best' Acquisition He Made During His Tenure with Disney," *CNBC,* December 22, 2021, online at https://www.cnbc.com/2021/12/21/disneys-bob-iger-says-pixar-was-probably-the-best-acquisition-as-ceo.html.

4. All quotes by Jeff Marrazzo are from the authors' October 2023 interview with him.

5. Here we add, with pride, that L.E.K.'s Pierre Jacquet and Eileen Coveney were invaluable advisers to both UPenn and CHOP.

6. See Spark's origin story in Malcolm Burnley, "Jeff Marrazzo's Big, Bold Philly Gene Therapy Vision," *Philadelphia,* February 25, 2023, online at https://www.phillymag.com/news/2023/02/25/jeff-marrazzo-gene-therapy.

Chapter 23

1. While there are always outliers, many drug development processes follow a similar pathway.

2. The Embraer website includes a concise corporate history, online at https://historicalcenter.embraer.com/global/en/history.

3. Ronaldo C. Parente, Alvaro Bruno Cyrino, Nicole Spohr, and Flavio Carvalho de Vasconcelos, "Lessons Learned from Brazilian Multinationals' Internationalization Strategies," *Business Horizons,* 2013, 453–63. Sales in the United States were modest: someone in Florida bought three Bandeirantes.

4. https://historicalcenter.embraer.com/global/en/history.

5. Parente et al., "Lessons Learned."

6. Pankaj Ghemawat, Gustavo A. Herrero, and Luiz Felipe Monteiro, "Embraer: The Global Leader in Regional Jets," HBS case #9-701-006, June 30, 2009.

7. "Embraer: The Global Leader in Regional Jets."

8. It was Bombardier that in 1992 introduced the first regional jet as a replacement for turboprop planes, forcing Embraer to respond in kind. See Fabiano Lopes et al., "Embraer: Shaking Up the Aircraft Manufacturing Market," Darden Business Publishing case #UV0802, 2007.

9. Gerry Yemon and Lynn A. Isabella, "Embraer E-Jets E2: Flying High," Darden Business Publishing case #UV8237, March 17, 2021.

10. Parente et al., "Lessons Learned."

11. https://embraer.com/global/en/about-us.

12. Yemon and Isabella, "Embraer E-Jets E2."

13. Derek Lowe, "Where Drugs Come From: The Numbers," *Science,* November 4, 2010.

Chapter 24

1. Patricia Callahan, "Fruit Additions Spoon Out New Life for Cereal Players," *The Wall Street Journal,* May 15, 2003, online at https://www.wsj.com/articles/SB105295323888157300.

2. This startling statistic comes from Statistica, online at https://www.statista.com/statistics/281797/us-households-usage-of-frozen-breakfast-entrees-sandwiches-trend/.

3. Niccolò Machiavelli, *The Prince and The Discourses* (Modern Library, 1950).

Chapter 25

1. From L.E.K.'s analysis of "Financial Times – Americas Fastest Growing Companies 2023."

2. Stuart Jackson, *Where Value Hides,* (Wiley, 2007), ch. 1.

3. From "State of Venture 2022 Report," *CB Insights,* January 11, 2023.

4. L.E.K. analysis of data in "PitchBook Analyst Note: Serial Entrepreneurs Raise More Capital, but at What Cost?," edited by Max Navas, September 1, 2022.

5. "PitchBook Analyst Note."

6. Paul A. Gompers, Josh Lerner, David Scharfstein, and Anna Kovner, "Performance Persistence in Entrepreneurship and Venture Capital," *Journal of Financial Economics,* April 2010, 18–32.

Index

Note: Page numbers in italic type indicate figures or tables.

FURTHER RESOURCES TO REACH THE FULL POTENTIAL OF YOUR INVESTMENT IN INNOVATION.

Visit PredictableWinners.com to access additional resources beyond the book, including:

Articles
References
Case Studies
Media
and more

PredictableWinners.com

The authorized representative in the EU for product safety and compliance is:
Mare Nostrum Group B.V.
Mauritskade 21D
1091 GC Amsterdam
The Netherlands
Email address: gpsr@mare-nostrum.co.uk

KVK chamber of commerce number: 96249943

The authorized representative in the EU for product safety and compliance is:
Mare Nostrum Group
B.V Doelen 72
4831 GR Breda
The Netherlands

www.ingramcontent.com/pod-product-compliance
Lightning Source LLC
Chambersburg PA
CBHW021501180326
41458CB00050B/6865/J